MATHYOGA9211

MATHYOGA9211

Patterns Do Wonders

Sanjay Kumar

PARTRIDGE

Print information available on the last page.

To order additional copies of this book, contact
Partridge India
000 800 10062 62
orders.india@partridgepublishing.com

www.partridgepublishing.com/india

GRATITUDE

I express my heartiest gratitude to my grandparents for ever inspiring me to do hard work. I express my heartiest gratitude to my mom and father for utmost devotion to my work. I express my love to my brothers, sisters in laws and sisters for providing me the sense of respect and affection. I express my heartiest gratitude to my all teachers for making my life purposeful. Special thanks to my wife Geeta and my children Manan and Naman for the being I am today. I extend my shake hand to all my friends and colleagues for their unconditional support and handholding in all ups and downs in life.

Sanjay Kumar
Delhi, India

TABLE OF CONTENT

PREFACE

Relaxed...... it's amazing...., pattern seeking is the natural phenomenon of human mind and it's as natural as waves in the ocean, musical nodes of an instrument and, landscapes which soothes our senses. All it's due to existence of some patterns in these phenomenons's which relax our senses. Systematic arrangement allows our senses to be relaxed, cool, and calm. To be harmonious is to be systematic and organized. Our activities are the reflection of our inside. Our activity reflects our patterns of mind. Are they haphazard or systematic? Understanding any phenomenon is simple as well as a complex process depends upon how the processing of information is done. That was done systematically or unsystematically. It's so simple. Mind always seeks patterns. Mind only understand the language of patterns. If we want anything may be easily understood by mind, the only way is to think like patterns, look like patterns, feels like patterns, behave like patterns and live like patterns. To be confident of our learning will directly improve our performance in our daily life activities and in examinations of life. We must be very confident that we will be able to visualise, express and apply our knowledge and information or our understanding in our life. It is almost same everywhere that people never try to visualizes their performance in advance before actual situations of performance. It's only about the visualising capacity of mind.

What we learn must be visualised in advance with closed eyes so that we go very confident while we have to perform. In our recording it is usually seen that we fail to visualizes and apply what we have learnt and understood previously in course of our performances. We can easily verify this in our daily lives. This program of mathemetisation of the mind with the help of simple patterns will be very useful to visualise our performance in advance so that we could go with full confidence in real time performance situations. The gap between our understandings, visualizing and expressing would be minimised with this simple process of patternising the mind by recognising and visualising these very simple patterns in numbers first and ultimately in life activities. All the deprievedness we faced while we perform like not confident, anxiousness, puzzleness, disharmonized mind and body can be minimised. This all is the resultant of that gap created due to our habit of non visualisation of our learning. If we visualise what we have learnt and understood prior to actual performance we will surely get rid of such type of illusions of daily life. This book is simply presenting something very natural to our mind and undoubtedly that is human capacity and power of seeking, observing and visualising patterns in all aspects of their course of life to live happily.

All the best
Good luck

Sanjay Kumar
Delhi, India

MATHYOGA9211

(CREATE WONDERS IN LIFE)

CHAPTER-I

INTRODUCTION

Mathyoga9211
(*Create wonders in life*)

My dear students, teachers and parents

I am going to help you to learn the process of mathemetisation of our mind. You will love to be associated to this amazing and wonderful process of mathemetisation of mind. This can create wonders in your life. If you listen, observe, recite, touch, taste and smell this process through simple patterns techniques the process of mathemetisation of your mind starts automatically. I am sure you will be enjoying your life fullest. Something beautiful will happens to you and the beauty is in calming. The more you adapt to mathyoga9211, the deeper you go within yourself. You will earn a kind of inner peace so strong that nothing in life will be able to shatter it.

Your body will benefit too. As time goes on, you will stay calm, cool, compose and productive for longer time. This mean that those process of the mind that makes our body harmonized will be strengthen. The body is designed to be healthy. It has its own healing mechanics. These mechanisms are blocked by untrained and unsystematic mind. Mathyoga9211is a procedure to control and direct mind. It will go a long way towards setting free the body's healing powers. When you learn to do this you will be at a level of mind where you will be able to free you imagination to search for beauties in nature through patterns, associations and symmetry.

Mathyoga9211: A journey of Visualization and intuition

Think about yourself and you prosperity. Right from the beginning practice visualization. This is central to mathyoga9211. This is for internalizing number pattern in particular and remaining in higher level of concentration and motivation in life in general. The better you learn to visualize the more powerful will be your association with body, mind and soul.

Mathyoga9211: It operates through psychological laws of happening:

Operate according to some very simple learning laws, so that the imaginary event will becomes real. What are at work are perfectly natural laws. Our minds are not confined to our heads but he reaches out and reaches out strongly and effectively. He should be motivated by desires, fuelled by belief and spark by expectancy.

Mathyoga9211: Follow psychological laws of learning

Desire for mathyoga9211:

You must desire that the following things will happen in my life:

- Mathyoga9211will be surely understood by me.
- Mathemetisation of mind is possible through mathyoga9211.
- Peoples will be more pleasant with me through mathyoga9211.
- Environment around me will be more conducive for me through mathyoga9211.
- I will be very happy, satisfied and agreeable tomorrow through mathyoga9211.
- I am going to be great at mathematics through mathyoga9211.

Belief for mathyoga9211:

You must believe that what you desire for mathyoga9211 will surely took place. Because if your mind is not going to believe your desire it will automatically dismiss and that pleasant learning environment can't took place because you mind will be working against its happening.

Expectation for mathyoga9211:

The law is sometimes called law of dynamics expectation because you must expect mathyoga9211 to take place because it is very much possible that your desire for it and simultaneously you can also believe it to take place and still not expect it to take place. You want your friends, parents, teachers, colleagues or well wishers to be very pleasant to you tomorrow. You know that it can be but you may still be some distance away from expecting it and this is where mathyoga9211 and effective visualization come in for help.

Goals achieved through mathyoga9211:

Introspective evaluation

You will be able to do evaluation of your learning. Step by step you can visualize what new you have learned. Are you capable of recalling at your will what you have learned? Based upon your Introspective evaluation you can find out all that. So day by day confidence on your recalling power at your will boost and solidify. For example if you have learned the table of 2 by forward and reverse patterns and able to see yourself visualizing the whole table as a process of repeated addition only then you will be able to apply/transfer that in further learning.

Boost concentration

Without concentration you cannot perform in mathyoga9211. Day by day by listening, observing, writing and reciting patterns again and again your concentration will boost

Motivation:

one successful pattern learning will motivate you to move to another pattern and so you will never be derailed because patterns is a never ending process and only you can limit you as per your requirement.

Curiosity, vigour and energy builder

The generating power of patterns increases a sense of inquisitiveness and inquiry in you because it is as harmonious as nature so in the process you will never feel exhausted. Your vigour, energy will boost tremendously.

Speedup mantel process

Your progress will all depend upon your concentration, motivation and energy level. All you are doing without the use of any paper and pen. So it will boost your capacity to hold information mentally and simultaneously able to use that. So all the process of visualization of patterns will certainly boost and strengthen your mental processes.

Sharp up estimation, imagination and visualization

Your imagination power will increase day by day as you progress. Estimation of the phenomenon will certainly boost.

Future orientation and intuition

Your capacity of intuition and future orientation will be highly increased and you will sense this in the process of mathemetisation through patterns.

CHAPTER-II

PATTERNS DO WONDERS

Patterns do wonders

Learning and living is all about mathemetisation of mind. Mathemetisation of mind is simply making our thinking (thought process) organized, systematic and applicable. Thought provoking and prompting are also a part of mathematised mind. This simply means that we have to challenge every bit of new information with salvating questions. Salvating questions are questions which lead you to transfer your learning in other areas of conflicts and peace. What are these salvating questions which can do magic in our life. They are the only questions which has the potential to transform your life.

These are the question which starts from:

Why
When
Which
How
Where
Whose
Whom
What

If your mind is in the process of mathemetisation or already mathematised then these transforming questions will certainly lead you to some rational and logical thinking. Our mind is very good in accepting, remembering and reviewing but only when it gained information through provocatation and prompting. This information will certainly guide, manage and facilitate us in our problem resolution and become successful and ultimately happy in life.

Patterns

Nature is nothing but a pattern or combination of patterns. Mathematised mind is the mind which is able to seek patterns in every phenomenon. Patterns itself are systematic, organized, symmetrical, goal oriented, progressive, live, intuitive and streamed in nature. So if properly practiced will makes us systematic, organized, symmetrical, goal oriented, progressive, live, intuitive and streamed in nature.

To understand more let us compare the qualities possessed by

- a mathematical mind
- a success full mind
- a happy mind
- a pattern: 1 2 3 4 5 6 7 8 9 10 11 1211 10 9 8 7 6 5 4 3 2 1

Sr. No.	Qualities/ characteristics	Posses by a mathema- tised mind	Posses by a success full mind	Posses by a happy mind	Posses by a pattern
1	like to find out solution of problems	Yes	yes	Yes	yes
2	remain content	Yes	yes	Yes	yes
3	enterprising	Yes	yes	Yes	yes
4	good at communication	Yes	yes	yes	yes
5	courageous		yes	yes	yes
6	speak economically	Yes	yes	yes	yes
7	never hesitate	Yes	yes	Yes	yes
8	Sober	Yes	yes	Yes	yes
9	aggressive	No	no	no	no
10	straight forward	Yes	Yes	yes	yes
11	daring	Yes	yes	yes	Yes
12	enthusiastic	Yes	yes	yes	yes
13	risk taking	Yes	calculated	calculated	calculated
14	bold	Yes	yes	yes	Yes
15	can take stress	Yes	Yes	yes	yes
16	dominant	No	no	no	No
17	influenced by facts than by feeling	Yes	Yes	yes	yes
18	Hard working	Yes	yes	yes	Yes
19	easy going never in hurry	Yes	yes	Yes	yes
20	quick decision	Yes	yes	yes	Yes
21	communicative	Yes	yes	Yes	yes
22	free from guilt	Yes	yes	yes	yes
23	never hesitate	Yes	yes	yes	yes
24	Secure	Yes	yes	Yes	yes
25	never act according to others	Yes	yes	yes	yes
26	capable of getting things done	Yes	yes	Yes	yes
27	assertive behaviour	Yes	yes	yes	yes

28	develop their own sets of rules	Yes	If required	If required	If required
29	self disciplined	Yes	yes	yes	Yes
30	abstract thinking	Yes	yes	Yes	yes
31	reliable behaviour	Yes	yes	yes	yes
32	Experimentive	Yes	yes	yes	yes
33	impulsive	No	no	no	no
34	self destructive	No	no	no	no
35	social	Yes	yes	yes	yes
36	cope with routine life	Yes	yes	yes	yes
37	highly self motivated	Yes	yes	Yes	yes
38	practical	Yes	yes	yes	yes
39	mindful	Yes	yes	yes	yes
40	lost in the world of dreams	Yes	no	no	no
41	participating	Yes	yes	yes	yes
42	Cautious	Yes	yes	Yes	yes
43	likes people	Yes	yes	yes	yes
44	open minded	Yes	yes	yes	yes
45	resolve conflicts	Yes	yes	Yes	yes
46	emotionally mature	Yes	yes	Yes	yes
47	realistic	Yes	yes	yes	yes
48	Cheerful	Yes	yes	Yes	yes
49	Intuitive	Yes	yes	yes	yes
50	keep things under control	Yes	yes	yes	yes
51	Competitor of self	Yes	yes	Yes	yes
52	self confident	Yes	yes	Yes	yes
53	Assertive	Yes	yes	Yes	yes
54	Mature	Yes	yes	Yes	yes
55	Relax	Yes	yes	Yes	yes
56	Adaptive	Yes	yes	Yes	yes
57	Flexible	Yes	yes	Yes	yes
58	open to change	Yes	yes	Yes	yes
59	accommodative	Yes	yes	Yes	yes
60	socially active	Yes	yes	Yes	yes
61	cultural interests	Yes	yes	Yes	yes
62	down to earth	Yes	yes	Yes	yes
63	friendly nature	Yes	yes	Yes	yes
64	Sociable	Yes	yes	Yes	yes
65	good reasoning	Yes	yes	Yes	yes
66	intelligent	Yes	yes	Yes	yes
67	hard to fool	Yes	yes	Yes	yes

This comparison conclude and confirmed that if a person posses a mathematised mind then there is maximum possibility to be a successful and a happy person in his/her life. The above characteristics are possessed by a pattern also. So what we want to inculcate in a child is possess by the patterns.

Characteristics possess by a pattern:

- Like to find out solution of problems

1	2	3	4	5	6	7	8	9	10
11	10	9	8	7	6	5	4	3	2
1									

Rationale: (pattern generate by +1 and -1)

- Remain content

1	2	3	4	5	6	7	8	9	10
11	10	9	8	7	6	5	4	3	2
1									

Rationale: (know how to generate, no doubt, no confusion)

- Enterprising

1	2	3	4	5	6	7	8	9	10
11	10	9	8	7	6	5	4	3	2
1									

Rationale: (ready to generate with confident)

- Good at communication

1	2	3	4	5	6	7	8	9	10
11	10	9	8	7	6	5	4	3	2
1									

Rationale: (how to generate is effectively communicated to other member of pattern)

- Courageous

1	2	3	4	5	6	7	8	9	10
11	10	9	8	7	6	5	4	3	2
1									

Rationale: (know how to generate, no doubt so act accordingly)

- Speak economically

1	2	3	4	5	6	7	8	9	10
11	10	9	8	7	6	5	4	3	2
1									

Rationale: (convey clearly what is to be conveyed)

- Never hesitate

1	2	3	4	5	6	7	8	9	10
11	10	9	8	7	6	5	4	3	2
1									

Rationale: (knowing how to generate, no hesitation to go forward)

- Sober

1	2	3	4	5	6	7	8	9	10
11	10	9	8	7	6	5	4	3	2
1									

Rationale: (systematic generation is itself a sober process)

- Aggressive

1	2	3	4	5	6	7	8	9	10
11	10	9	8	7	6	5	4	3	2
1									

Rationale: (no one can stop him now to generate)

- Straight forward

1	2	3	4	5	6	7	8	9	10
11	10	9	8	7	6	5	4	3	2
1									

Rationale: (no hidden agenda you can watch the process of generation)

- Daring

1	2	3	4	5	6	7	8	9	10
11	10	9	8	7	6	5	4	3	2
1									

Rationale: (dare to generate as expected)

- Enthusiastic/optimistic

1	2	3	4	5	6	7	8	9	10
11	10	9	8	7	6	5	4	3	2
1									

Rationale: (no doubt in his doing and responsibilities)

- Calculated risk taking

1	2	3	4	5	6	7	8	9	10
11	10	9	8	7	6	5	4	3	2
1									

Rationale: (go on a journey with confidence)

- Bold

1	2	3	4	5	6	7	8	9	10
11	10	9	8	7	6	5	4	3	2
1									

Rationale: (no hidden process so opens to debate and discuss)

- Can take stress

1	2	3	4	5	6	7	8	9	10
11	10	9	8	7	6	5	4	3	2
1									

Rationale: (enjoy the generation process so there cannot be any stress if something comes on the way ready to enjoy)

- Dominant

1	2	3	4	5	6	7	8	9	10
11	10	9	8	7	6	5	4	3	2
1									

Rationale: (after taking action become dominant on distraction)

- Influenced by facts than by feeling

1	2	3	4	5	6	7	8	9	10
11	10	9	8	7	6	5	4	3	2
1									

Rationale: (never swayed away by emotion only stands on the basis of solid rationality behind every action)

- Hard working

1	2	3	4	5	6	7	8	9	10
11	10	9	8	7	6	5	4	3	2
1									

Rationale: (pattern generate by +1 and -1 in a regular manner require lot of hard work)

- Easy going

1	2	3	4	5	6	7	8	9	10
11	10	9	8	7	6	5	4	3	2
1									

Rationale: (pattern generate its member in a very systematic and organized way)

- Quick decision

1	2	3	4	5	6	7	8	9	10
11	10	9	8	7	6	5	4	3	2
1									

Rationale: (systematic and organized so no confusion)

- Free from guilt

1	2	3	4	5	6	7	8	9	10
11	10	9	8	7	6	5	4	3	2
1									

Rationale: (pattern knows what is going on so no question of guilt)

- Assertive behaviour

1	2	3	4	5	6	7	8	9	10
11	10	9	8	7	6	5	4	3	2
1									

Rationale: (all is well)

- Self disciplined

1	2	3	4	5	6	7	8	9	10
11	10	9	8	7	6	5	4	3	2
1									

Rationale: (streamed)

- Abstract thinking

1	2	3	4	5	6	7	8	9	10
11	10	9	8	7	6	5	4	3	2
1									

Rationale: (goal oriented and intuitive)

- Reliable behaviour

1	2	3	4	5	6	7	8	9	10
11	10	9	8	7	6	5	4	3	2
1									

Rationale: (pattern generate by +1 and -1)

- Experimentive

1	2	3	4	5	6	7	8	9	10
11	10	9	8	7	6	5	4	3	2
1									

Rationale: (pattern generate by +1 and -1)

- Highly goal oriented and motivated

1	2	3	4	5	6	7	8	9	10
11	10	9	8	7	6	5	4	3	2
1									

Rationale: (pattern generate by +1 and -1)

- Practical

1	2	3	4	5	6	7	8	9	10
11	10	9	8	7	6	5	4	3	2
1									

Rationale: (pattern generate by +1 and -1)

- Participating

1	2	3	4	5	6	7	8	9	10
11	10	9	8	7	6	5	4	3	2
1									

Rationale: (pattern generate by +1 and -1)

- Realistic

1	2	3	4	5	6	7	8	9	10
11	10	9	8	7	6	5	4	3	2
1									

Rationale: (pattern generate by +1 and -1)

- Intuitive

1	2	3	4	5	6	7	8	9	10
11	10	9	8	7	6	5	4	3	2
1									

Rationale: (pattern generate by +1 and -1)

- Self confident

1	2	3	4	5	6	7	8	9	10
11	10	9	8	7	6	5	4	3	2
1									

Rationale: (pattern generate by +1 and -1)

- Good reasoning

1	2	3	4	5	6	7	8	9	10
11	10	9	8	7	6	5	4	3	2
1									

Rationale: (pattern generate by +1 and -1)

- Intelligent

1	2	3	4	5	6	7	8	9	10
11	10	9	8	7	6	5	4	3	2
1									

Rationale: (pattern generate by +1 and -1)

Ultimate aim of mathyoga9211 is to activate the process of mathemetisation of mind:

If you are learning how to count from 1-10 then first step for mathemetisation of mind is to seek patterns and finally reach to some generalization. Learning counting is much more than simply recitation from1-10.this process must be salvating in nature. The learner must able to transfer her learning in different situations of adoption and adaptations in life? This means that learner must search for the answers of questions as following:

Why we do counting: one to one grouping, ordering group, classification, matching, to know the volume of quantity, selection etc.

When we do counting: need based situations

Which we count: systems of counting, things of counting

How we count: ways of counting-one-to-one, in different groups

Where we do counting: situations of counting

Whose we count: things of counting

Whom we count: things of counting

What we count: things of counting

CHAPTER-III

EXERCISING MATHYOGA9211

Procedure of doing mathyoga9211:-

Exercising a pattern:

Direction:

Practioners are advised to follow the steps.

Be comfortable and sit at ease and follow the steps given below.

Record the pattern in your mobile phone or recording gadget.

1. Listen the pattern 5 times keeping eyes closed.
2. Listen and observe the written pattern 5 times.
3. Write the pattern 5 times.
4. Recite the pattern loudly 5 times.

5.   Recite the pattern 5 times loudly keeping eyes closed.
6.   Visualize the pattern 5 times while reciting the pattern keeping mum and eyes closed.

Keep on Observing (KOO) the positivity of following thoughts while you are listening or observing or writing or reciting or visualising the patterns

- I like to find out solution of problems,
- I always remain content,
- I am always enterprising,
- I am good at communication,
- I am courageous,
- I always speak economically,
- I never hesitate,
- I am Sober,
- I am not aggressive,
- I am straight forward,
- I am daring,
- I am enthusiastic,
- I am risk taking,
- I am bold,
- I can take stress,
- I am not dominant,
- I am influenced by facts than by feeling,
- I am hard working,
- I am easy going,
- I am never in hurry,
- I am free from guilt,
- I feel Secure,
- I never act according to others,
- I am capable of getting things done,

- I am assertive,
- I am self disciplined,
- I am reliable,
- I am experimentive,
- I am social,
- I am able to cope with routine life,
- I am highly self motivated,
- I am practical,
- I am mindful,
- I am participating,
- I am Cautious,
- I likes people,
- I am open minded,
- I am able to resolve conflicts,
- I am emotionally mature,
- I am realistic,
- I am Cheerful,
- I am intuitive,
- I keep things under control,
- I am Competitor of self,
- I am self confident,
- I am Relaxed,
- I am Adaptive,
- I am Flexible,
- I am open to change,
- I am accommodative,
- I am socially active,
- I take cultural interests,
- I am down to earth,
- I am friendly nature
- and so on.........

Time schedule for exercising a pattern:

- A gap of 1 second between the two counts will be suitable.
- Gap can be extended while you practised advanced patterns.

CHAPTER-IV

COUNTING BY ONE'S

Group: 1: counting by one's

1	2	3	4	5	6	7	8	9	10
11	12	13	14	15	16	17	18	19	20
21	22	23	24	25	26	27	28	29	30
31	32	33	34	35	36	37	38	39	40
41	42	43	44	45	46	47	48	49	50
51	52	53	54	55	56	57	58	59	60
61	62	63	64	65	66	67	68	69	70
71	72	73	74	75	76	77	78	79	80
81	82	83	84	85	86	87	88	89	90
91	92	93	94	95	96	97	98	99	100

PATTERN: 1

CYCLE-1

1	2	1							

Keep On Observing (KOO):

I like to find out solution of problems, I always remain content, I am always enterprising, I am good at communication, I am courageous, I always speak economically, I never hesitate, I am Sober, I am not aggressive, I am straight forward, I am daring, I am enthusiastic, I am risk taking, I am bold, I can take stress, I am not dominant, I am influenced by facts than by feeling, I am hard working, I am easy going, I am never in hurry, I am free from guilt, I feel Secure, I never act according to others, I am capable of getting things done, I am assertive, I am self disciplined, I am reliable, I am experimentive, I am social, I am able to cope with routine life, I am highly self motivated, I am practical, I am mindful, I am participating, I am Cautious, I likes people, I am open minded, I am able to resolve conflicts, I am emotionally mature, I am realistic, I am Cheerful, I am intuitive, I keep things under control, I am Competitor of self, I am self confident, I am Relaxed, I am Adaptive, I am Flexible, I am open to change, I am accommodative, I am socially active, I take cultural interests, I am down to earth, I am friendly nature and so on.........

CYCLE-2

1	2	3	2	1					

Keep On Observing (KOO):

I like to find out solution of problems, I always remain content, I am always enterprising, I am good at communication, I am courageous, I always speak economically, I never hesitate, I am Sober, I am not aggressive, I am straight forward, I am daring, I am enthusiastic, I am risk taking, I am bold, I can take stress, I am not dominant, I am influenced by facts than by feeling, I am hard working, I am easy going, I am never in hurry, I am free from guilt, I feel Secure, I never act according to others, I am capable of getting things done, I am assertive, I am self disciplined, I am reliable, I am experimentive, I am social, I am able to cope with routine life, I am highly self motivated, I am practical, I am mindful, I am participating, I am Cautious, I likes people, I am open minded, I am able to resolve conflicts, I am emotionally mature, I am realistic, I am Cheerful, I am intuitive, I keep things under control, I am Competitor of self, I am self confident, I am Relaxed, I am Adaptive, I am Flexible, I am open to change, I am accommodative, I am socially active, I take cultural interests, I am down to earth, I am friendly nature and so on.........

CYCLE-3

1	2	3	4	3	2	1			

Keep On Observing (KOO):

I like to find out solution of problems, I always remain content, I am always enterprising, I am good at communication, I am courageous, I always speak economically, I never hesitate, I am sober, I am not aggressive and so on....

CYCLE-4

1	2	3	4	5	4	3	2	1	

Keep On Observing (KOO):

I like to find out solution of problems, I always remain content, I am always enterprising, I am good at communication, I am courageous, I always speak economically, I never hesitate, I am sober, I am not aggressive and so on....

CYCLE-5

1	2	3	4	5	6	5	4	3	2
1									

Keep On Observing (KOO):

I like to find out solution of problems, I always remain content, I am always enterprising, I am good at communication, I am courageous, I always speak economically, I never hesitate, I am sober, I am not aggressive and so on....

CYCLE-6

1	2	3	4	5	6	7	6	5	4
3	2	1							

Keep On Observing (KOO):

I like to find out solution of problems, I always remain content, I am always enterprising, I am good at communication, I am courageous, I always speak economically, I never hesitate, I am sober, I am not aggressive and so on....

CYCLE-7

1	2	3	4	5	6	7	8	7	6
5	4	3	2	1					

Keep On Observing (KOO):

I like to find out solution of problems, I always remain content, I am always enterprising, I am good at communication, I am courageous, I always speak economically, I never hesitate, I am sober, I am not aggressive and so on....

CYCLE-8

1	2	3	4	5	6	7	8	9	8
6	5	4	3	2	1				

Keep On Observing (KOO):

I like to find out solution of problems, I always remain content, I am always enterprising, I am good at communication, I am courageous, I always speak economically, I never hesitate, I am sober, I am not aggressive and so on....

CYCLE-9

1	2	3	4	5	6	7	8	9	10
9	8	7	6	5	4	3	2	1	

Keep On Observing (KOO):

I like to find out solution of problems, I always remain content, I am always enterprising, I am good at communication, I am courageous, I always speak economically, I never hesitate, I am sober, I am not aggressive and so on....

CYCLE-10

1	2	3	4	5	6	7	8	9	10
11	10	9	8	7	6	5	4	3	2
1									

Keep On Observing (KOO):

I like to find out solution of problems, I always remain content, I am always enterprising, I am good at communication, I am courageous, I always speak economically, I never hesitate, I am sober, I am not aggressive and so on....

CYCLE-11

1	2	3	4	5	6	7	8	9	10
11	12	11	10	9	8	7	6	5	4
3	2	1							

Keep On Observing (KOO):

I like to find out solution of problems, I always remain content, I am always enterprising, I am good at communication, I am courageous, I always speak economically, I never hesitate, I am sober, I am not aggressive and so on....

CYCLE-12

1	2	3	4	5	6	7	8	9	10
11	12	13	12	11	10	9	8	7	6
5	4	3	2	1					

Keep On Observing (KOO):

I like to find out solution of problems, I always remain content, I am always enterprising, I am good at communication, I am courageous, I always speak economically, I never hesitate, I am sober, I am not aggressive and so on....

CYCLE-13

1	2	3	4	5	6	7	8	9	10
11	12	13	14	13	12	11	10	9	8
7	6	5	4	3	2	1			

Keep On Observing (KOO):

I like to find out solution of problems, I always remain content, I am always enterprising, I am good at communication, I am courageous, I always speak economically, I never hesitate, I am sober, I am not aggressive and so on....

CYCLE-14

1	2	3	4	5	6	7	8	9	10
11	12	13	14	15	14	13	12	11	10
9	8	7	6	5	5	4	3	2	1

Keep On Observing (KOO):

I like to find out solution of problems, I always remain content, I am always enterprising, I am good at communication, I am courageous, I always speak economically, I never hesitate, I am sober, I am not aggressive and so on....

CYCLE-15

1	2	3	4	5	6	7	8	9	10
11	12	13	14	15	16	15	14	13	12
11	10	9	8	7	6	5	4	3	2
1									

Keep On Observing (KOO):

I like to find out solution of problems, I always remain content, I am always enterprising, I am good at communication,

I am courageous, I always speak economically, I never hesitate, I am sober, I am not aggressive and so on....

CYCLE-16

1	2	3	4	5	6	7	8	9	10
11	12	13	14	15	16	17	16	15	14
13	12	11	10	9	8	7	6	5	4
3	2	1							

Keep On Observing (KOO):

I like to find out solution of problems, I always remain content, I am always enterprising, I am good at communication, I am courageous, I always speak economically, I never hesitate, I am sober, I am not aggressive and so on....

CYCLE-17

1	2	3	4	5	6	7	8	9	10
11	12	13	14	15	16	17	18	*	*
*	*	17	16	15	14	13	12	11	10
9	8	7	6	5	4	3	2	1	

Keep On Observing (KOO):

I like to find out solution of problems, I always remain content, I am always enterprising, I am good at communication, I am courageous, I always speak economically, I never hesitate, I am sober, I am not aggressive and so on....

CYCLE-18

1	2	3	4	5	6	7	8	9	10
11	12	13	14	15	16	17	18	19	*
*	18	17	16	15	14	13	12	11	10
9	8	7	6	5	4	3	2	1	

Keep On Observing (KOO):

I like to find out solution of problems, I always remain content, I am always enterprising, I am good at communication, I am courageous, I always speak economically, I never hesitate, I am sober, I am not aggressive and so on....

CYCLE-19

1	2	3	4	5	6	7	8	9	10
11	12	13	14	15	16	17	18	19	20
19	18	17	16	15	14	13	12	11	10
9	8	7	6	5	4	3	2	1	

Keep On Observing (KOO):

I like to find out solution of problems, I always remain content, I am always enterprising, I am good at communication, I am courageous, I always speak economically, I never hesitate, I am sober, I am not aggressive and so on....

CYCLE-20

1	2	3	4	5	6	7	8	9	10
11	12	13	14	15	16	17	18	19	20
21									
									20
19	18	17	16	15	14	13	12	11	10
9	8	7	6	5	4	3	2	1	

Keep On Observing (KOO):

I like to find out solution of problems, I always remain content, I am always enterprising, I am good at communication, I am courageous, I always speak economically, I never hesitate, I am sober, I am not aggressive and so on....

CYCLE-21

1	2	3	4	5	6	7	8	9	10
11	12	13	14	15	16	17	18	19	20
21	22								
								21	20
19	18	17	16	15	14	13	12	11	10
9	8	7	6	5	4	3	2	1	

Keep On Observing (KOO):

I like to find out solution of problems, I always remain content, I am always enterprising, I am good at communication, I am courageous, I always speak economically, I never hesitate, I am sober, I am not aggressive and so on....

CYCLE-22

1	2	3	4	5	6	7	8	9	10
11	12	13	14	15	16	17	18	19	20
21	22	23							
							22	21	20
19	18	17	16	15	14	13	12	11	10
9	8	7	6	5	4	3	2	1	

Keep On Observing (KOO):

I like to find out solution of problems, I always remain content, I am always enterprising, I am good at communication, I am courageous, I always speak economically, I never hesitate, I am sober, I am not aggressive and so on....

CYCLE-23

1	2	3	4	5	6	7	8	9	10
11	12	13	14	15	16	17	18	19	20
21	22	23	24						
						23	22	21	20
19	18	17	16	15	14	13	12	11	10
9	8	7	6	5	4	3	2	1	

Keep On Observing (KOO):

I like to find out solution of problems, I always remain content, I am always enterprising, I am good at communication, I am courageous, I always speak economically, I never hesitate, I am sober, I am not aggressive and so on....

CYCLE-24

1	2	3	4	5	6	7	8	9	10
11	12	13	14	15	16	17	18	19	20
21	22	23	24	25					
					24	23	22	21	20
19	18	17	16	15	14	13	12	11	10
9	8	7	6	5	4	3	2	1	

Keep On Observing (KOO):

I like to find out solution of problems, I always remain content, I am always enterprising, I am good at communication, I am courageous, I always speak economically, I never hesitate, I am sober, I am not aggressive and so on....

CYCLE-25

1	2	3	4	5	6	7	8	9	10
11	12	13	14	15	16	17	18	19	20
21	22	23	24	25	26				
				25	24	23	22	21	20
19	18	17	16	15	14	13	12	11	10
9	8	7	6	5	4	3	2	1	

Keep On Observing (KOO):

I like to find out solution of problems, I always remain content, I am always enterprising, I am good at communication, I am courageous, I always speak economically, I never hesitate, I am sober, I am not aggressive and so on....

CYCLE-26

1	2	3	4	5	6	7	8	9	10
11	12	13	14	15	16	17	18	19	20
21	22	23	24	25	26	27			
			26	25	24	23	22	21	20
19	18	17	16	15	14	13	12	11	10
9	8	7	6	5	4	3	2	1	

Keep On Observing (KOO):

I like to find out solution of problems, I always remain content, I am always enterprising, I am good at communication, I am courageous, I always speak economically, I never hesitate, I am sober, I am not aggressive and so on....

CYCLE-27

1	2	3	4	5	6	7	8	9	10
11	12	13	14	15	16	17	18	19	20
21	22	23	24	25	26	27	28	■	■
■	■	■	26	25	24	23	22	21	20
19	18	17	16	15	14	13	12	11	10
9	8	7	6	5	4	3	2	1	

Keep On Observing (KOO):

I like to find out solution of problems, I always remain content, I am always enterprising, I am good at communication, I am courageous, I always speak economically, I never hesitate, I am sober, I am not aggressive and so on....

CYCLE-28

1	2	3	4	5	6	7	8	9	10
11	12	13	14	15	16	17	18	19	20
21	22	23	24	25	26	27	28	29	■
■	28	27	26	25	24	23	22	21	20
19	18	17	16	15	14	13	12	11	10
9	8	7	6	5	4	3	2	1	

Keep On Observing (KOO):

I like to find out solution of problems, I always remain content, I am always enterprising, I am good at communication, I am courageous, I always speak economically, I never hesitate, I am sober, I am not aggressive and so on....

CYCLE-29

1	2	3	4	5	6	7	8	9	10
11	12	13	14	15	16	17	18	19	20
21	22	23	24	25	26	27	28	29	30
29	28	27	26	25	24	23	22	21	20
19	18	17	16	15	14	13	12	11	10
9	8	7	6	5	4	3	2	1	

Keep On Observing (KOO):

I like to find out solution of problems, I always remain content, I am always enterprising, I am good at communication, I am courageous, I always speak economically, I never hesitate, I am sober, I am not aggressive and so on....

CYCLE-30

1	2	3	4	5	6	7	8	9	10
11	12	13	14	15	16	17	18	19	20
21	22	23	24	25	26	27	28	29	30
31									
									30
29	28	27	26	25	24	23	22	21	20
19	18	17	16	15	14	13	12	11	10
9	8	7	6	5	4	3	2	1	

Keep On Observing (KOO):

I like to find out solution of problems, I always remain content, I am always enterprising, I am good at communication, I am courageous, I always speak economically, I never hesitate, I am sober, I am not aggressive and so on....

CYCLE-31

1	2	3	4	5	6	7	8	9	10
11	12	13	14	15	16	17	18	19	20
21	22	23	24	25	26	27	28	29	30
31	32								
								31	30
29	28	27	26	25	24	23	22	21	20
19	18	17	16	15	14	13	12	11	10
9	8	7	6	5	4	3	2	1	

Keep On Observing (KOO):

I like to find out solution of problems, I always remain content, I am always enterprising, I am good at communication, I am courageous, I always speak economically, I never hesitate, I am sober, I am not aggressive and so on....

CYCLE-32

1	2	3	4	5	6	7	8	9	10
11	12	13	14	15	16	17	18	19	20
21	22	23	24	25	26	27	28	29	30
31	32	33							
							32	31	30
29	28	27	26	25	24	23	22	21	20
19	18	17	16	15	14	13	12	11	10
9	8	7	6	5	4	3	2	1	

Keep On Observing (KOO):

I like to find out solution of problems, I always remain content, I am always enterprising, I am good at communication, I am courageous, I always speak economically, I never hesitate, I am sober, I am not aggressive and so on....

CYCLE-33

1	2	3	4	5	6	7	8	9	10
11	12	13	14	15	16	17	18	19	20
21	22	23	24	25	26	27	28	29	30
31	32	33	34						
						33	32	31	30
29	28	27	26	25	24	23	22	21	20
19	18	17	16	15	14	13	12	11	10
9	8	7	6	5	4	3	2	1	

Keep On Observing (KOO):

I like to find out solution of problems, I always remain content, I am always enterprising, I am good at communication, I am courageous, I always speak economically, I never hesitate, I am sober, I am not aggressive and so on....

CYCLE-34

1	2	3	4	5	6	7	8	9	10
11	12	13	14	15	16	17	18	19	20
21	22	23	24	25	26	27	28	29	30
31	32	33	34	35					
					34	33	32	31	30
29	28	27	26	25	24	23	22	21	20
19	18	17	16	15	14	13	12	11	10
9	8	7	6	5	4	3	2	1	

Keep On Observing (KOO):

I like to find out solution of problems, I always remain content, I am always enterprising, I am good at communication, I am courageous, I always speak economically, I never hesitate, I am sober, I am not aggressive and so on....

CYCLE-35

1	2	3	4	5	6	7	8	9	10
11	12	13	14	15	16	17	18	19	20
21	22	23	24	25	26	27	28	29	30
31	32	33	34	35	36	███	███	███	███
███	███	███	███	35	34	33	32	31	30
29	28	27	26	25	24	23	22	21	20
19	18	17	16	15	14	13	12	11	10
9	8	7	6	5	4	3	2	1	

Keep On Observing (KOO):

I like to find out solution of problems, I always remain content, I am always enterprising, I am good at communication, I am courageous, I always speak economically, I never hesitate, I am sober, I am not aggressive and so on....

CYCLE-36

1	2	3	4	5	6	7	8	9	10
11	12	13	14	15	16	17	18	19	20
21	22	23	24	25	26	27	28	29	30
31	32	33	34	35	36	37	███	███	███
███	███	███	36	35	34	33	32	31	30
29	28	27	26	25	24	23	22	21	20
19	18	17	16	15	14	13	12	11	10
9	8	7	6	5	4	3	2	1	

Keep On Observing (KOO):

I like to find out solution of problems, I always remain content, I am always enterprising, I am good at communication, I am courageous, I always speak economically, I never hesitate, I am sober, I am not aggressive and so on....

CYCLE-37

1	2	3	4	5	6	7	8	9	10
11	12	13	14	15	16	17	18	19	20
21	22	23	24	25	26	27	28	29	30
31	32	33	34	35	36	37	38	■	■
■	37	36	35	34	33	32	31	30	
29	28	27	26	25	24	23	22	21	20
19	18	17	16	15	14	13	12	11	10
9	8	7	6	5	4	3	2	1	

Keep On Observing (KOO):

I like to find out solution of problems, I always remain content, I am always enterprising, I am good at communication, I am courageous, I always speak economically, I never hesitate, I am sober, I am not aggressive and so on....

CYCLE-38

1	2	3	4	5	6	7	8	9	10
11	12	13	14	15	16	17	18	19	20
21	22	23	24	25	26	27	28	29	30
31	32	33	34	35	36	37	38	39	■
■	38	37	36	35	34	33	32	31	30
29	28	27	26	25	24	23	22	21	20
19	18	17	16	15	14	13	12	11	10
9	8	7	6	5	4	3	2	1	

Keep On Observing (KOO):

I like to find out solution of problems, I always remain content, I am always enterprising, I am good at communication, I am courageous, I always speak economically, I never hesitate, I am sober, I am not aggressive and so on....

CYCLE-39

1	2	3	4	5	6	7	8	9	10
11	12	13	14	15	16	17	18	19	20
21	22	23	24	25	26	27	28	29	30
31	32	33	34	35	36	37	38	39	40
39	38	37	36	35	34	33	32	31	30
29	28	27	26	25	24	23	22	21	20
19	18	17	16	15	14	13	12	11	10
9	8	7	6	5	4	3	2	1	

Keep On Observing (KOO):

I like to find out solution of problems, I always remain content, I am always enterprising, I am good at communication, I am courageous, I always speak economically, I never hesitate, I am sober, I am not aggressive and so on....

CYCLE-40

1	2	3	4	5	6	7	8	9	10
11	12	13	14	15	16	17	18	19	20
21	22	23	24	25	26	27	28	29	30
31	32	33	34	35	36	37	38	39	40
41									
									40
39	38	37	36	35	34	33	32	31	30
29	28	27	26	25	24	23	22	21	20
19	18	17	16	15	14	13	12	11	10
9	8	7	6	5	4	3	2	1	

Keep On Observing (KOO):

I like to find out solution of problems, I always remain content, I am always enterprising, I am good at communication, I am courageous, I always speak economically, I never hesitate, I am sober, I am not aggressive and so on....

CYCLE-41

1	2	3	4	5	6	7	8	9	10
11	12	13	14	15	16	17	18	19	20
21	22	23	24	25	26	27	28	29	30
31	32	33	34	35	36	37	38	39	40
41	42								
								41	40
39	38	37	36	35	34	33	32	31	30
29	28	27	26	25	24	23	22	21	20
19	18	17	16	15	14	13	12	11	10
9	8	7	6	5	4	3	2	1	

Keep On Observing (KOO):

I like to find out solution of problems, I always remain content, I am always enterprising, I am good at communication, I am courageous, I always speak economically, I never hesitate, I am sober, I am not aggressive and so on....

CYCLE-42

1	2	3	4	5	6	7	8	9	10
11	12	13	14	15	16	17	18	19	20
21	22	23	24	25	26	27	28	29	30
31	32	33	34	35	36	37	38	39	40
41	42	43							
							42	41	40
39	38	37	36	35	34	33	32	31	30
29	28	27	26	25	24	23	22	21	20
19	18	17	16	15	14	13	12	11	10
9	8	7	6	5	4	3	2	1	

Keep On Observing (KOO):

I like to find out solution of problems, I always remain content, I am always enterprising, I am good at communication, I am courageous, I always speak economically, I never hesitate, I am sober, I am not aggressive and so on....

CYCLE-43

1	2	3	4	5	6	7	8	9	10
11	12	13	14	15	16	17	18	19	20
21	22	23	24	25	26	27	28	29	30
31	32	33	34	35	36	37	38	39	40
41	42	43	44						
						43	42	41	40
39	38	37	36	35	34	33	32	31	30
29	28	27	26	25	24	23	22	21	20
19	18	17	16	15	14	13	12	11	10
9	8	7	6	5	4	3	2	1	

Keep On Observing (KOO):

I like to find out solution of problems, I always remain content, I am always enterprising, I am good at communication, I am courageous, I always speak economically, I never hesitate, I am sober, I am not aggressive and so on....

CYCLE-44

1	2	3	4	5	6	7	8	9	10
11	12	13	14	15	16	17	18	19	20
21	22	23	24	25	26	27	28	29	30
31	32	33	34	35	36	37	38	39	40
41	42	43	44	45					
					44	43	42	41	40
39	38	37	36	35	34	33	32	31	30
29	28	27	26	25	24	23	22	21	20
19	18	17	16	15	14	13	12	11	10
9	8	7	6	5	4	3	2	1	

Keep On Observing (KOO):

I like to find out solution of problems, I always remain content, I am always enterprising, I am good at communication, I am courageous, I always speak economically, I never hesitate, I am sober, I am not aggressive and so on....

CYCLE-45

1	2	3	4	5	6	7	8	9	10
11	12	13	14	15	16	17	18	19	20
21	22	23	24	25	26	27	28	29	30
31	32	33	34	35	36	37	38	39	40
41	42	43	44	45	46	███	███	███	███
███	███	███	███	45	44	43	42	41	40
39	38	37	36	35	34	33	32	31	30
29	28	27	26	25	24	23	22	21	20
19	18	17	16	15	14	13	12	11	10
9	8	7	6	5	4	3	2	1	

Keep On Observing (KOO):

I like to find out solution of problems, I always remain content, I am always enterprising, I am good at communication, I am courageous, I always speak economically, I never hesitate, I am sober, I am not aggressive and so on....

CYCLE-46

1	2	3	4	5	6	7	8	9	10
11	12	13	14	15	16	17	18	19	20
21	22	23	24	25	26	27	28	29	30
31	32	33	34	35	36	37	38	39	40
41	42	43	44	45	46	47	███	███	███
███	███	███	46	45	44	43	42	41	40
39	38	37	36	35	34	33	32	31	30
29	28	27	26	25	24	23	22	21	20
19	18	17	16	15	14	13	12	11	10
9	8	7	6	5	4	3	2	1	

Keep On Observing (KOO):

I like to find out solution of problems, I always remain content, I am always enterprising, I am good at communication, I am courageous, I always speak economically, I never hesitate, I am sober, I am not aggressive and so on....

CYCLE-47

1	2	3	4	5	6	7	8	9	10
11	12	13	14	15	16	17	18	19	20
21	22	23	24	25	26	27	28	29	30
31	32	33	34	35	36	37	38	39	40
41	42	43	44	45	46	47	48		
		47	46	45	44	43	42	41	40
39	38	37	36	35	34	33	32	31	30
29	28	27	26	25	24	23	22	21	20
19	18	17	16	15	14	13	12	11	10
9	8	7	6	5	4	3	2	1	

Keep On Observing (KOO):

I like to find out solution of problems, I always remain content, I am always enterprising, I am good at communication, I am courageous, I always speak economically, I never hesitate, I am sober, I am not aggressive and so on....

CYCLE-48

1	2	3	4	5	6	7	8	9	10
11	12	13	14	15	16	17	18	19	20
21	22	23	24	25	26	27	28	29	30
31	32	33	34	35	36	37	38	39	40
41	42	43	44	45	46	47	48	49	
	48	47	46	45	44	43	42	41	40
39	38	37	36	35	34	33	32	31	30
29	28	27	26	25	24	23	22	21	20
19	18	17	16	15	14	13	12	11	10
9	8	7	6	5	4	3	2	1	

Keep On Observing (KOO):

I like to find out solution of problems, I always remain content, I am always enterprising, I am good at communication,

I am courageous, I always speak economically, I never hesitate, I am sober, I am not aggressive and so on....

CYCLE-49

1	2	3	4	5	6	7	8	9	10
11	12	13	14	15	16	17	18	19	20
21	22	23	24	25	26	27	28	29	30
31	32	33	34	35	36	37	38	39	40
41	42	43	44	45	46	47	48	49	50
49	48	47	46	45	44	43	42	41	40
39	38	37	36	35	34	33	32	31	30
29	28	27	26	25	24	23	22	21	20
19	18	17	16	15	14	13	12	11	10
9	8	7	6	5	4	3	2	1	

Keep On Observing (KOO):

I like to find out solution of problems, I always remain content, I am always enterprising, I am good at communication, I am courageous, I always speak economically, I never hesitate, I am sober, I am not aggressive and so on....

CYCLE-50

1	2	3	4	5	6	7	8	9	10
11	12	13	14	15	16	17	18	19	20
21	22	23	24	25	26	27	28	29	30
31	32	33	34	35	36	37	38	39	40
41	42	43	44	45	46	47	48	49	50
51									
									50
49	48	47	46	45	44	43	42	41	40
39	38	37	36	35	34	33	32	31	30
29	28	27	26	25	24	23	22	21	20
19	18	17	16	15	14	13	12	11	10
9	8	7	6	5	4	3	2	1	

Keep On Observing (KOO):

I like to find out solution of problems, I always remain content, I am always enterprising, I am good at communication, I am courageous, I always speak economically, I never hesitate, I am sober, I am not aggressive and so on....

CYCLE-51

1	2	3	4	5	6	7	8	9	10
11	12	13	14	15	16	17	18	19	20
21	22	23	24	25	26	27	28	29	30
31	32	33	34	35	36	37	38	39	40
41	42	43	44	45	46	47	48	49	50
51	52								
								51	50
49	48	47	46	45	44	43	42	41	40
39	38	37	36	35	34	33	32	31	30
29	28	27	26	25	24	23	22	21	20
19	18	17	16	15	14	13	12	11	10
9	8	7	6	5	4	3	2	1	

Keep On Observing (KOO):

I like to find out solution of problems, I always remain content, I am always enterprising, I am good at communication, I am courageous, I always speak economically, I never hesitate, I am sober, I am not aggressive and so on....

CYCLE-52

1	2	3	4	5	6	7	8	9	10
11	12	13	14	15	16	17	18	19	20
21	22	23	24	25	26	27	28	29	30
31	32	33	34	35	36	37	38	39	40
41	42	43	44	45	46	47	48	49	50
51	52	53							
							52	51	50
49	48	47	46	45	44	43	42	41	40
39	38	37	36	35	34	33	32	31	30
29	28	27	26	25	24	23	22	21	20
19	18	17	16	15	14	13	12	11	10
9	8	7	6	5	4	3	2	1	

Keep On Observing (KOO):

I like to find out solution of problems, I always remain content, I am always enterprising, I am good at communication, I am courageous, I always speak economically, I never hesitate, I am sober, I am not aggressive and so on....

CYCLE-53

1	2	3	4	5	6	7	8	9	10
11	12	13	14	15	16	17	18	19	20
21	22	23	24	25	26	27	28	29	30
31	32	33	34	35	36	37	38	39	40
41	42	43	44	45	46	47	48	49	50
51	52	53	54						
						53	52	51	50
49	48	47	46	45	44	43	42	41	40
39	38	37	36	35	34	33	32	31	30
29	28	27	26	25	24	23	22	21	20
19	18	17	16	15	14	13	12	11	10
9	8	7	6	5	4	3	2	1	

Keep On Observing (KOO):

I like to find out solution of problems, I always remain content, I am always enterprising, I am good at communication, I am courageous, I always speak economically, I never hesitate, I am sober, I am not aggressive and so on....

CYCLE-54

1	2	3	4	5	6	7	8	9	10
11	12	13	14	15	16	17	18	19	20
21	22	23	24	25	26	27	28	29	30
31	32	33	34	35	36	37	38	39	40
41	42	43	44	45	46	47	48	49	50
51	52	53	54	55					
					54	53	52	51	50
49	48	47	46	45	44	43	42	41	40
39	38	37	36	35	34	33	32	31	30
29	28	27	26	25	24	23	22	21	20
19	18	17	16	15	14	13	12	11	10
9	8	7	6	5	4	3	2	1	

Keep On Observing (KOO):

I like to find out solution of problems, I always remain content, I am always enterprising, I am good at communication, I am courageous, I always speak economically, I never hesitate, I am sober, I am not aggressive and so on....

CYCLE-55

1	2	3	4	5	6	7	8	9	10
11	12	13	14	15	16	17	18	19	20
21	22	23	24	25	26	27	28	29	30
31	32	33	34	35	36	37	38	39	40
41	42	43	44	45	46	47	48	49	50
51	52	53	54	55	56	■	■	■	■
■	■	■	■	55	54	53	52	51	50
49	48	47	46	45	44	43	42	41	40
39	38	37	36	35	34	33	32	31	30
29	28	27	26	25	24	23	22	21	20
19	18	17	16	15	14	13	12	11	10
9	8	7	6	5	4	3	2	1	

Keep On Observing (KOO):

I like to find out solution of problems, I always remain content, I am always enterprising, I am good at communication, I am courageous, I always speak economically, I never hesitate, I am sober, I am not aggressive and so on....

CYCLE-56

1	2	3	4	5	6	7	8	9	10
11	12	13	14	15	16	17	18	19	20
21	22	23	24	25	26	27	28	29	30
31	32	33	34	35	36	37	38	39	40
41	42	43	44	45	46	47	48	49	50
51	52	53	54	55	56	57	■	■	■
■	■	■	56	55	54	53	52	51	50
49	48	47	46	45	44	43	42	41	40
39	38	37	36	35	34	33	32	31	30
29	28	27	26	25	24	23	22	21	20
19	18	17	16	15	14	13	12	11	10
9	8	7	6	5	4	3	2	1	

Keep On Observing (KOO):

I like to find out solution of problems, I always remain content, I am always enterprising, I am good at communication, I am courageous, I always speak economically, I never hesitate, I am sober, I am not aggressive and so on....

CYCLE-57

1	2	3	4	5	6	7	8	9	10
11	12	13	14	15	16	17	18	19	20
21	22	23	24	25	26	27	28	29	30
31	32	33	34	35	36	37	38	39	40
41	42	43	44	45	46	47	48	49	50
51	52	53	54	55	56	57	58	■	■
■	■	57	56	55	54	53	52	51	50
49	48	47	46	45	44	43	42	41	40
39	38	37	36	35	34	33	32	31	30
29	28	27	26	25	24	23	22	21	20
19	18	17	16	15	14	13	12	11	10
9	8	7	6	5	4	3	2	1	

Keep On Observing (KOO):

I like to find out solution of problems, I always remain content, I am always enterprising, I am good at communication, I am courageous, I always speak economically, I never hesitate, I am sober, I am not aggressive and so on....

CYCLE-58

1	2	3	4	5	6	7	8	9	10
11	12	13	14	15	16	17	18	19	20
21	22	23	24	25	26	27	28	29	30
31	32	33	34	35	36	37	38	39	40
41	42	43	44	45	46	47	48	49	50
51	52	53	54	55	56	57	58	59	■
■	58	57	56	55	54	53	52	51	50
49	48	47	46	45	44	43	42	41	40
39	38	37	36	35	34	33	32	31	30
29	28	27	26	25	24	23	22	21	20
19	18	17	16	15	14	13	12	11	10
9	8	7	6	5	4	3	2	1	

Keep On Observing (KOO):

I like to find out solution of problems, I always remain content, I am always enterprising, I am good at communication, I am courageous, I always speak economically, I never hesitate, I am sober, I am not aggressive and so on....

CYCLE-59

1	2	3	4	5	6	7	8	9	10
11	12	13	14	15	16	17	18	19	20
21	22	23	24	25	26	27	28	29	30
31	32	33	34	35	36	37	38	39	40
41	42	43	44	45	46	47	48	49	50
51	52	53	54	55	56	57	58	59	60
59	58	57	56	55	54	53	52	51	50
49	48	47	46	45	44	43	42	41	40
39	38	37	36	35	34	33	32	31	30
29	28	27	26	25	24	23	22	21	20
19	18	17	16	15	14	13	12	11	10
9	8	7	6	5	4	3	2	1	

Keep On Observing (KOO):

I like to find out solution of problems, I always remain content, I am always enterprising, I am good at communication, I am courageous, I always speak economically, I never hesitate, I am sober, I am not aggressive and so on....

CYCLE-60

1	2	3	4	5	6	7	8	9	10
11	12	13	14	15	16	17	18	19	20
21	22	23	24	25	26	27	28	29	30
31	32	33	34	35	36	37	38	39	40
41	42	43	44	45	46	47	48	49	50
51	52	53	54	55	56	57	58	59	60
61									
									60
59	58	57	56	55	54	53	52	51	50
49	48	47	46	45	44	43	42	41	40
39	38	37	36	35	34	33	32	31	30
29	28	27	26	25	24	23	22	21	20
19	18	17	16	15	14	13	12	11	10
9	8	7	6	5	4	3	2	1	

Keep On Observing (KOO):

I like to find out solution of problems, I always remain content, I am always enterprising, I am good at communication, I am courageous, I always speak economically, I never hesitate, I am sober, I am not aggressive and so on....

CYCLE-61

1	2	3	4	5	6	7	8	9	10
11	12	13	14	15	16	17	18	19	20
21	22	23	24	25	26	27	28	29	30
31	32	33	34	35	36	37	38	39	40
41	42	43	44	45	46	47	48	49	50
51	52	53	54	55	56	57	58	59	60
61	62								
								61	60
59	58	57	56	55	54	53	52	51	50
49	48	47	46	45	44	43	42	41	40
39	38	37	36	35	34	33	32	31	30
29	28	27	26	25	24	23	22	21	20
19	18	17	16	15	14	13	12	11	10
9	8	7	6	5	4	3	2	1	

Keep On Observing (KOO):

I like to find out solution of problems, I always remain content, I am always enterprising, I am good at communication, I am courageous, I always speak economically, I never hesitate, I am sober, I am not aggressive and so on....

CYCLE-62

1	2	3	4	5	6	7	8	9	10
11	12	13	14	15	16	17	18	19	20
21	22	23	24	25	26	27	28	29	30
31	32	33	34	35	36	37	38	39	40
41	42	43	44	45	46	47	48	49	50
51	52	53	54	55	56	57	58	59	60
61	62	63							
							62	61	60
59	58	57	56	55	54	53	52	51	50
49	48	47	46	45	44	43	42	41	40
39	38	37	36	35	34	33	32	31	30
29	28	27	26	25	24	23	22	21	20
19	18	17	16	15	14	13	12	11	10
9	8	7	6	5	4	3	2	1	

Keep On Observing (KOO):

I like to find out solution of problems, I always remain content, I am always enterprising, I am good at communication, I am courageous, I always speak economically, I never hesitate, I am sober, I am not aggressive and so on....

CYCLE-63

1	2	3	4	5	6	7	8	9	10
11	12	13	14	15	16	17	18	19	20
21	22	23	24	25	26	27	28	29	30
31	32	33	34	35	36	37	38	39	40
41	42	43	44	45	46	47	48	49	50
51	52	53	54	55	56	57	58	59	60
61	62	63	64						
						63	62	61	60
59	58	57	56	55	54	53	52	51	50
49	48	47	46	45	44	43	42	41	40
39	38	37	36	35	34	33	32	31	30
29	28	27	26	25	24	23	22	21	20
19	18	17	16	15	14	13	12	11	10
9	8	7	6	5	4	3	2	1	

Keep On Observing (KOO):

I like to find out solution of problems, I always remain content, I am always enterprising, I am good at communication, I am courageous, I always speak economically, I never hesitate, I am sober, I am not aggressive and so on....

CYCLE-64

1	2	3	4	5	6	7	8	9	10
11	12	13	14	15	16	17	18	19	20
21	22	23	24	25	26	27	28	29	30
31	32	33	34	35	36	37	38	39	40
41	42	43	44	45	46	47	48	49	50
51	52	53	54	55	56	57	58	59	60
61	62	63	64	65					
					64	63	62	61	60
59	58	57	56	55	54	53	52	51	50
49	48	47	46	45	44	43	42	41	40
39	38	37	36	35	34	33	32	31	30
29	28	27	26	25	24	23	22	21	20
19	18	17	16	15	14	13	12	11	10
9	8	7	6	5	4	3	2	1	

Keep On Observing (KOO):

I like to find out solution of problems, I always remain content, I am always enterprising, I am good at communication, I am courageous, I always speak economically, I never hesitate, I am sober, I am not aggressive and so on....

CYCLE-65

1	2	3	4	5	6	7	8	9	10
11	12	13	14	15	16	17	18	19	20
21	22	23	24	25	26	27	28	29	30
31	32	33	34	35	36	37	38	39	40
41	42	43	44	45	46	47	48	49	50
51	52	53	54	55	56	57	58	59	60
61	62	63	64	65	66				
					65	64	63	62	61	60
59	58	57	56	55	54	53	52	51	50
49	48	47	46	45	44	43	42	41	40
39	38	37	36	35	34	33	32	31	30
29	28	27	26	25	24	23	22	21	20
19	18	17	16	15	14	13	12	11	10
9	8	7	6	5	4	3	2	1	

Keep On Observing (KOO):

I like to find out solution of problems, I always remain content, I am always enterprising, I am good at communication, I am courageous, I always speak economically, I never hesitate, I am sober, I am not aggressive and so on....

CYCLE-66

1	2	3	4	5	6	7	8	9	10
11	12	13	14	15	16	17	18	19	20
21	22	23	24	25	26	27	28	29	30
31	32	33	34	35	36	37	38	39	40
41	42	43	44	45	46	47	48	49	50
51	52	53	54	55	56	57	58	59	60
61	62	63	64	65	66	67	■	■	■
■	■	■	66	65	64	63	62	61	60
59	58	57	56	55	54	53	52	51	50
49	48	47	46	45	44	43	42	41	40
39	38	37	36	35	34	33	32	31	30
29	28	27	26	25	24	23	22	21	20
19	18	17	16	15	14	13	12	11	10
9	8	7	6	5	4	3	2	1	

Keep On Observing (KOO):

I like to find out solution of problems, I always remain content, I am always enterprising, I am good at communication, I am courageous, I always speak economically, I never hesitate, I am sober, I am not aggressive and so on....

CYCLE-67

1	2	3	4	5	6	7	8	9	10
11	12	13	14	15	16	17	18	19	20
21	22	23	24	25	26	27	28	29	30
31	32	33	34	35	36	37	38	39	40
41	42	43	44	45	46	47	48	49	50
51	52	53	54	55	56	57	58	59	60
61	62	63	64	65	66	67	68	■	
■	67	66	65	64	63	62	61	60	
59	58	57	56	55	54	53	52	51	50
49	48	47	46	45	44	43	42	41	40
39	38	37	36	35	34	33	32	31	30
29	28	27	26	25	24	23	22	21	20
19	18	17	16	15	14	13	12	11	10
9	8	7	6	5	4	3	2	1	

Keep On Observing (KOO):

I like to find out solution of problems, I always remain content, I am always enterprising, I am good at communication, I am courageous, I always speak economically, I never hesitate, I am sober, I am not aggressive and so on....

CYCLE-68

1	2	3	4	5	6	7	8	9	10
11	12	13	14	15	16	17	18	19	20
21	22	23	24	25	26	27	28	29	30
31	32	33	34	35	36	37	38	39	40
41	42	43	44	45	46	47	48	49	50
51	52	53	54	55	56	57	58	59	60
61	62	63	64	65	66	67	68	69	■
■	68	67	66	65	64	63	62	61	60
59	58	57	56	55	54	53	52	51	50
49	48	47	46	45	44	43	42	41	40
39	38	37	36	35	34	33	32	31	30
29	28	27	26	25	24	23	22	21	20
19	18	17	16	15	14	13	12	11	10
9	8	7	6	5	4	3	2	1	

Keep On Observing (KOO):

I like to find out solution of problems, I always remain content, I am always enterprising, I am good at communication, I am courageous, I always speak economically, I never hesitate, I am sober, I am not aggressive and so on....

CYCLE-69

1	2	3	4	5	6	7	8	9	10
11	12	13	14	15	16	17	18	19	20
21	22	23	24	25	26	27	28	29	30
31	32	33	34	35	36	37	38	39	40
41	42	43	44	45	46	47	48	49	50
51	52	53	54	55	56	57	58	59	60
61	62	63	64	65	66	67	68	69	70
69	68	67	66	65	64	63	62	61	60
59	58	57	56	55	54	53	52	51	50
49	48	47	46	45	44	43	42	41	40
39	38	37	36	35	34	33	32	31	30
29	28	27	26	25	24	23	22	21	20
19	18	17	16	15	14	13	12	11	10
9	8	7	6	5	4	3	2	1	

Keep On Observing (KOO):

I like to find out solution of problems, I always remain content, I am always enterprising, I am good at communication, I am courageous, I always speak economically, I never hesitate, I am sober, I am not aggressive and so on....

CYCLE-70

1	2	3	4	5	6	7	8	9	10
11	12	13	14	15	16	17	18	19	20
21	22	23	24	25	26	27	28	29	30
31	32	33	34	35	36	37	38	39	40
41	42	43	44	45	46	47	48	49	50
51	52	53	54	55	56	57	58	59	60
61	62	63	64	65	66	67	68	69	70
71									
									70
69	68	67	66	65	64	63	62	61	60
59	58	57	56	55	54	53	52	51	50
49	48	47	46	45	44	43	42	41	40
39	38	37	36	35	34	33	32	31	30
29	28	27	26	25	24	23	22	21	20
19	18	17	16	15	14	13	12	11	10
9	8	7	6	5	4	3	2	1	

Keep On Observing (KOO):

I like to find out solution of problems, I always remain content, I am always enterprising, I am good at communication, I am courageous, I always speak economically, I never hesitate, I am sober, I am not aggressive and so on....

CYCLE-71

1	2	3	4	5	6	7	8	9	10
11	12	13	14	15	16	17	18	19	20
21	22	23	24	25	26	27	28	29	30
31	32	33	34	35	36	37	38	39	40
41	42	43	44	45	46	47	48	49	50
51	52	53	54	55	56	57	58	59	60
61	62	63	64	65	66	67	68	69	70
71	72								
								71	70
69	68	67	66	65	64	63	62	61	60
59	58	57	56	55	54	53	52	51	50
49	48	47	46	45	44	43	42	41	40
39	38	37	36	35	34	33	32	31	30
29	28	27	26	25	24	23	22	21	20
19	18	17	16	15	14	13	12	11	10
9	8	7	6	5	4	3	2	1	

Keep On Observing (KOO):

I like to find out solution of problems, I always remain content, I am always enterprising, I am good at communication, I am courageous, I always speak economically, I never hesitate, I am sober, I am not aggressive and so on....

CYCLE-72

1	2	3	4	5	6	7	8	9	10
11	12	13	14	15	16	17	18	19	20
21	22	23	24	25	26	27	28	29	30
31	32	33	34	35	36	37	38	39	40
41	42	43	44	45	46	47	48	49	50
51	52	53	54	55	56	57	58	59	60
61	62	63	64	65	66	67	68	69	70
71	72	73							
							72	71	70
69	68	67	66	65	64	63	62	61	60
59	58	57	56	55	54	53	52	51	50
49	48	47	46	45	44	43	42	41	40
39	38	37	36	35	34	33	32	31	30
29	28	27	26	25	24	23	22	21	20
19	18	17	16	15	14	13	12	11	10
9	8	7	6	5	4	3	2	1	

Keep On Observing (KOO):

I like to find out solution of problems, I always remain content, I am always enterprising, I am good at communication, I am courageous, I always speak economically, I never hesitate, I am sober, I am not aggressive and so on....

CYCLE-73

1	2	3	4	5	6	7	8	9	10
11	12	13	14	15	16	17	18	19	20
21	22	23	24	25	26	27	28	29	30
31	32	33	34	35	36	37	38	39	40
41	42	43	44	45	46	47	48	49	50
51	52	53	54	55	56	57	58	59	60
61	62	63	64	65	66	67	68	69	70
71	72	73	74						
							73	72	71	70
69	68	67	66	65	64	63	62	61	60
59	58	57	56	55	54	53	52	51	50
49	48	47	46	45	44	43	42	41	40
39	38	37	36	35	34	33	32	31	30
29	28	27	26	25	24	23	22	21	20
19	18	17	16	15	14	13	12	11	10
9	8	7	6	5	4	3	2	1	

Keep On Observing (KOO):

I like to find out solution of problems, I always remain content, I am always enterprising, I am good at communication, I am courageous, I always speak economically, I never hesitate, I am sober, I am not aggressive and so on....

CYCLE-74

1	2	3	4	5	6	7	8	9	10
11	12	13	14	15	16	17	18	19	20
21	22	23	24	25	26	27	28	29	30
31	32	33	34	35	36	37	38	39	40
41	42	43	44	45	46	47	48	49	50
51	52	53	54	55	56	57	58	59	60
61	62	63	64	65	66	67	68	69	70
71	72	73	74	75					
					74	73	72	71	70
69	68	67	66	65	64	63	62	61	60
59	58	57	56	55	54	53	52	51	50
49	48	47	46	45	44	43	42	41	40
39	38	37	36	35	34	33	32	31	30
29	28	27	26	25	24	23	22	21	20
19	18	17	16	15	14	13	12	11	10
9	8	7	6	5	4	3	2	1	

Keep On Observing (KOO):

I like to find out solution of problems, I always remain content, I am always enterprising, I am good at communication, I am courageous, I always speak economically, I never hesitate, I am sober, I am not aggressive and so on....

CYCLE-75

1	2	3	4	5	6	7	8	9	10
11	12	13	14	15	16	17	18	19	20
21	22	23	24	25	26	27	28	29	30
31	32	33	34	35	36	37	38	39	40
41	42	43	44	45	46	47	48	49	50
51	52	53	54	55	56	57	58	59	60
61	62	63	64	65	66	67	68	69	70
71	72	73	74	75	76				
				75	74	73	72	71	70
69	68	67	66	65	64	63	62	61	60
59	58	57	56	55	54	53	52	51	50
49	48	47	46	45	44	43	42	41	40
39	38	37	36	35	34	33	32	31	30
29	28	27	26	25	24	23	22	21	20
19	18	17	16	15	14	13	12	11	10
9	8	7	6	5	4	3	2	1	

Keep On Observing (KOO):

I like to find out solution of problems, I always remain content, I am always enterprising, I am good at communication, I am courageous, I always speak economically, I never hesitate, I am sober, I am not aggressive and so on....

CYCLE-76

1	2	3	4	5	6	7	8	9	10
11	12	13	14	15	16	17	18	19	20
21	22	23	24	25	26	27	28	29	30
31	32	33	34	35	36	37	38	39	40
41	42	43	44	45	46	47	48	49	50
51	52	53	54	55	56	57	58	59	60
61	62	63	64	65	66	67	68	69	70
71	72	73	74	75	76	77			
			76	75	74	73	72	71	70
69	68	67	66	65	64	63	62	61	60
59	58	57	56	55	54	53	52	51	50
49	48	47	46	45	44	43	42	41	40
39	38	37	36	35	34	33	32	31	30
29	28	27	26	25	24	23	22	21	20
19	18	17	16	15	14	13	12	11	10
9	8	7	6	5	4	3	2	1	

Keep On Observing (KOO):

I like to find out solution of problems, I always remain content, I am always enterprising, I am good at communication, I am courageous, I always speak economically, I never hesitate, I am sober, I am not aggressive and so on....

CYCLE-77

1	2	3	4	5	6	7	8	9	10
11	12	13	14	15	16	17	18	19	20
21	22	23	24	25	26	27	28	29	30
31	32	33	34	35	36	37	38	39	40
41	42	43	44	45	46	47	48	49	50
51	52	53	54	55	56	57	58	59	60
61	62	63	64	65	66	67	68	69	70
71	72	73	74	75	76	77	78		

		77	76	75	74	73	72	71	70
69	68	67	66	65	64	63	62	61	60
59	58	57	56	55	54	53	52	51	50
49	48	47	46	45	44	43	42	41	40
39	38	37	36	35	34	33	32	31	30
29	28	27	26	25	24	23	22	21	20
19	18	17	16	15	14	13	12	11	10
9	8	7	6	5	4	3	2	1	

Keep On Observing (KOO):

I like to find out solution of problems, I always remain content, I am always enterprising, I am good at communication, I am courageous, I always speak economically, I never hesitate, I am sober, I am not aggressive and so on....

CYCLE-78

1	2	3	4	5	6	7	8	9	10
11	12	13	14	15	16	17	18	19	20
21	22	23	24	25	26	27	28	29	30
31	32	33	34	35	36	37	38	39	40
41	42	43	44	45	46	47	48	49	50
51	52	53	54	55	56	57	58	59	60
61	62	63	64	65	66	67	68	69	70
71	72	73	74	75	76	77	78	79	
	78	77	76	75	74	73	72	71	70
69	68	67	66	65	64	63	62	61	60
59	58	57	56	55	54	53	52	51	50
49	48	47	46	45	44	43	42	41	40
39	38	37	36	35	34	33	32	31	30
29	28	27	26	25	24	23	22	21	20
19	18	17	16	15	14	13	12	11	10
9	8	7	6	5	4	3	2	1	

Keep On Observing (KOO):

I like to find out solution of problems, I always remain content, I am always enterprising, I am good at communication, I am courageous, I always speak economically, I never hesitate, I am sober, I am not aggressive and so on....

CYCLE-79

1	2	3	4	5	6	7	8	9	10
11	12	13	14	15	16	17	18	19	20
21	22	23	24	25	26	27	28	29	30
31	32	33	34	35	36	37	38	39	40
41	42	43	44	45	46	47	48	49	50
51	52	53	54	55	56	57	58	59	60
61	62	63	64	65	66	67	68	69	70
71	72	73	74	75	76	77	78	79	80
79	78	77	76	75	74	73	72	71	70
69	68	67	66	65	64	63	62	61	60
59	58	57	56	55	54	53	52	51	50
49	48	47	46	45	44	43	42	41	40
39	38	37	36	35	34	33	32	31	30
29	28	27	26	25	24	23	22	21	20
19	18	17	16	15	14	13	12	11	10
9	8	7	6	5	4	3	2	1	

Keep On Observing (KOO):

I like to find out solution of problems, I always remain content, I am always enterprising, I am good at communication, I am courageous, I always speak economically, I never hesitate, I am sober, I am not aggressive and so on....

CYCLE-80

1	2	3	4	5	6	7	8	9	10
11	12	13	14	15	16	17	18	19	20
21	22	23	24	25	26	27	28	29	30
31	32	33	34	35	36	37	38	39	40
41	42	43	44	45	46	47	48	49	50
51	52	53	54	55	56	57	58	59	60
61	62	63	64	65	66	67	68	69	70
71	72	73	74	75	76	77	78	79	80
81									
									80
79	78	77	76	75	74	73	72	71	70
69	68	67	66	65	64	63	62	61	60
59	58	57	56	55	54	53	52	51	50
49	48	47	46	45	44	43	42	41	40
39	38	37	36	35	34	33	32	31	30
29	28	27	26	25	24	23	22	21	20
19	18	17	16	15	14	13	12	11	10
9	8	7	6	5	4	3	2	1	

Keep On Observing (KOO):

I like to find out solution of problems, I always remain content, I am always enterprising, I am good at communication, I am courageous, I always speak economically, I never hesitate, I am sober, I am not aggressive and so on....

CYCLE-81

1	2	3	4	5	6	7	8	9	10
11	12	13	14	15	16	17	18	19	20
21	22	23	24	25	26	27	28	29	30
31	32	33	34	35	36	37	38	39	40
41	42	43	44	45	46	47	48	49	50
51	52	53	54	55	56	57	58	59	60
61	62	63	64	65	66	67	68	69	70
71	72	73	74	75	76	77	78	79	80
81	82								
								81	80
79	78	77	76	75	74	73	72	71	70
69	68	67	66	65	64	63	62	61	60
59	58	57	56	55	54	53	52	51	50
49	48	47	46	45	44	43	42	41	40
39	38	37	36	35	34	33	32	31	30
29	28	27	26	25	24	23	22	21	20
19	18	17	16	15	14	13	12	11	10
9	8	7	6	5	4	3	2	1	

Keep On Observing (KOO):

I like to find out solution of problems, I always remain content, I am always enterprising, I am good at communication, I am courageous, I always speak economically, I never hesitate, I am sober, I am not aggressive and so on....

CYCLE-82

1	2	3	4	5	6	7	8	9	10
11	12	13	14	15	16	17	18	19	20
21	22	23	24	25	26	27	28	29	30
31	32	33	34	35	36	37	38	39	40
41	42	43	44	45	46	47	48	49	50
51	52	53	54	55	56	57	58	59	60
61	62	63	64	65	66	67	68	69	70
71	72	73	74	75	76	77	78	79	80
81	82	83							
							82	81	80
79	78	77	76	75	74	73	72	71	70
69	68	67	66	65	64	63	62	61	60
59	58	57	56	55	54	53	52	51	50
49	48	47	46	45	44	43	42	41	40
39	38	37	36	35	34	33	32	31	30
29	28	27	26	25	24	23	22	21	20
19	18	17	16	15	14	13	12	11	10
9	8	7	6	5	4	3	2	1	

Keep On Observing (KOO):

I like to find out solution of problems, I always remain content, I am always enterprising, I am good at communication, I am courageous, I always speak economically, I never hesitate, I am sober, I am not aggressive and so on....

CYCLE-83

1	2	3	4	5	6	7	8	9	10
11	12	13	14	15	16	17	18	19	20
21	22	23	24	25	26	27	28	29	30
31	32	33	34	35	36	37	38	39	40
41	42	43	44	45	46	47	48	49	50
51	52	53	54	55	56	57	58	59	60
61	62	63	64	65	66	67	68	69	70
71	72	73	74	75	76	77	78	79	80
81	82	83	84						
						83	82	81	80
79	78	77	76	75	74	73	72	71	70
69	68	67	66	65	64	63	62	61	60
59	58	57	56	55	54	53	52	51	50
49	48	47	46	45	44	43	42	41	40
39	38	37	36	35	34	33	32	31	30
29	28	27	26	25	24	23	22	21	20
19	18	17	16	15	14	13	12	11	10
9	8	7	6	5	4	3	2	1	

Keep On Observing (KOO):

I like to find out solution of problems, I always remain content, I am always enterprising, I am good at communication, I am courageous, I always speak economically, I never hesitate, I am sober, I am not aggressive and so on....

CYCLE-84

1	2	3	4	5	6	7	8	9	10
11	12	13	14	15	16	17	18	19	20
21	22	23	24	25	26	27	28	29	30
31	32	33	34	35	36	37	38	39	40
41	42	43	44	45	46	47	48	49	50
51	52	53	54	55	56	57	58	59	60
61	62	63	64	65	66	67	68	69	70
71	72	73	74	75	76	77	78	79	80
81	82	83	84	85					
					84	83	82	81	80
79	78	77	76	75	74	73	72	71	70
69	68	67	66	65	64	63	62	61	60
59	58	57	56	55	54	53	52	51	50
49	48	47	46	45	44	43	42	41	40
39	38	37	36	35	34	33	32	31	30
29	28	27	26	25	24	23	22	21	20
19	18	17	16	15	14	13	12	11	10
9	8	7	6	5	4	3	2	1	

Keep On Observing (KOO):

I like to find out solution of problems, I always remain content, I am always enterprising, I am good at communication, I am courageous, I always speak economically, I never hesitate, I am sober, I am not aggressive and so on....

CYCLE-85

1	2	3	4	5	6	7	8	9	10
11	12	13	14	15	16	17	18	19	20
21	22	23	24	25	26	27	28	29	30
31	32	33	34	35	36	37	38	39	40
41	42	43	44	45	46	47	48	49	50
51	52	53	54	55	56	57	58	59	60
61	62	63	64	65	66	67	68	69	70
71	72	73	74	75	76	77	78	79	80
81	82	83	84	85	86				
				85	84	83	82	81	80
79	78	77	76	75	74	73	72	71	70
69	68	67	66	65	64	63	62	61	60
59	58	57	56	55	54	53	52	51	50
49	48	47	46	45	44	43	42	41	40
39	38	37	36	35	34	33	32	31	30
29	28	27	26	25	24	23	22	21	20
19	18	17	16	15	14	13	12	11	10
9	8	7	6	5	4	3	2	1	

Keep On Observing (KOO):

I like to find out solution of problems, I always remain content, I am always enterprising, I am good at communication, I am courageous, I always speak economically, I never hesitate, I am sober, I am not aggressive and so on....

CYCLE-86

1	2	3	4	5	6	7	8	9	10
11	12	13	14	15	16	17	18	19	20
21	22	23	24	25	26	27	28	29	30
31	32	33	34	35	36	37	38	39	40
41	42	43	44	45	46	47	48	49	50
51	52	53	54	55	56	57	58	59	60
61	62	63	64	65	66	67	68	69	70
71	72	73	74	75	76	77	78	79	80
81	82	83	84	85	86	87			
			86	85	84	83	82	81	80
79	78	77	76	75	74	73	72	71	70
69	68	67	66	65	64	63	62	61	60
59	58	57	56	55	54	53	52	51	50
49	48	47	46	45	44	43	42	41	40
39	38	37	36	35	34	33	32	31	30
29	28	27	26	25	24	23	22	21	20
19	18	17	16	15	14	13	12	11	10
9	8	7	6	5	4	3	2	1	

Keep On Observing (KOO):

I like to find out solution of problems, I always remain content, I am always enterprising, I am good at communication, I am courageous, I always speak economically, I never hesitate, I am sober, I am not aggressive and so on....

CYCLE-87

1	2	3	4	5	6	7	8	9	10
11	12	13	14	15	16	17	18	19	20
21	22	23	24	25	26	27	28	29	30
31	32	33	34	35	36	37	38	39	40
41	42	43	44	45	46	47	48	49	50
51	52	53	54	55	56	57	58	59	60
61	62	63	64	65	66	67	68	69	70
71	72	73	74	75	76	77	78	79	80
81	82	83	84	85	86	87	88		
		87	86	85	84	83	82	81	80
79	78	77	76	75	74	73	72	71	70
69	68	67	66	65	64	63	62	61	60
59	58	57	56	55	54	53	52	51	50
49	48	47	46	45	44	43	42	41	40
39	38	37	36	35	34	33	32	31	30
29	28	27	26	25	24	23	22	21	20
19	18	17	16	15	14	13	12	11	10
9	8	7	6	5	4	3	2	1	

Keep On Observing (KOO):

I like to find out solution of problems, I always remain content, I am always enterprising, I am good at communication, I am courageous, I always speak economically, I never hesitate, I am sober, I am not aggressive and so on....

CYCLE-88

1	2	3	4	5	6	7	8	9	10
11	12	13	14	15	16	17	18	19	20
21	22	23	24	25	26	27	28	29	30
31	32	33	34	35	36	37	38	39	40
41	42	43	44	45	46	47	48	49	50
51	52	53	54	55	56	57	58	59	60
61	62	63	64	65	66	67	68	69	70
71	72	73	74	75	76	77	78	79	80
81	82	83	84	85	86	87	88	89	
	88	87	86	85	84	83	82	81	80
79	78	77	76	75	74	73	72	71	70
69	68	67	66	65	64	63	62	61	60
59	58	57	56	55	54	53	52	51	50
49	48	47	46	45	44	43	42	41	40
39	38	37	36	35	34	33	32	31	30
29	28	27	26	25	24	23	22	21	20
19	18	17	16	15	14	13	12	11	10
9	8	7	6	5	4	3	2	1	

Keep On Observing (KOO):

I like to find out solution of problems, I always remain content, I am always enterprising, I am good at communication, I am courageous, I always speak economically, I never hesitate, I am sober, I am not aggressive and so on....

CYCLE-89

1	2	3	4	5	6	7	8	9	10
11	12	13	14	15	16	17	18	19	20
21	22	23	24	25	26	27	28	29	30
31	32	33	34	35	36	37	38	39	40
41	42	43	44	45	46	47	48	49	50
51	52	53	54	55	56	57	58	59	60
61	62	63	64	65	66	67	68	69	70
71	72	73	74	75	76	77	78	79	80
81	82	83	84	85	86	87	88	89	90
89	88	87	86	85	84	83	82	81	80
79	78	77	76	75	74	73	72	71	70
69	68	67	66	65	64	63	62	61	60
59	58	57	56	55	54	53	52	51	50
49	48	47	46	45	44	43	42	41	40
39	38	37	36	35	34	33	32	31	30
29	28	27	26	25	24	23	22	21	20
19	18	17	16	15	14	13	12	11	10
9	8	7	6	5	4	3	2	1	

Keep On Observing (KOO):

I like to find out solution of problems, I always remain content, I am always enterprising, I am good at communication, I am courageous, I always speak economically, I never hesitate, I am sober, I am not aggressive and so on....

CYCLE-90

1	2	3	4	5	6	7	8	9	10
11	12	13	14	15	16	17	18	19	20
21	22	23	24	25	26	27	28	29	30
31	32	33	34	35	36	37	38	39	40
41	42	43	44	45	46	47	48	49	50
51	52	53	54	55	56	57	58	59	60
61	62	63	64	65	66	67	68	69	70
71	72	73	74	75	76	77	78	79	80
81	82	83	84	85	86	87	88	89	90
91									
									90
89	88	87	86	85	84	83	82	81	80
79	78	77	76	75	74	73	72	71	70
69	68	67	66	65	64	63	62	61	60
59	58	57	56	55	54	53	52	51	50
49	48	47	46	45	44	43	42	41	40
39	38	37	36	35	34	33	32	31	30
29	28	27	26	25	24	23	22	21	20
19	18	17	16	15	14	13	12	11	10
9	8	7	6	5	4	3	2	1	

Keep On Observing (KOO):

I like to find out solution of problems, I always remain content, I am always enterprising, I am good at communication, I am courageous, I always speak economically, I never hesitate, I am sober, I am not aggressive and so on....

CYCLE-91

1	2	3	4	5	6	7	8	9	10
11	12	13	14	15	16	17	18	19	20
21	22	23	24	25	26	27	28	29	30
31	32	33	34	35	36	37	38	39	40
41	42	43	44	45	46	47	48	49	50
51	52	53	54	55	56	57	58	59	60
61	62	63	64	65	66	67	68	69	70
71	72	73	74	75	76	77	78	79	80
81	82	83	84	85	86	87	88	89	90
91	92								
								91	90
89	88	87	86	85	84	83	82	81	80
79	78	77	76	75	74	73	72	71	70
69	68	67	66	65	64	63	62	61	60
59	58	57	56	55	54	53	52	51	50
49	48	47	46	45	44	43	42	41	40
39	38	37	36	35	34	33	32	31	30
29	28	27	26	25	24	23	22	21	20
19	18	17	16	15	14	13	12	11	10
9	8	7	6	5	4	3	2	1	

Keep On Observing (KOO):

I like to find out solution of problems, I always remain content, I am always enterprising, I am good at communication, I am courageous, I always speak economically, I never hesitate, I am sober, I am not aggressive and so on....speak economically, I never hesitate, I am sober, I am not aggressive and so on....

CYCLE-92

1	2	3	4	5	6	7	8	9	10
11	12	13	14	15	16	17	18	19	20
21	22	23	24	25	26	27	28	29	30
31	32	33	34	35	36	37	38	39	40
41	42	43	44	45	46	47	48	49	50
51	52	53	54	55	56	57	58	59	60
61	62	63	64	65	66	67	68	69	70
71	72	73	74	75	76	77	78	79	80
81	82	83	84	85	86	87	88	89	90
91	92	93							
							92	91	90
89	88	87	86	85	84	83	82	81	80
79	78	77	76	75	74	73	72	71	70
69	68	67	66	65	64	63	62	61	60
59	58	57	56	55	54	53	52	51	50
49	48	47	46	45	44	43	42	41	40
39	38	37	36	35	34	33	32	31	30
29	28	27	26	25	24	23	22	21	20
19	18	17	16	15	14	13	12	11	10
9	8	7	6	5	4	3	2	1	

Keep On Observing (KOO):

I like to find out solution of problems, I always remain content, I am always enterprising, I am good at communication, I am courageous, I always speak economically, I never hesitate, I am sober, I am not aggressive and so on....

CYCLE-93

1	2	3	4	5	6	7	8	9	10
11	12	13	14	15	16	17	18	19	20
21	22	23	24	25	26	27	28	29	30
31	32	33	34	35	36	37	38	39	40
41	42	43	44	45	46	47	48	49	50
51	52	53	54	55	56	57	58	59	60
61	62	63	64	65	66	67	68	69	70
71	72	73	74	75	76	77	78	79	80
81	82	83	84	85	86	87	88	89	90
91	92	93	94						
						93	92	91	90
89	88	87	86	85	84	83	82	81	80
79	78	77	76	75	74	73	72	71	70
69	68	67	66	65	64	63	62	61	60
59	58	57	56	55	54	53	52	51	50
49	48	47	46	45	44	43	42	41	40
39	38	37	36	35	34	33	32	31	30
29	28	27	26	25	24	23	22	21	20
19	18	17	16	15	14	13	12	11	10
9	8	7	6	5	4	3	2	1	

Keep On Observing (KOO):

I like to find out solution of problems, I always remain content, I am always enterprising, I am good at communication, I am courageous, I always speak economically, I never hesitate, I am sober, I am not aggressive and so on....

CYCLE- 94

1	2	3	4	5	6	7	8	9	10
11	12	13	14	15	16	17	18	19	20
21	22	23	24	25	26	27	28	29	30
31	32	33	34	35	36	37	38	39	40
41	42	43	44	45	46	47	48	49	50
51	52	53	54	55	56	57	58	59	60
61	62	63	64	65	66	67	68	69	70
71	72	73	74	75	76	77	78	79	80
81	82	83	84	85	86	87	88	89	90
91	92	93	94	95					
					94	93	92	91	90
89	88	87	86	85	84	83	82	81	80
79	78	77	76	75	74	73	72	71	70
69	68	67	66	65	64	63	62	61	60
59	58	57	56	55	54	53	52	51	50
49	48	47	46	45	44	43	42	41	40
39	38	37	36	35	34	33	32	31	30
29	28	27	26	25	24	23	22	21	20
19	18	17	16	15	14	13	12	11	10
9	8	7	6	5	4	3	2	1	

Keep On Observing (KOO):

I like to find out solution of problems, I always remain content, I am always enterprising, I am good at communication, I am courageous, I always speak economically, I never hesitate, I am sober, I am not aggressive and so on.......

CYCLE-95

1	2	3	4	5	6	7	8	9	10
11	12	13	14	15	16	17	18	19	20
21	22	23	24	25	26	27	28	29	30
31	32	33	34	35	36	37	38	39	40
41	42	43	44	45	46	47	48	49	50
51	52	53	54	55	56	57	58	59	60
61	62	63	64	65	66	67	68	69	70
71	72	73	74	75	76	77	78	79	80
81	82	83	84	85	86	87	88	89	90
91	92	93	94	95	96				
				95	94	93	92	91	90
89	88	87	86	85	84	83	82	81	80
79	78	77	76	75	74	73	72	71	70
69	68	67	66	65	64	63	62	61	60
59	58	57	56	55	54	53	52	51	50
49	48	47	46	45	44	43	42	41	40
39	38	37	36	35	34	33	32	31	30
29	28	27	26	25	24	23	22	21	20
19	18	17	16	15	14	13	12	11	10
9	8	7	6	5	4	3	2	1	

Keep On Observing (KOO):

I like to find out solution of problems, I always remain content, I am always enterprising, I am good at communication, I am courageous, I always speak economically, I never hesitate, I am sober, I am not aggressive and so on....

CYCLE-96

1	2	3	4	5	6	7	8	9	10
11	12	13	14	15	16	17	18	19	20
21	22	23	24	25	26	27	28	29	30
31	32	33	34	35	36	37	38	39	40
41	42	43	44	45	46	47	48	49	50
51	52	53	54	55	56	57	58	59	60
61	62	63	64	65	66	67	68	69	70
71	72	73	74	75	76	77	78	79	80
81	82	83	84	85	86	87	88	89	90
91	92	93	94	95	96	97			
			96	95	94	93	92	91	90
89	88	87	86	85	84	83	82	81	80
79	78	77	76	75	74	73	72	71	70
69	68	67	66	65	64	63	62	61	60
59	58	57	56	55	54	53	52	51	50
49	48	47	46	45	44	43	42	41	40
39	38	37	36	35	34	33	32	31	30
29	28	27	26	25	24	23	22	21	20
19	18	17	16	15	14	13	12	11	10
9	8	7	6	5	4	3	2	1	

Keep On Observing (KOO):

I like to find out solution of problems, I always remain content, I am always enterprising, I am good at communication, I am courageous, I always speak economically, I never hesitate, I am sober, I am not aggressive and so on....

CYCLE-97

1	2	3	4	5	6	7	8	9	10
11	12	13	14	15	16	17	18	19	20
21	22	23	24	25	26	27	28	29	30
31	32	33	34	35	36	37	38	39	40
41	42	43	44	45	46	47	48	49	50
51	52	53	54	55	56	57	58	59	60
61	62	63	64	65	66	67	68	69	70
71	72	73	74	75	76	77	78	79	80
81	82	83	84	85	86	87	88	89	90
91	92	93	94	95	96	97	98		
		97	96	95	94	93	92	91	90
89	88	87	86	85	84	83	82	81	80
79	78	77	76	75	74	73	72	71	70
69	68	67	66	65	64	63	62	61	60
59	58	57	56	55	54	53	52	51	50
49	48	47	46	45	44	43	42	41	40
39	38	37	36	35	34	33	32	31	30
29	28	27	26	25	24	23	22	21	20
19	18	17	16	15	14	13	12	11	10
9	8	7	6	5	4	3	2	1	

Keep On Observing (KOO):

I like to find out solution of problems, I always remain content, I am always enterprising, I am good at communication, I am courageous, I always speak economically, I never hesitate, I am sober, I am not aggressive and so on....

CYCLE-98

1	2	3	4	5	6	7	8	9	10
11	12	13	14	15	16	17	18	19	20
21	22	23	24	25	26	27	28	29	30
31	32	33	34	35	36	37	38	39	40
41	42	43	44	45	46	47	48	49	50
51	52	53	54	55	56	57	58	59	60
61	62	63	64	65	66	67	68	69	70
71	72	73	74	75	76	77	78	79	80
81	82	83	84	85	86	87	88	89	90
91	92	93	94	95	96	97	98	99	
	98	97	96	95	94	93	92	91	90
89	88	87	86	85	84	83	82	81	80
79	78	77	76	75	74	73	72	71	70
69	68	67	66	65	64	63	62	61	60
59	58	57	56	55	54	53	52	51	50
49	48	47	46	45	44	43	42	41	40
39	38	37	36	35	34	33	32	31	30
29	28	27	26	25	24	23	22	21	20
19	18	17	16	15	14	13	12	11	10
9	8	7	6	5	4	3	2	1	

Keep On Observing (KOO):

I like to find out solution of problems, I always remain content, I am always enterprising, I am good at communication, I am courageous, I always speak economically, I never hesitate, I am sober, I am not aggressive and so on....

CYCLE-99

1	2	3	4	5	6	7	8	9	10
11	12	13	14	15	16	17	18	19	20
21	22	23	24	25	26	27	28	29	30
31	32	33	34	35	36	37	38	39	40
41	42	43	44	45	46	47	48	49	50
51	52	53	54	55	56	57	58	59	60
61	62	63	64	65	66	67	68	69	70
71	72	73	74	75	76	77	78	79	80
81	82	83	84	85	86	87	88	89	90
91	92	93	94	95	96	97	98	99	100
99	98	97	96	95	94	93	92	91	90
89	88	87	86	85	84	83	82	81	80
79	78	77	76	75	74	73	72	71	70
69	68	67	66	65	64	63	62	61	60
59	58	57	56	55	54	53	52	51	50
49	48	47	46	45	44	43	42	41	40
39	38	37	36	35	34	33	32	31	30
29	28	27	26	25	24	23	22	21	20
19	18	17	16	15	14	13	12	11	10
9	8	7	6	5	4	3	2	1	

Keep On Observing (KOO):

I like to find out solution of problems, I always remain content, I am always enterprising, I am good at communication, I am courageous, I always speak economically, I never hesitate, I am sober, I am not aggressive and so on....

CHAPTER-V

INTROSPECTION

What you will achieve after successful exercising these patterns, for that you have to do an introspective exercise time and again regularly:

Please check what you achieved and able to exercise now in your life

Sr. No.	Qualities/ characteristics	Posses by a mathe- matised mind	Posses by a success full mind	Posses by a happy mind	Posses by a pattern	Posses by you		
						Begin- ning	Con- soli- dating	Exer- cising
1	like to find out solution of problems	yes	yes	Yes	yes			
2	remain content	yes	yes	Yes	yes			
3	enterprising	yes	yes	Yes	yes			
4	good at communication	yes	yes	Yes	yes			
5	courageous	yes	yes	Yes	yes			
6	speak economically	yes	yes	Yes	yes			
7	never hesitate	yes	yes	Yes	yes			
8	Sober	yes	yes	Yes	yes			
9	aggressive	no	no	No	no			
10	straight forward	yes	Yes	Yes	yes			
11	daring	yes	yes	Yes	Yes			
12	enthusiastic	yes	yes	Yes	yes			
13	risk taking	yes	calcu- lated	calcu- lated	calcu- lated			
14	bold	yes	yes	Yes	Yes			
15	can take stress	yes	Yes	Yes	yes			
16	dominant	yes	no	No	No			
17	influenced by facts than by feeling	yes	Yes	Yes	yes			
18	Hard working	yes	yes	yes	Yes			
19	easy going never in hurry	yes	yes	Yes	yes			
20	quick decision	yes	yes	yes	Yes			
21	communicative	yes	yes	Yes	yes			
22	free from guilt	yes	yes	yes	yes			
23	never hesitate	yes	yes	yes	yes			
24	Secure	yes	yes	Yes	yes			
25	never act according to others	yes	yes	yes	yes			
26	capable of getting things done	yes	yes	Yes	yes			
27	assertive behaviour	yes	yes	yes	yes			
28	develop their own sets of rules	yes	If re- quired	If re- quired	If re- quired			

29	self disciplined	yes	yes	yes	Yes			
30	abstract thinking	yes	yes	Yes	yes			
31	reliable behaviour	yes	yes	yes	yes			
32	experimentive	yes	yes	yes	yes			
33	impulsive	yes	no	no	no			
34	self destructive	no	no	no	no			
35	social	yes	yes	yes	yes			
36	cope with routine life		yes	yes	yes			
37	highly self motivated	yes	yes	Yes	yes			
38	practical	yes	yes	yes	yes			
39	mindful	yes	yes	yes	yes			
40	lost in the world of dreams	no	no	no	no			
41	participating	yes	yes	yes	yes			
42	Cautious	yes	yes	Yes	yes			
43	likes people	yes	yes	yes	yes			
44	open minded	yes	yes	yes	yes			
45	resolve conflicts	yes	yes	Yes	yes			
46	emotionally mature	yes	yes	Yes	yes			
47	realistic	yes	yes	yes	yes			
48	Cheerful	yes	yes	Yes	yes			
49	Intuitive	yes	yes	yes	yes			
50	keep things under control	yes	yes	yes	yes			
51	Competitor of self	yes	yes	Yes	yes			
52	self confident	yes	yes	Yes	yes			
53	Assertive	yes	yes	Yes	yes			
54	Mature	yes	yes	Yes	yes			
55	Relax	yes	yes	Yes	yes			
56	Adaptive	yes	yes	Yes	yes			
57	Flexible	yes	yes	Yes	yes			
58	open to change	yes	yes	Yes	yes			
59	accommodative	yes	yes	Yes	yes			
60	socially active	yes	yes	Yes	yes			
61	cultural interests	yes	yes	Yes	yes			
62	down to earth	yes	yes	Yes	yes			
63	friendly nature	yes	yes	Yes	yes			
64	Sociable	yes	yes	Yes	yes			
65	good reasoning	yes	yes	Yes	yes			
66	intelligent	yes	yes	Yes	yes			
67	hard to fool	yes	yes	Yes	yes			

Express your feeling about your accomplishments through mathyogs9211:

....
....
....
....
....
....
....
....
....
....
....
....
....
....
....
....
....
....
....
....
....
....
....
....
....
....
....
....
....
....

CHAPTER-VI

COUNTING BY TWO'S

Group 2: Counting by two's

PATTERN-1	PATTERN-2
1	2
3	4
5	6
7	8
9	10
11	12
13	14
15	16
17	18
19	20
21	22
23	24
25	26
27	28
29	30
31	32
33	34

35	36
37	38
39	40
41	42
43	44
45	46
47	48
49	50
51	52
53	54
55	56
57	58
59	60
61	62
63	64
65	66
67	68
69	70
71	72
73	74
75	76
77	78
79	80
81	82
83	84
85	86
87	88
89	90
91	92
93	94
95	96
97	98
99	100

PATTERN-1

CYCLE-1

1	3	1							

Keep On Observing (KOO):

I like to find out solution of problems, I always remain content, I am always enterprising, I am good at communication, I am courageous, I always speak economically, I never hesitate, I am sober, I am not aggressive and so on....

CYCLE-2

1	3	5	3	1					

Keep On Observing (KOO):

I like to find out solution of problems, I always remain content, I am always enterprising, I am good at communication, I am courageous, I always speak economically, I never hesitate, I am sober, I am not aggressive and so on....

CYCLE-3

1	3	5	7	5	3	1			

Keep On Observing (KOO):

I like to find out solution of problems, I always remain content, I am always enterprising, I am good at communication, I am courageous, I always speak economically, I never hesitate, I am sober, I am not aggressive and so on....

CYCLE-4

1	3	5	7	9	7	5	3	1	

Keep On Observing (KOO):

I like to find out solution of problems, I always remain content, I am always enterprising, I am good at communication, I am courageous, I always speak economically, I never hesitate, I am sober, I am not aggressive and so on....

CYCLE-5

1	3	5	7	9	11	9	7	5	3
1									

Keep On Observing (KOO):

I like to find out solution of problems, I always remain content, I am always enterprising, I am good at communication, I am courageous, I always speak economically, I never hesitate, I am sober, I am not aggressive and so on.....

CYCLE-6

1	3	5	7	9	11	13	11	9	7
5	3	1							

Keep On Observing (KOO):

I like to find out solution of problems, I always remain content, I am always enterprising, I am good at communication, I am courageous, I always speak economically, I never hesitate, I am sober, I am not aggressive and so on....

CYCLE-7

1	3	5	7	9	11	13	15	13	11
9	7	5	3	1					

Keep On Observing (KOO):

I like to find out solution of problems, I always remain content, I am always enterprising, I am good at communication, I am courageous, I always speak economically, I never hesitate, I am sober, I am not aggressive and so on....

CYCLE-8

1	3	5	7	9	11	13	15	17	15
13	11	9	7	5	3	1			

Keep On Observing (KOO):

I like to find out solution of problems, I always remain content, I am always enterprising, I am good at communication, I am courageous, I always speak economically, I never hesitate, I am sober, I am not aggressive and so on....

CYCLE-9

1	3	5	7	9	11	13	15	17	19
									17
15	13	11	9	7	5	3	1		

Keep On Observing (KOO):

I like to find out solution of problems, I always remain content, I am always enterprising, I am good at communication, I am courageous, I always speak economically, I never hesitate, I am sober, I am not aggressive and so on....

CYCLE-10

1	3	5	7	9	11	13	15	17	19
21									
								19	17
25	23	21	19	17	15	13	11	9	7
15	13	11	9	7	5	3	1		

Keep On Observing (KOO):

I like to find out solution of problems, I always remain content, I am always enterprising, I am good at communication, I am courageous, I always speak economically, I never hesitate, I am sober, I am not aggressive and so on....

CYCLE-11

1	3	5	7	9	11	13	15	17	19
21	23								
		21	19	17	15	13	11	9	7
15	13	11	9	7	5	3	1		

Keep On Observing (KOO):

I like to find out solution of problems, I always remain content, I am always enterprising, I am good at communication, I am courageous, I always speak economically, I never hesitate, I am sober, I am not aggressive and so on....

CYCLE-12

1	3	5	7	9	11	13	15	17	19
21	23	25							
	23	21	19	17	15	13	11	9	7
15	13	11	9	7	5	3	1		

Keep On Observing (KOO):

I like to find out solution of problems, I always remain content, I am always enterprising, I am good at communication, I am courageous, I always speak economically, I never hesitate, I am sober, I am not aggressive and so on....

CYCLE-13

1	3	5	7	9	11	13	15	17	19
21	23	25	27						
25	23	21	19	17	15	13	11	9	7
15	13	11	9	7	5	3	1		

Keep On Observing (KOO):

I like to find out solution of problems, I always remain content, I am always enterprising, I am good at communication, I am courageous, I always speak economically, I never hesitate, I am sober, I am not aggressive and so on....

CYCLE-14

1	3	5	7	9	11	13	15	17	19
21	23	25	27	29					
									27
25	23	21	19	17	15	13	11	9	7
15	13	11	9	7	5	3	1		

Keep On Observing (KOO):

I like to find out solution of problems, I always remain content, I am always enterprising, I am good at communication, I am courageous, I always speak economically, I never hesitate, I am sober, I am not aggressive and so on....

CYCLE-15

1	3	5	7	9	11	13	15	17	19
21	23	25	27	29	31				
								29	27
25	23	21	19	17	15	13	11	9	7
15	13	11	9	7	5	3	1		

Keep On Observing (KOO):

I like to find out solution of problems, I always remain content, I am always enterprising, I am good at communication, I am courageous, I always speak economically, I never hesitate, I am sober, I am not aggressive and so on....

CYCLE-16

1	3	5	7	9	11	13	15	17	19
21	23	25	27	29	31	33			
							31	29	27
25	23	21	19	17	15	13	11	9	7
15	13	11	9	7	5	3	1		

Keep On Observing (KOO):

I like to find out solution of problems, I always remain content, I am always enterprising, I am good at communication, I am courageous, I always speak economically, I never hesitate, I am sober, I am not aggressive and so on....

CYCLE-17

1	3	5	7	9	11	13	15	17	19
21	23	25	27	29	31	33	35		
						33	31	29	27
25	23	21	19	17	15	13	11	9	7
15	13	11	9	7	5	3	1		

Keep On Observing (KOO):

I like to find out solution of problems, I always remain content, I am always enterprising, I am good at communication, I am courageous, I always speak economically, I never hesitate, I am sober, I am not aggressive and so on....

CYCLE-18

1	3	5	7	9	11	13	15	17	19
21	23	25	27	29	31	33	35	37	
					35	33	31	29	27
25	23	21	19	17	15	13	11	9	7
15	13	11	9	7	5	3	1		

Keep On Observing (KOO):

I like to find out solution of problems, I always remain content, I am always enterprising, I am good at communication, I am courageous, I always speak economically, I never hesitate, I am sober, I am not aggressive and so on....

CYCLE-19

1	3	5	7	9	11	13	15	17	19
21	23	25	27	29	31	33	35	37	39
				37	35	33	31	29	27
25	23	21	19	17	15	13	11	9	7
15	13	11	9	7	5	3	1		

Keep On Observing (KOO):

I like to find out solution of problems, I always remain content, I am always enterprising, I am good at communication, I am courageous, I always speak economically, I never hesitate, I am sober, I am not aggressive and so on....

CYCLE-20

1	3	5	7	9	11	13	15	17	19
21	23	25	27	29	31	33	35	37	39
41									
		39	37	35	33	31	29	27	
25	23	21	19	17	15	13	11	9	7
15	13	11	9	7	5	3	1		

Keep On Observing (KOO):

I like to find out solution of problems, I always remain content, I am always enterprising, I am good at communication, I am courageous, I always speak economically, I never hesitate, I am sober, I am not aggressive and so on....

CYCLE-21

1	3	5	7	9	11	13	15	17	19
21	23	25	27	29	31	33	35	37	39
41	43								
		41	39	37	35	33	31	29	27
25	23	21	19	17	15	13	11	9	7
15	13	11	9	7	5	3	1		

Keep On Observing (KOO):

I like to find out solution of problems, I always remain content, I am always enterprising, I am good at communication, I am courageous, I always speak economically, I never hesitate, I am sober, I am not aggressive and so on....

CYCLE-23

1	3	5	7	9	11	13	15	17	19
21	23	25	27	29	31	33	35	37	39
41	43	45							
	43	41	39	37	35	33	31	29	27
25	23	21	19	17	15	13	11	9	7
15	13	11	9	7	5	3	1		

Keep On Observing (KOO):

I like to find out solution of problems, I always remain content, I am always enterprising, I am good at communication, I am courageous, I always speak economically, I never hesitate, I am sober, I am not aggressive and so on....

CYCLE-24

1	3	5	7	9	11	13	15	17	19
21	23	25	27	29	31	33	35	37	39
41	43	45	47						
45	43	41	39	37	35	33	31	29	27
25	23	21	19	17	15	13	11	9	7
15	13	11	9	7	5	3	1		

Keep On Observing (KOO):

I like to find out solution of problems, I always remain content, I am always enterprising, I am good at communication, I am courageous, I always speak economically, I never hesitate, I am sober, I am not aggressive and so on....

CYCLE-25

1	3	5	7	9	11	13	15	17	19
21	23	25	27	29	31	33	35	37	39
41	43	45	47	49					
									47
45	43	41	39	37	35	33	31	29	27
25	23	21	19	17	15	13	11	9	7
15	13	11	9	7	5	3	1		

Keep On Observing (KOO):

I like to find out solution of problems, I always remain content, I am always enterprising, I am good at communication, I am courageous, I always speak economically, I never hesitate, I am sober, I am not aggressive and so on....

CYCLE-26

1	3	5	7	9	11	13	15	17	19
21	23	25	27	29	31	33	35	37	39
41	43	45	47	49	51				
								49	47
45	43	41	39	37	35	33	31	29	27
25	23	21	19	17	15	13	11	9	7
15	13	11	9	7	5	3	1		

Keep On Observing (KOO):

I like to find out solution of problems, I always remain content, I am always enterprising, I am good at communication, I am courageous, I always speak economically, I never hesitate, I am sober, I am not aggressive and so on....

CYCLE-27

1	3	5	7	9	11	13	15	17	19
21	23	25	27	29	31	33	35	37	39
41	43	45	47	49	51	53			
							51	49	47
45	43	41	39	37	35	33	31	29	27
25	23	21	19	17	15	13	11	9	7
15	13	11	9	7	5	3	1		

Keep On Observing (KOO):

I like to find out solution of problems, I always remain content, I am always enterprising, I am good at communication, I am courageous, I always speak economically, I never hesitate, I am sober, I am not aggressive and so on....

CYCLE-28

1	3	5	7	9	11	13	15	17	19
21	23	25	27	29	31	33	35	37	39
41	43	45	47	49	51	53	55		
						53	51	49	47
45	43	41	39	37	35	33	31	29	27
25	23	21	19	17	15	13	11	9	7
15	13	11	9	7	5	3	1		

Keep On Observing (KOO):

I like to find out solution of problems, I always remain content, I am always enterprising, I am good at communication, I am courageous, I always speak economically, I never hesitate, I am sober, I am not aggressive and so on....

CYCLE-29

1	3	5	7	9	11	13	15	17	19
21	23	25	27	29	31	33	35	37	39
41	43	45	47	49	51	53	55	57	
					55	53	51	49	47
45	43	41	39	37	35	33	31	29	27
25	23	21	19	17	15	13	11	9	7
15	13	11	9	7	5	3	1		

Keep On Observing (KOO):

I like to find out solution of problems, I always remain content, I am always enterprising, I am good at communication, I am courageous, I always speak economically, I never hesitate, I am sober, I am not aggressive and so on....

CYCLE-30

1	3	5	7	9	11	13	15	17	19
21	23	25	27	29	31	33	35	37	39
41	43	45	47	49	51	53	55	57	59
				57	55	53	51	49	47
45	43	41	39	37	35	33	31	29	27
25	23	21	19	17	15	13	11	9	7
15	13	11	9	7	5	3	1		

Keep On Observing (KOO):

I like to find out solution of problems, I always remain content, I am always enterprising, I am good at communication, I am courageous, I always speak economically, I never hesitate, I am sober, I am not aggressive and so on....

CYCLE-31

1	3	5	7	9	11	13	15	17	19
21	23	25	27	29	31	33	35	37	39
41	43	45	47	49	51	53	55	57	59
61									
			59	57	55	53	51	49	47
45	43	41	39	37	35	33	31	29	27
25	23	21	19	17	15	13	11	9	7
15	13	11	9	7	5	3	1		

Keep On Observing (KOO):

I like to find out solution of problems, I always remain content, I am always enterprising, I am good at communication, I am courageous, I always speak economically, I never hesitate, I am sober, I am not aggressive and so on....

CYCLE-32

1	3	5	7	9	11	13	15	17	19
21	23	25	27	29	31	33	35	37	39
41	43	45	47	49	51	53	55	57	59
61	63								
		61	59	57	55	53	51	49	47
45	43	41	39	37	35	33	31	29	27
25	23	21	19	17	15	13	11	9	7
15	13	11	9	7	5	3	1		

Keep On Observing (KOO):

I like to find out solution of problems, I always remain content, I am always enterprising, I am good at communication, I am courageous, I always speak economically, I never hesitate, I am sober, I am not aggressive and so on....

CYCLE-33

1	3	5	7	9	11	13	15	17	19
21	23	25	27	29	31	33	35	37	39
41	43	45	47	49	51	53	55	57	59
61	63	65							
	63	61	59	57	55	53	51	49	47
45	43	41	39	37	35	33	31	29	27
25	23	21	19	17	15	13	11	9	7
15	13	11	9	7	5	3	1		

Keep On Observing (KOO):

I like to find out solution of problems, I always remain content, I am always enterprising, I am good at communication, I am courageous, I always speak economically, I never hesitate, I am sober, I am not aggressive and so on....

CYCLE-34

1	3	5	7	9	11	13	15	17	19
21	23	25	27	29	31	33	35	37	39
41	43	45	47	49	51	53	55	57	59
61	63	65	67						
65	63	61	59	57	55	53	51	49	47
45	43	41	39	37	35	33	31	29	27
25	23	21	19	17	15	13	11	9	7
15	13	11	9	7	5	3	1		

Keep On Observing (KOO):

I like to find out solution of problems, I always remain content, I am always enterprising, I am good at communication, I am courageous, I always speak economically, I never hesitate, I am sober, I am not aggressive and so on....

CYCLE-35

1	3	5	7	9	11	13	15	17	19
21	23	25	27	29	31	33	35	37	39
41	43	45	47	49	51	53	55	57	59
61	63	65	67	69					
									67
65	63	61	59	57	55	53	51	49	47
45	43	41	39	37	35	33	31	29	27
25	23	21	19	17	15	13	11	9	7
15	13	11	9	7	5	3	1		

Keep On Observing (KOO):

I like to find out solution of problems, I always remain content, I am always enterprising, I am good at communication, I am courageous, I always speak economically, I never hesitate, I am sober, I am not aggressive and so on....

CYCLE-36

1	3	5	7	9	11	13	15	17	19
21	23	25	27	29	31	33	35	37	39
41	43	45	47	49	51	53	55	57	59
61	63	65	67	69	71				
								69	67
65	63	61	59	57	55	53	51	49	47
45	43	41	39	37	35	33	31	29	27
25	23	21	19	17	15	13	11	9	7
15	13	11	9	7	5	3	1		

Keep On Observing (KOO):

I like to find out solution of problems, I always remain content, I am always enterprising, I am good at communication, I am courageous, I always speak economically, I never hesitate, I am sober, I am not aggressive and so on....

CYCLE-37

1	3	5	7	9	11	13	15	17	19
21	23	25	27	29	31	33	35	37	39
41	43	45	47	49	51	53	55	57	59
61	63	65	67	69	71	73			
							71	69	67
65	63	61	59	57	55	53	51	49	47
45	43	41	39	37	35	33	31	29	27
25	23	21	19	17	15	13	11	9	7
15	13	11	9	7	5	3	1		

Keep On Observing (KOO):

I like to find out solution of problems, I always remain content, I am always enterprising, I am good at communication, I am courageous, I always speak economically, I never hesitate, I am sober, I am not aggressive and so on....

CYCLE-38

1	3	5	7	9	11	13	15	17	19
21	23	25	27	29	31	33	35	37	39
41	43	45	47	49	51	53	55	57	59
61	63	65	67	69	71	73	75		
						73	71	69	67
65	63	61	59	57	55	53	51	49	47
45	43	41	39	37	35	33	31	29	27
25	23	21	19	17	15	13	11	9	7
15	13	11	9	7	5	3	1		

Keep On Observing (KOO):

I like to find out solution of problems, I always remain content, I am always enterprising, I am good at communication, I am courageous, I always speak economically, I never hesitate, I am sober, I am not aggressive and so on....

CYCLE-39

1	3	5	7	9	11	13	15	17	19
21	23	25	27	29	31	33	35	37	39
41	43	45	47	49	51	53	55	57	59
61	63	65	67	69	71	73	75	77	
				75	73	71	69	67	
65	63	61	59	57	55	53	51	49	47
45	43	41	39	37	35	33	31	29	27
25	23	21	19	17	15	13	11	9	7
15	13	11	9	7	5	3	1		

Keep On Observing (KOO):

I like to find out solution of problems, I always remain content, I am always enterprising, I am good at communication, I am courageous, I always speak economically, I never hesitate, I am sober, I am not aggressive and so on....

CYCLE-40

1	3	5	7	9	11	13	15	17	19
21	23	25	27	29	31	33	35	37	39
41	43	45	47	49	51	53	55	57	59
61	63	65	67	69	71	73	75	77	79
				77	75	73	71	69	67
65	63	61	59	57	55	53	51	49	47
45	43	41	39	37	35	33	31	29	27
25	23	21	19	17	15	13	11	9	7
15	13	11	9	7	5	3	1		

Keep On Observing (KOO):

I like to find out solution of problems, I always remain content, I am always enterprising, I am good at communication, I am courageous, I always speak economically, I never hesitate, I am sober, I am not aggressive and so on....

CYCLE-41

1	3	5	7	9	11	13	15	17	19
21	23	25	27	29	31	33	35	37	39
41	43	45	47	49	51	53	55	57	59
61	63	65	67	69	71	73	75	77	79
81									
			79	77	75	73	71	69	67
65	63	61	59	57	55	53	51	49	47
45	43	41	39	37	35	33	31	29	27
25	23	21	19	17	15	13	11	9	7
15	13	11	9	7	5	3	1		

Keep On Observing (KOO):

I like to find out solution of problems, I always remain content, I am always enterprising, I am good at communication, I am courageous, I always speak economically, I never hesitate, I am sober, I am not aggressive and so on....

CYCLE-42

1	3	5	7	9	11	13	15	17	19
21	23	25	27	29	31	33	35	37	39
41	43	45	47	49	51	53	55	57	59
61	63	65	67	69	71	73	75	77	79
81	83								
		81	79	77	75	73	71	69	67
65	63	61	59	57	55	53	51	49	47
45	43	41	39	37	35	33	31	29	27
25	23	21	19	17	15	13	11	9	7
15	13	11	9	7	5	3	1		

Keep On Observing (KOO):

I like to find out solution of problems, I always remain content, I am always enterprising, I am good at communication, I am courageous, I always speak economically, I never hesitate, I am sober, I am not aggressive and so on....

CYCLE-43

1	3	5	7	9	11	13	15	17	19
21	23	25	27	29	31	33	35	37	39
41	43	45	47	49	51	53	55	57	59
61	63	65	67	69	71	73	75	77	79
81	83	85							
	83	81	79	77	75	73	71	69	67
65	63	61	59	57	55	53	51	49	47
45	43	41	39	37	35	33	31	29	27
25	23	21	19	17	15	13	11	9	7
15	13	11	9	7	5	3	1		

Keep On Observing (KOO):

I like to find out solution of problems, I always remain content, I am always enterprising, I am good at communication, I am courageous, I always speak economically, I never hesitate, I am sober, I am not aggressive and so on....

CYCLE-44

1	3	5	7	9	11	13	15	17	19
21	23	25	27	29	31	33	35	37	39
41	43	45	47	49	51	53	55	57	59
61	63	65	67	69	71	73	75	77	79
81	83	85	87						
85	83	81	79	77	75	73	71	69	67
65	63	61	59	57	55	53	51	49	47
45	43	41	39	37	35	33	31	29	27
25	23	21	19	17	15	13	11	9	7
15	13	11	9	7	5	3	1		

Keep On Observing (KOO):

I like to find out solution of problems, I always remain content, I am always enterprising, I am good at communication, I am courageous, I always speak economically, I never hesitate, I am sober, I am not aggressive and so on....

CYCLE-45

1	3	5	7	9	11	13	15	17	19
21	23	25	27	29	31	33	35	37	39
41	43	45	47	49	51	53	55	57	59
61	63	65	67	69	71	73	75	77	79
81	83	85	87	89					
									87
85	83	81	79	77	75	73	71	69	67
65	63	61	59	57	55	53	51	49	47
45	43	41	39	37	35	33	31	29	27
25	23	21	19	17	15	13	11	9	7
15	13	11	9	7	5	3	1		

Keep On Observing (KOO):

I like to find out solution of problems, I always remain content, I am always enterprising, I am good at communication, I am courageous, I always speak economically, I never hesitate, I am sober, I am not aggressive and so on....

CYCLE-46

1	3	5	7	9	11	13	15	17	19
21	23	25	27	29	31	33	35	37	39
41	43	45	47	49	51	53	55	57	59
61	63	65	67	69	71	73	75	77	79
81	83	85	87	89	91				
								89	87
85	83	81	79	77	75	73	71	69	67
65	63	61	59	57	55	53	51	49	47
45	43	41	39	37	35	33	31	29	27
25	23	21	19	17	15	13	11	9	7
15	13	11	9	7	5	3	1		

Keep On Observing (KOO):

I like to find out solution of problems, I always remain content, I am always enterprising, I am good at communication, I am courageous, I always speak economically, I never hesitate, I am sober, I am not aggressive and so on......

CYCLE-47

1	3	5	7	9	11	13	15	17	19
21	23	25	27	29	31	33	35	37	39
41	43	45	47	49	51	53	55	57	59
61	63	65	67	69	71	73	75	77	79
81	83	85	87	89	91	93			
								91	87
85	83	81	79	77	75	73	71	69	67
65	63	61	59	57	55	53	51	49	47
45	43	41	39	37	35	33	31	29	27
25	23	21	19	17	15	13	11	9	7
15	13	11	9	7	5	3	1		

Keep On Observing (KOO):

I like to find out solution of problems, I always remain content, I am always enterprising, I am good at communication, I am courageous, I always speak economically, I never hesitate, I am sober, I am not aggressive and so on....

CYCLE-48

1	3	5	7	9	11	13	15	17	19
21	23	25	27	29	31	33	35	37	39
41	43	45	47	49	51	53	55	57	59
61	63	65	67	69	71	73	75	77	79
81	83	85	87	89	91	93	95		
							93	91	87
85	83	81	79	77	75	73	71	69	67
65	63	61	59	57	55	53	51	49	47
45	43	41	39	37	35	33	31	29	27
25	23	21	19	17	15	13	11	9	7
15	13	11	9	7	5	3	1		

Keep On Observing (KOO):

I like to find out solution of problems, I always remain content, I am always enterprising, I am good at communication, I am courageous, I always speak economically, I never hesitate, I am sober, I am not aggressive and so on....

CYCLE-49

1	3	5	7	9	11	13	15	17	19
21	23	25	27	29	31	33	35	37	39
41	43	45	47	49	51	53	55	57	59
61	63	65	67	69	71	73	75	77	79
81	83	85	87	89	91	93	95	97	
						95	93	91	87
85	83	81	79	77	75	73	71	69	67
65	63	61	59	57	55	53	51	49	47
45	43	41	39	37	35	33	31	29	27
25	23	21	19	17	15	13	11	9	7
15	13	11	9	7	5	3	1		

Keep On Observing (KOO):

I like to find out solution of problems, I always remain content, I am always enterprising, I am good at communication, I am courageous, I always speak economically, I never hesitate, I am sober, I am not aggressive and so on....

CYCLE-50

1	3	5	7	9	11	13	15	17	19
21	23	25	27	29	31	33	35	37	39
41	43	45	47	49	51	53	55	57	59
61	63	65	67	69	71	73	75	77	79
81	83	85	87	89	91	93	95	97	99
101				99	97	95	93	91	87
85	83	81	79	77	75	73	71	69	67
65	63	61	59	57	55	53	51	49	47
45	43	41	39	37	35	33	31	29	27
25	23	21	19	17	15	13	11	9	7
15	13	11	9	7	5	3	1		

Keep On Observing (KOO):

I like to find out solution of problems, I always remain content, I am always enterprising, I am good at communication, I am courageous, I always speak economically, I never hesitate, I am sober, I am not aggressive and so on....

PATTERN-2

CYCLE-1

2	4								
								2	

Keep On Observing (KOO):

I like to find out solution of problems, I always remain content, I am always enterprising, I am good at communication, I am courageous, I always speak economically, I never hesitate, I am sober, I am not aggressive and so on....

CYCLE-2

2	4	6							
							4	2	

Keep On Observing (KOO):

I like to find out solution of problems, I always remain content, I am always enterprising, I am good at communication, I am courageous, I always speak economically, I never hesitate, I am sober, I am not aggressive and so on....

CYCLE-3

2	4	6	8						
						6	4	2	

Keep On Observing (KOO):

I like to find out solution of problems, I always remain content, I am always enterprising, I am good at communication, I am courageous, I always speak economically, I never hesitate, I am sober, I am not aggressive and so on....

CYCLE-4

2	4	6	8	10					
					8	6	4	2	

Keep On Observing (KOO):

I like to find out solution of problems, I always remain content, I am always enterprising, I am good at communication, I am courageous, I always speak economically, I never hesitate, I am sober, I am not aggressive and so on....

CYCLE-5

2	4	6	8	10	12				
				10	8	6	4	2	

Keep On Observing (KOO):

I like to find out solution of problems, I always remain content, I am always enterprising, I am good at communication, I am courageous, I always speak economically, I never hesitate, I am sober, I am not aggressive and so on....

CYCLE-6

2	4	6	8	10	12	14			
			12	10	8	6	4	2	

Keep On Observing (KOO):

I like to find out solution of problems, I always remain content, I am always enterprising, I am good at communication, I am courageous, I always speak economically, I never hesitate, I am sober, I am not aggressive and so on....

CYCLE-7

2	4	6	8	10	12	14	16	
		14	12	10	8	6	4	2	

Keep On Observing (KOO):

I like to find out solution of problems, I always remain content, I am always enterprising, I am good at communication, I am courageous, I always speak economically, I never hesitate, I am sober, I am not aggressive and so on....

CYCLE-8

2	4	6	8	10	12	14	16	18	
	16	14	12	10	8	6	4	2	

Keep On Observing (KOO):

I like to find out solution of problems, I always remain content, I am always enterprising, I am good at communication, I am courageous, I always speak economically, I never hesitate, I am sober, I am not aggressive and so on....

CYCLE-9

2	4	6	8	10	12	14	16	18	20
18	16	14	12	10	8	6	4	2	

Keep On Observing (KOO):

I like to find out solution of problems, I always remain content, I am always enterprising, I am good at communication, I am courageous, I always speak economically, I never hesitate, I am sober, I am not aggressive and so on....

CYCLE-10

2	4	6	8	10	12	14	16	18	20
22									
									20
18	16	14	12	10	8	6	4	2	

Keep On Observing (KOO):

I like to find out solution of problems, I always remain content, I am always enterprising, I am good at communication, I am courageous, I always speak economically, I never hesitate, I am sober, I am not aggressive and so on....

CYCLE-11

2	4	6	8	10	12	14	16	18	20
22	24								
									20
18	16	14	12	10	8	6	4	2	

Keep On Observing (KOO):

I like to find out solution of problems, I always remain content, I am always enterprising, I am good at communication, I am courageous, I always speak economically, I never hesitate, I am sober, I am not aggressive and so on....

CYCLE-12

2	4	6	8	10	12	14	16	18	20
22	24	26							
							24	22	20
18	16	14	12	10	8	6	4	2	

Keep On Observing (KOO):

I like to find out solution of problems, I always remain content, I am always enterprising, I am good at communication, I am courageous, I always speak economically, I never hesitate, I am sober, I am not aggressive and so on.....

CYCLE-13

2	4	6	8	10	12	14	16	18	20
22	24	26	28						
						26	24	22	20
18	16	14	12	10	8	6	4	2	

Keep On Observing (KOO):

I like to find out solution of problems, I always remain content, I am always enterprising, I am good at communication, I am courageous, I always speak economically, I never hesitate, I am sober, I am not aggressive and so on....

CYCLE-14

2	4	6	8	10	12	14	16	18	20
22	24	26	28	30					
					28	26	24	22	20
18	16	14	12	10	8	6	4	2	

Keep On Observing (KOO):

I like to find out solution of problems, I always remain content, I am always enterprising, I am good at communication, I am courageous, I always speak economically, I never hesitate, I am sober, I am not aggressive and so on....

CYCLE-15

2	4	6	8	10	12	14	16	18	20
22	24	26	28	30	32				
				30	28	26	24	22	20
18	16	14	12	10	8	6	4	2	

Keep On Observing (KOO):

I like to find out solution of problems, I always remain content, I am always enterprising, I am good at communication, I am courageous, I always speak economically, I never hesitate, I am sober, I am not aggressive and so on....

CYCLE-16

2	4	6	8	10	12	14	16	18	20
22	24	26	28	30	32	34			
			32	30	28	26	24	22	20
18	16	14	12	10	8	6	4	2	

Keep On Observing (KOO):

I like to find out solution of problems, I always remain content, I am always enterprising, I am good at communication, I am courageous, I always speak economically, I never hesitate, I am sober, I am not aggressive and so on.....

CYCLE-17

2	4	6	8	10	12	14	16	18	20
22	24	26	28	30	32	34	36		
		34	32	30	28	26	24	22	20
18	16	14	12	10	8	6	4	2	

Keep On Observing (KOO):

I like to find out solution of problems, I always remain content, I am always enterprising, I am good at communication, I am courageous, I always speak economically, I never hesitate, I am sober, I am not aggressive and so on....

CYCLE-18

2	4	6	8	10	12	14	16	18	20
22	24	26	28	30	32	34	36	38	
	36	34	32	30	28	26	24	22	20
18	16	14	12	10	8	6	4	2	

Keep On Observing (KOO):

I like to find out solution of problems, I always remain content, I am always enterprising, I am good at communication, I am courageous, I always speak economically, I never hesitate, I am sober, I am not aggressive and so on....

CYCLE-19

2	4	6	8	10	12	14	16	18	20
22	24	26	28	30	32	34	36	38	40
38	36	34	32	30	28	26	24	22	20
18	16	14	12	10	8	6	4	2	

Keep On Observing (KOO):

I like to find out solution of problems, I always remain content, I am always enterprising, I am good at communication, I am courageous, I always speak economically, I never hesitate, I am sober, I am not aggressive and so on....

CYCLE-20

2	4	6	8	10	12	14	16	18	20
22	24	26	28	30	32	34	36	38	40
42									
									40
38	36	34	32	30	28	26	24	22	20
18	16	14	12	10	8	6	4	2	

Keep On Observing (KOO):

I like to find out solution of problems, I always remain content, I am always enterprising, I am good at communication, I am courageous, I always speak economically, I never hesitate, I am sober, I am not aggressive and so on....

CYCLE-21

2	4	6	8	10	12	14	16	18	20
22	24	26	28	30	32	34	36	38	40
42	44								
								42	40
38	36	34	32	30	28	26	24	22	20
18	16	14	12	10	8	6	4	2	

Keep On Observing (KOO):

I like to find out solution of problems, I always remain content, I am always enterprising, I am good at communication, I am courageous, I always speak economically, I never hesitate, I am sober, I am not aggressive and so on....

CYCLE-22

2	4	6	8	10	12	14	16	18	20
22	24	26	28	30	32	34	36	38	40
42	44	46							
							44	42	40
38	36	34	32	30	28	26	24	22	20
18	16	14	12	10	8	6	4	2	

Keep On Observing (KOO):

I like to find out solution of problems, I always remain content, I am always enterprising, I am good at communication, I am courageous, I always speak economically, I never hesitate, I am sober, I am not aggressive and so on....

CYCLE-23

2	4	6	8	10	12	14	16	18	20
22	24	26	28	30	32	34	36	38	40
42	44	46	48						
						46	44	42	40
38	36	34	32	30	28	26	24	22	20
18	16	14	12	10	8	6	4	2	

Keep On Observing (KOO):

I like to find out solution of problems, I always remain content, I am always enterprising, I am good at communication, I am courageous, I always speak economically, I never hesitate, I am sober, I am not aggressive and so on....

CYCLE-24

2	4	6	8	10	12	14	16	18	20
22	24	26	28	30	32	34	36	38	40
42	44	46	48	50					
					48	46	44	42	40
38	36	34	32	30	28	26	24	22	20
18	16	14	12	10	8	6	4	2	

Keep On Observing (KOO):

I like to find out solution of problems, I always remain content, I am always enterprising, I am good at communication, I am courageous, I always speak economically, I never hesitate, I am sober, I am not aggressive and so on....

CYCLE-25

2	4	6	8	10	12	14	16	18	20
22	24	26	28	30	32	34	36	38	40
42	44	46	48	50	52				
				50	48	46	44	42	40
38	36	34	32	30	28	26	24	22	20
18	16	14	12	10	8	6	4	2	

Keep On Observing (KOO):

I like to find out solution of problems, I always remain content, I am always enterprising, I am good at communication, I am courageous, I always speak economically, I never hesitate, I am sober, I am not aggressive and so on....

CYCLE-26

2	4	6	8	10	12	14	16	18	20
22	24	26	28	30	32	34	36	38	40
42	44	46	48	50	52	54			
			52	50	48	46	44	42	40
38	36	34	32	30	28	26	24	22	20
18	16	14	12	10	8	6	4	2	

Keep On Observing (KOO):

I like to find out solution of problems, I always remain content, I am always enterprising, I am good at communication, I am courageous, I always speak economically, I never hesitate, I am sober, I am not aggressive and so on....

CYCLE-27

2	4	6	8	10	12	14	16	18	20
22	24	26	28	30	32	34	36	38	40
42	44	46	48	50	52	54	56		
		54	52	50	48	46	44	42	40
38	36	34	32	30	28	26	24	22	20
18	16	14	12	10	8	6	4	2	

Keep On Observing (KOO):

I like to find out solution of problems, I always remain content, I am always enterprising, I am good at communication, I am courageous, I always speak economically, I never hesitate, I am sober, I am not aggressive and so on....

CYCLE-28

2	4	6	8	10	12	14	16	18	20
22	24	26	28	30	32	34	36	38	40
42	44	46	48	50	52	54	56	58	
	56	54	52	50	48	46	44	42	40
38	36	34	32	30	28	26	24	22	20
18	16	14	12	10	8	6	4	2	

Keep On Observing (KOO):

I like to find out solution of problems, I always remain content, I am always enterprising, I am good at communication, I am courageous, I always speak economically, I never hesitate, I am sober, I am not aggressive and so on....

CYCLE-29

2	4	6	8	10	12	14	16	18	20
22	24	26	28	30	32	34	36	38	40
42	44	46	48	50	52	54	56	58	60
58	56	54	52	50	48	46	44	42	40
38	36	34	32	30	28	26	24	22	20
18	16	14	12	10	8	6	4	2	

Keep On Observing (KOO):

I like to find out solution of problems, I always remain content, I am always enterprising, I am good at communication, I am courageous, I always speak economically, I never hesitate, I am sober, I am not aggressive and so on....

CYCLE-30

2	4	6	8	10	12	14	16	18	20
22	24	26	28	30	32	34	36	38	40
42	44	46	48	50	52	54	56	58	60
62									
									60
58	56	54	52	50	48	46	44	42	40
38	36	34	32	30	28	26	24	22	20
18	16	14	12	10	8	6	4	2	

Keep On Observing (KOO):

I like to find out solution of problems, I always remain content, I am always enterprising, I am good at communication, I am courageous, I always speak economically, I never hesitate, I am sober, I am not aggressive and so on....

CYCLE-31

2	4	6	8	10	12	14	16	18	20
22	24	26	28	30	32	34	36	38	40
42	44	46	48	50	52	54	56	58	60
62	64								
								62	60
58	56	54	52	50	48	46	44	42	40
38	36	34	32	30	28	26	24	22	20
18	16	14	12	10	8	6	4	2	

Keep On Observing (KOO):

I like to find out solution of problems, I always remain content, I am always enterprising, I am good at communication, I am courageous, I always speak economically, I never hesitate, I am sober, I am not aggressive and so on....

CYCLE-32

2	4	6	8	10	12	14	16	18	20
22	24	26	28	30	32	34	36	38	40
42	44	46	48	50	52	54	56	58	60
62	64	66							
							64	62	60
58	56	54	52	50	48	46	44	42	40
38	36	34	32	30	28	26	24	22	20
18	16	14	12	10	8	6	4	2	

Keep On Observing (KOO):

I like to find out solution of problems, I always remain content, I am always enterprising, I am good at communication, I am courageous, I always speak economically, I never hesitate, I am sober, I am not aggressive and so on....

CYCLE-33

2	4	6	8	10	12	14	16	18	20
22	24	26	28	30	32	34	36	38	40
42	44	46	48	50	52	54	56	58	60
62	64	66	68						
						66	64	62	60
58	56	54	52	50	48	46	44	42	40
38	36	34	32	30	28	26	24	22	20
18	16	14	12	10	8	6	4	2	

Keep On Observing (KOO):

I like to find out solution of problems, I always remain content, I am always enterprising, I am good at communication, I am courageous, I always speak economically, I never hesitate, I am sober, I am not aggressive and so on....

CYCLE-34

2	4	6	8	10	12	14	16	18	20
22	24	26	28	30	32	34	36	38	40
42	44	46	48	50	52	54	56	58	60
62	64	66	68	70					
					68	66	64	62	60
58	56	54	52	50	48	46	44	42	40
38	36	34	32	30	28	26	24	22	20
18	16	14	12	10	8	6	4	2	

Keep On Observing (KOO):

I like to find out solution of problems, I always remain content, I am always enterprising, I am good at communication, I am courageous, I always speak economically, I never hesitate, I am sober, I am not aggressive and so on....

CYCLE-35

2	4	6	8	10	12	14	16	18	20
22	24	26	28	30	32	34	36	38	40
42	44	46	48	50	52	54	56	58	60
62	64	66	68	70	72				
				70	68	66	64	62	60
58	56	54	52	50	48	46	44	42	40
38	36	34	32	30	28	26	24	22	20
18	16	14	12	10	8	6	4	2	

Keep On Observing (KOO):

I like to find out solution of problems, I always remain content, I am always enterprising, I am good at communication, I am courageous, I always speak economically, I never hesitate, I am sober, I am not aggressive and so on....

CYCLE-36

2	4	6	8	10	12	14	16	18	20
22	24	26	28	30	32	34	36	38	40
42	44	46	48	50	52	54	56	58	60
62	64	66	68	70	72	74			
			72	70	68	66	64	62	60
58	56	54	52	50	48	46	44	42	40
38	36	34	32	30	28	26	24	22	20
18	16	14	12	10	8	6	4	2	

Keep On Observing (KOO):

I like to find out solution of problems, I always remain content, I am always enterprising, I am good at communication, I am courageous, I always speak economically, I never hesitate, I am sober, I am not aggressive and so on....

CYCLE-37

2	4	6	8	10	12	14	16	18	20
22	24	26	28	30	32	34	36	38	40
42	44	46	48	50	52	54	56	58	60
62	64	66	68	70	72	74	76		
		74	72	70	68	66	64	62	60
58	56	54	52	50	48	46	44	42	40
38	36	34	32	30	28	26	24	22	20
18	16	14	12	10	8	6	4	2	

Keep On Observing (KOO):

I like to find out solution of problems, I always remain content, I am always enterprising, I am good at communication, I am courageous, I always speak economically, I never hesitate, I am sober, I am not aggressive and so on....

CYCLE-38

2	4	6	8	10	12	14	16	18	20
22	24	26	28	30	32	34	36	38	40
42	44	46	48	50	52	54	56	58	60
62	64	66	68	70	72	74	76	78	
	76	74	72	70	68	66	64	62	60
58	56	54	52	50	48	46	44	42	40
38	36	34	32	30	28	26	24	22	20
18	16	14	12	10	8	6	4	2	

Keep On Observing (KOO):

I like to find out solution of problems, I always remain content, I am always enterprising, I am good at communication, I am courageous, I always speak economically, I never hesitate, I am sober, I am not aggressive and so on....

CYCLE-39

2	4	6	8	10	12	14	16	18	20
22	24	26	28	30	32	34	36	38	40
42	44	46	48	50	52	54	56	58	60
62	64	66	68	70	72	74	76	78	80
78	76	74	72	70	68	66	64	62	60
58	56	54	52	50	48	46	44	42	40
38	36	34	32	30	28	26	24	22	20
18	16	14	12	10	8	6	4	2	

Keep On Observing (KOO):

I like to find out solution of problems, I always remain content, I am always enterprising, I am good at communication, I am courageous, I always speak economically, I never hesitate, I am sober, I am not aggressive and so on....

CYCLE-40

2	4	6	8	10	12	14	16	18	20
22	24	26	28	30	32	34	36	38	40
42	44	46	48	50	52	54	56	58	60
62	64	66	68	70	72	74	76	78	80
82									
									80
78	76	74	72	70	68	66	64	62	60
58	56	54	52	50	48	46	44	42	40
38	36	34	32	30	28	26	24	22	20
18	16	14	12	10	8	6	4	2	

Keep On Observing (KOO):

I like to find out solution of problems, I always remain content, I am always enterprising, I am good at communication, I am courageous, I always speak economically, I never hesitate, I am sober, I am not aggressive and so on....

CYCLE-41

2	4	6	8	10	12	14	16	18	20
22	24	26	28	30	32	34	36	38	40
42	44	46	48	50	52	54	56	58	60
62	64	66	68	70	72	74	76	78	80
82	84								
								82	80
78	76	74	72	70	68	66	64	62	60
58	56	54	52	50	48	46	44	42	40
38	36	34	32	30	28	26	24	22	20
18	16	14	12	10	8	6	4	2	

Keep On Observing (KOO):

I like to find out solution of problems, I always remain content, I am always enterprising, I am good at communication, I am courageous, I always speak economically, I never hesitate, I am sober, I am not aggressive and so on....

CYCLE-42

2	4	6	8	10	12	14	16	18	20
22	24	26	28	30	32	34	36	38	40
42	44	46	48	50	52	54	56	58	60
62	64	66	68	70	72	74	76	78	80
82	84	86							
							84	82	80
78	76	74	72	70	68	66	64	62	60
58	56	54	52	50	48	46	44	42	40
38	36	34	32	30	28	26	24	22	20
18	16	14	12	10	8	6	4	2	

Keep On Observing (KOO):

I like to find out solution of problems, I always remain content, I am always enterprising, I am good at communication, I am courageous, I always speak economically, I never hesitate, I am sober, I am not aggressive and so on....

CYCLE-43

2	4	6	8	10	12	14	16	18	20
22	24	26	28	30	32	34	36	38	40
42	44	46	48	50	52	54	56	58	60
62	64	66	68	70	72	74	76	78	80
82	84	86	88						
						86	84	82	80
78	76	74	72	70	68	66	64	62	60
58	56	54	52	50	48	46	44	42	40
38	36	34	32	30	28	26	24	22	20
18	16	14	12	10	8	6	4	2	

Keep On Observing (KOO):

I like to find out solution of problems, I always remain content, I am always enterprising, I am good at communication, I am courageous, I always speak economically, I never hesitate, I am sober, I am not aggressive and so on......

CYCLE-44

2	4	6	8	10	12	14	16	18	20
22	24	26	28	30	32	34	36	38	40
42	44	46	48	50	52	54	56	58	60
62	64	66	68	70	72	74	76	78	80
82	84	86	88	90					
					88	86	84	82	80
78	76	74	72	70	68	66	64	62	60
58	56	54	52	50	48	46	44	42	40
38	36	34	32	30	28	26	24	22	20
18	16	14	12	10	8	6	4	2	

Keep On Observing (KOO):

I like to find out solution of problems, I always remain content, I am always enterprising, I am good at communication, I am courageous, I always speak economically, I never hesitate, I am sober, I am not aggressive and so on....

CYCLE-45

2	4	6	8	10	12	14	16	18	20
22	24	26	28	30	32	34	36	38	40
42	44	46	48	50	52	54	56	58	60
62	64	66	68	70	72	74	76	78	80
82	84	86	88	90	92				
				90	88	86	84	82	80
78	76	74	72	70	68	66	64	62	60
58	56	54	52	50	48	46	44	42	40
38	36	34	32	30	28	26	24	22	20
18	16	14	12	10	8	6	4	2	

Keep On Observing (KOO):

I like to find out solution of problems, I always remain content, I am always enterprising, I am good at communication, I am courageous, I always speak economically, I never hesitate, I am sober, I am not aggressive and so on....

CYCLE-46

2	4	6	8	10	12	14	16	18	20
22	24	26	28	30	32	34	36	38	40
42	44	46	48	50	52	54	56	58	60
62	64	66	68	70	72	74	76	78	80
82	84	86	88	90	92	94			
			92	90	88	86	84	82	80
78	76	74	72	70	68	66	64	62	60
58	56	54	52	50	48	46	44	42	40
38	36	34	32	30	28	26	24	22	20
18	16	14	12	10	8	6	4	2	

Keep On Observing (KOO):

I like to find out solution of problems, I always remain content, I am always enterprising, I am good at communication, I am courageous, I always speak economically, I never hesitate, I am sober, I am not aggressive and so on....

CYCLE-47

2	4	6	8	10	12	14	16	18	20
22	24	26	28	30	32	34	36	38	40
42	44	46	48	50	52	54	56	58	60
62	64	66	68	70	72	74	76	78	80
82	84	86	88	90	92	94	96		
		94	92	90	88	86	84	82	80
78	76	74	72	70	68	66	64	62	60
58	56	54	52	50	48	46	44	42	40
38	36	34	32	30	28	26	24	22	20
18	16	14	12	10	8	6	4	2	

Keep On Observing (KOO):

I like to find out solution of problems, I always remain content, I am always enterprising, I am good at communication, I am courageous, I always speak economically, I never hesitate, I am sober, I am not aggressive and so on....

CYCLE-48

2	4	6	8	10	12	14	16	18	20
22	24	26	28	30	32	34	36	38	40
42	44	46	48	50	52	54	56	58	60
62	64	66	68	70	72	74	76	78	80
82	84	86	88	90	92	94	96	98	
	96	94	92	90	88	86	84	82	80
78	76	74	72	70	68	66	64	62	60
58	56	54	52	50	48	46	44	42	40
38	36	34	32	30	28	26	24	22	20
18	16	14	12	10	8	6	4	2	

Keep On Observing (KOO):

I like to find out solution of problems, I always remain content, I am always enterprising, I am good at communication, I am courageous, I always speak economically, I never hesitate, I am sober, I am not aggressive and so on....

CYCLE-49

2	4	6	8	10	12	14	16	18	20
22	24	26	28	30	32	34	36	38	40
42	44	46	48	50	52	54	56	58	60
62	64	66	68	70	72	74	76	78	80
82	84	86	88	90	92	94	96	98	100
98	96	94	92	90	88	86	84	82	80
78	76	74	72	70	68	66	64	62	60
58	56	54	52	50	48	46	44	42	40
38	36	34	32	30	28	26	24	22	20
18	16	14	12	10	8	6	4	2	

Keep On Observing (KOO):

I like to find out solution of problems, I always remain content, I am always enterprising, I am good at communication, I am courageous, I always speak economically, I never hesitate, I am sober, I am not aggressive and so on....

Let's do an introspective exercise:

Please check what you achieved and able to exercise now in your life

Sr. No.	Qualities/ characteristics	Posses by a mathe- matised mind	Posses by a success full mind	Posses by a happy mind	Posses by a pat- tern	Posses by you		
						Begin- ning	Con- soli- dating	Exer- cising
1	like to find out solution of problems	yes	yes	Yes	yes			
2	remain content	yes	yes	Yes	yes			
3	enterprising	yes	yes	Yes	yes			
4	good at communication	yes	yes	Yes	yes			
5	courageous	yes	yes	Yes	yes			
6	speak economically	yes	yes	Yes	yes			
7	never hesitate	yes	yes	Yes	yes			
8	Sober	yes	yes	Yes	yes			
9	aggressive	no	no	No	no			
10	straight forward	yes	Yes	Yes	yes			
11	daring	yes	yes	Yes	Yes			
12	enthusiastic	yes	yes	Yes	yes			
13	risk taking	yes	calcu- lated	calcu- lated	calcu- lated			
14	bold	yes	yes	Yes	Yes			
15	can take stress	yes	Yes	Yes	yes			
16	dominant	yes	no	No	No			
17	influenced by facts than by feeling	yes	Yes	Yes	yes			
18	Hard working	yes	yes	yes	Yes			
19	easy going never in hurry	yes	yes	Yes	yes			
20	quick decision	yes	yes	yes	Yes			
21	communicative	yes	yes	Yes	yes			
22	free from guilt	yes	yes	yes	yes			
23	never hesitate	yes	yes	yes	yes			
24	Secure	yes	yes	Yes	yes			
25	never act according to others	yes	yes	yes	yes			
26	capable of getting things done	yes	yes	Yes	yes			
27	assertive behaviour	yes	yes	yes	yes			

28	develop their own sets of rules	yes	If required	If required	If required			
29	self disciplined	yes	yes	yes	Yes			
30	abstract thinking	yes	yes	Yes	yes			
31	reliable behaviour	yes	yes	yes	yes			
32	experementive	yes	yes	yes	yes			
33	impulsive	yes	no	no	no			
34	self destructive	no	no	no	no			
35	social	yes	yes	yes	yes			
36	cope with routine life		yes	yes	yes			
37	highly self motivated	yes	yes	Yes	yes			
38	practical	yes	yes	yes	yes			
39	mindful	yes	yes	yes	yes			
40	lost in the world of dreams	no	no	no	no			
41	participating	yes	yes	yes	yes			
42	Cautious	yes	yes	Yes	yes			
43	likes people	yes	yes	yes	yes			
44	open minded	yes	yes	yes	yes			
45	resolve conflicts	yes	yes	Yes	yes			
46	emotionally mature	yes	yes	Yes	yes			
47	realistic	yes	yes	yes	yes			
48	Cheerful	yes	yes	Yes	yes			
49	Intuitive	yes	yes	yes	yes			
50	keep things under control	yes	yes	yes	yes			
51	Competitor of self	yes	yes	Yes	yes			
52	self confident	yes	yes	Yes	yes			
53	Assertive	yes	yes	Yes	yes			
54	Mature	yes	yes	Yes	yes			
55	Relax	yes	yes	Yes	yes			
56	Adaptive	yes	yes	Yes	yes			
57	Flexible	yes	yes	Yes	yes			
58	open to change	yes	yes	Yes	yes			
59	accommodative	yes	yes	Yes	yes			
60	socially active	yes	yes	Yes	yes			
61	cultural interests	yes	yes	Yes	yes			
62	down to earth	yes	yes	Yes	yes			
63	friendly nature	yes	yes	Yes	yes			
64	Sociable	yes	yes	Yes	yes			
65	good reasoning	yes	yes	Yes	yes			
66	intelligent	yes	yes	Yes	yes			
67	hard to fool	yes	yes	Yes	yes			

Express your feeling about your accomplishments through mathyogs9211:

....
....
....
....
....
....
....
....
....
....
....
....
....
....
....
....
....
....
....
....
....
....
....
....
....
....
....
....
....
....
....
....
....

CHAPTER-VII

COUNTING BY THREE'S

Group 3: Counting by three's

Sr. No.	GROUP III		
Term	PATTERN-1	PATTERN-2	PATTERN-3
1	1	2	3
2	4	5	6
3	7	8	9
4	10	11	12
5	13	14	15
6	16	17	18
7	19	20	21
8	22	23	24
9	25	26	27
10	28	29	30
11	31	32	33
12	34	35	36
13	37	38	39
14	40	41	42
15	43	44	45
16	46	47	48

17	49	50	51
18	52	53	54
19	55	56	57
20	58	59	60
21	61	62	63
22	64	65	66
23	67	68	69
24	70	71	72
25	73	74	75
26	76	77	78
27	79	80	81
28	82	83	84
29	85	86	87
30	88	89	90
31	91	92	93
32	94	95	96
33	97	98	99

PATTERN-1

CYCLE-1

1	4	1							

Keep On Observing (KOO):

I like to find out solution of problems, I always remain content, I am always enterprising, I am good at communication, I am courageous, I always speak economically, I never hesitate, I am sober, I am not aggressive and so on....

CYCLE-2

1	4	7	4	1					

Keep On Observing (KOO):

I like to find out solution of problems, I always remain content, I am always enterprising, I am good at communication, I am courageous, I always speak economically, I never hesitate, I am sober, I am not aggressive and so on....

CYCLE-3

1	4	7	10	7	4	1	

Keep On Observing (KOO):

I like to find out solution of problems, I always remain content, I am always enterprising, I am good at communication, I am courageous, I always speak economically, I never hesitate, I am sober, I am not aggressive and so on....

CYCLE-4

1	4	7	10	13	10	7	4	1	

Keep On Observing (KOO):

I like to find out solution of problems, I always remain content, I am always enterprising, I am good at communication, I am courageous, I always speak economically, I never hesitate, I am sober, I am not aggressive and so on....

CYCLE-5

1	4	7	10	13	16	13	10	7	1

1   4   7   10   13   16   13   10   7   4   1

Keep On Observing (KOO):

I like to find out solution of problems, I always remain content, I am always enterprising, I am good at communication, I am courageous, I always speak economically, I never hesitate, I am sober, I am not aggressive and so on....

CYCLE-6

1	4	7	10	13	16	19	16	13	10
7	1								

Keep On Observing (KOO):

I like to find out solution of problems, I always remain content, I am always enterprising, I am good at communication, I am courageous, I always speak economically, I never hesitate, I am sober, I am not aggressive and so on....

CYCLE-7

1	4	7	10	13	16	19	22	19	16
13	10	7	4	1					

Keep On Observing (KOO):

I like to find out solution of problems, I always remain content, I am always enterprising, I am good at communication, I am courageous, I always speak economically, I never hesitate, I am sober, I am not aggressive and so on....

CYCLE-8

1	4	7	10	13	16	19	22	25	22
19	16	13	10	7	4	1			

Keep On Observing (KOO):

I like to find out solution of problems, I always remain content, I am always enterprising, I am good at communication, I am courageous, I always speak economically, I never hesitate, I am sober, I am not aggressive and so on....

CYCLE-9

1	4	7	10	13	16	19	22	25	28
25	22	19	16	13	10	7	4	1	

Keep On Observing (KOO):

I like to find out solution of problems, I always remain content, I am always enterprising, I am good at communication, I am courageous, I always speak economically, I never hesitate, I am sober, I am not aggressive and so on....

CYCLE-10

1	4	7	10	13	16	19	22	25	28
31	28	25	22	19	16	13	10	7	4
1									

Keep On Observing (KOO):

I like to find out solution of problems, I always remain content, I am always enterprising, I am good at communication, I am courageous, I always speak economically, I never hesitate, I am sober, I am not aggressive and so on....

CYCLE-11

1	4	7	10	13	16	19	22	25	28
31	34	31	28	25	22	19	16	13	10
7	4	1							

Keep On Observing (KOO):

I like to find out solution of problems, I always remain content, I am always enterprising, I am good at communication, I am courageous, I always speak economically, I never hesitate, I am sober, I am not aggressive and so on....

CYCLE-12

1	4	7	10	13	16	19	22	25	28
31	34	37	34	31	28	25	22	19	16
13	10	7	4	1					

Keep On Observing (KOO):

I like to find out solution of problems, I always remain content, I am always enterprising, I am good at communication,

I am courageous, I always speak economically, I never hesitate, I am sober, I am not aggressive and so on....

CYCLE-13

1	4	7	10	13	16	19	22	25	28
31	34	37	40	37	34	31	28	25	22
19	16	13	10	7	4	1			

Keep On Observing (KOO):

I like to find out solution of problems, I always remain content, I am always enterprising, I am good at communication, I am courageous, I always speak economically, I never hesitate, I am sober, I am not aggressive and so on....

CYCLE-14

1	4	7	10	13	16	19	22	25	28
31	34	37	40	43	40	37	34	31	28
25	22	19	16	13	10	7	4	1	

Keep On Observing (KOO):

I like to find out solution of problems, I always remain content, I am always enterprising, I am good at communication, I am courageous, I always speak economically, I never hesitate, I am sober, I am not aggressive and so on....

CYCLE-15

1	4	7	10	13	16	19	22	25	28
31	34	37	40	43	46	43	40	37	34
31	28	25	22	19	16	13	10	7	4
1									

Keep On Observing (KOO):

I like to find out solution of problems, I always remain content, I am always enterprising, I am good at communication, I am courageous, I always speak economically, I never hesitate, I am sober, I am not aggressive and so on....

CYCLE-16

1	4	7	10	13	16	19	22	25	28
31	34	37	40	43	46	49	46	43	40
37	34	31	28	25	22	19	16	13	10
7	4	1							

Keep On Observing (KOO):

I like to find out solution of problems, I always remain content, I am always enterprising, I am good at communication, I am courageous, I always speak economically, I never hesitate, I am sober, I am not aggressive and so on....

CYCLE-17

1	4	7	10	13	16	19	22	25	28
31	34	37	40	43	46	49	52	49	46
43	40	37	34	31	28	25	22	19	16
13	10	7	4	1					

Keep On Observing (KOO):

I like to find out solution of problems, I always remain content, I am always enterprising, I am good at communication, I am courageous, I always speak economically, I never hesitate, I am sober, I am not aggressive and so on....

CYCLE-18

1	4	7	10	13	16	19	22	25	28
31	34	37	40	43	46	49	52	55	52
49	46	43	40	37	34	31	28	25	22
19	16	13	10	7	4	1			

Keep On Observing (KOO):

I like to find out solution of problems, I always remain content, I am always enterprising, I am good at communication, I am courageous, I always speak economically, I never hesitate, I am sober, I am not aggressive and so on....

CYCLE-19

1	4	7	10	13	16	19	22	25	28
31	34	37	40	43	46	49	52	55	58
55	52	49	46	43	40	37	34	31	28
25	22	19	16	13	10	7	4	1	

Keep On Observing (KOO):

I like to find out solution of problems, I always remain content, I am always enterprising, I am good at communication, I am courageous, I always speak economically, I never hesitate, I am sober, I am not aggressive and so on....

CYCLE-20

1	4	7	10	13	16	19	22	25	28
31	34	37	40	43	46	49	52	55	58
61	58	55	52	49	46	43	40	37	34
31	28	25	22	19	16	13	10	7	4
1									

Keep On Observing (KOO):

I like to find out solution of problems, I always remain content, I am always enterprising, I am good at communication, I am courageous, I always speak economically, I never hesitate, I am sober, I am not aggressive and so on....

CYCLE-21

1	4	7	10	13	16	19	22	25	28
31	34	37	40	43	46	49	52	55	58
61	64	61	58	55	52	49	46	43	40
37	34	31	28	25	22	19	16	13	10
7	4	1							

Keep On Observing (KOO):

I like to find out solution of problems, I always remain content, I am always enterprising, I am good at communication, I am courageous, I always speak economically, I never hesitate, I am sober, I am not aggressive and so on....

CYCLE-22

1	4	7	10	13	16	19	22	25	28
31	34	37	40	43	46	49	52	55	58
61	64	67	64	61	58	55	52	49	46
43	40	37	34	31	28	25	22	19	16
13	10	7	4	1					

Keep On Observing (KOO):

I like to find out solution of problems, I always remain content, I am always enterprising, I am good at communication, I am courageous, I always speak economically, I never hesitate, I am sober, I am not aggressive and so on....

CYCLE-23

1	4	7	10	13	16	19	22	25	28
31	34	37	40	43	46	49	52	55	58
61	64	67	70	67	64	61	58	55	52
49	46	43	40	37	34	31	28	25	22
19	16	13	10	7	4	1			

Keep On Observing (KOO):

I like to find out solution of problems, I always remain content, I am always enterprising, I am good at communication, I am courageous, I always speak economically, I never hesitate, I am sober, I am not aggressive and so on....

CYCLE-24

1	4	7	10	13	16	19	22	25	28
31	34	37	40	43	46	49	52	55	58
61	64	67	70	73		70	67	64	61
58	55	52	49	46	43	40	37	34	31
28	25	22	19	16	13	10	7	4	1

Keep On Observing (KOO):

I like to find out solution of problems, I always remain content, I am always enterprising, I am good at communication, I am courageous, I always speak economically, I never hesitate, I am sober, I am not aggressive and so on....

CYCLE-25

1	4	7	10	13	16	19	22	25	28
31	34	37	40	43	46	49	52	55	58
61	64	67	70	73	76	73	70	67	64
61	58	55	52	49	46	43	40	37	34
31	28	25	22	19	16	13	10	7	4
1									

Keep On Observing (KOO):

I like to find out solution of problems, I always remain content, I am always enterprising, I am good at communication, I am courageous, I always speak economically, I never hesitate, I am sober, I am not aggressive and so on....

CYCLE-26

1	4	7	10	13	16	19	22	25	28
31	34	37	40	43	46	49	52	55	58
61	64	67	70	73	76	79	76	73	70
67	64	61	58	55	52	49	46	43	40
37	34	31	28	25	22	19	16	13	10
7	4	1							

Keep On Observing (KOO):

I like to find out solution of problems, I always remain content, I am always enterprising, I am good at communication, I am courageous, I always speak economically, I never hesitate, I am sober, I am not aggressive and so on....

CYCLE-27

1	4	7	10	13	16	19	22	25	28
31	34	37	40	43	46	49	52	55	58
61	64	67	70	73	76	79	82	79	76
73	70	67	64	61	58	55	52	49	46
43	40	37	34	31	28	25	22	19	16
13	10	7	4	1					

Keep On Observing (KOO):

I like to find out solution of problems, I always remain content, I am always enterprising, I am good at communication, I am courageous, I always speak economically, I never hesitate, I am sober, I am not aggressive and so on........

CYCLE-28

1	4	7	10	13	16	19	22	25	28
31	34	37	40	43	46	49	52	55	58
61	64	67	70	73	76	79	82	85	82
79	76	73	70	67	64	61	58	55	52
49	46	43	40	37	34	31	28	25	22
19	16	13	10	7	4	1			

Keep On Observing (KOO):

I like to find out solution of problems, I always remain content, I am always enterprising, I am good at communication, I am courageous, I always speak economically, I never hesitate, I am sober, I am not aggressive and so on....

CYCLE-29

1	4	7	10	13	16	19	22	25	28
31	34	37	40	43	46	49	52	55	58
61	64	67	70	73	76	79	82	85	88
85	82	79	76	73	70	67	64	61	58
55	52	49	46	43	40	37	34	31	28
25	22	19	16	13	10	7	4	1	

Keep On Observing (KOO):

I like to find out solution of problems, I always remain content, I am always enterprising, I am good at communication, I am courageous, I always speak economically, I never hesitate, I am sober, I am not aggressive and so on....

CYCLE-30

1	4	7	10	13	16	19	22	25	28
31	34	37	40	43	46	49	52	55	58
61	64	67	70	73	76	79	82	85	88
91	88	85	82	79	76	73	70	67	64
61	58	55	52	49	46	43	40	37	34
31	28	25	22	19	16	13	10	7	4
1									

Keep On Observing (KOO):

I like to find out solution of problems, I always remain content, I am always enterprising, I am good at communication, I am courageous, I always speak economically, I never hesitate, I am sober, I am not aggressive and so on....

CYCLE-31

1	4	7	10	13	16	19	22	25	28
31	34	37	40	43	46	49	52	55	58
61	64	67	70	73	76	79	82	85	88
91	94	91	88	85	82	79	76	73	70
67	64	61	58	55	52	49	46	43	40
37	34	31	28	25	22	19	16	13	10
7	4	1							

Keep On Observing (KOO):

I like to find out solution of problems, I always remain content, I am always enterprising, I am good at communication, I am courageous, I always speak economically, I never hesitate, I am sober, I am not aggressive and so on....

CYCLE-32

1	4	7	10	13	16	19	22	25	28
31	34	37	40	43	46	49	52	55	58
61	64	67	70	73	76	79	82	85	88
91	94	97	94	91	88	85	82	79	76
73	70	67	64	61	58	55	52	49	46
43	40	37	34	31	28	25	22	19	16
13	10	7	4	1					

Keep On Observing (KOO):

I like to find out solution of problems, I always remain content, I am always enterprising, I am good at communication, I am courageous, I always speak economically, I never hesitate, I am sober, I am not aggressive and so on....

PATTERN 2

CYCLE-1

2	5	2							

Keep On Observing (KOO):

I like to find out solution of problems, I always remain content, I am always enterprising, I am good at communication, I am courageous, I always speak economically, I never hesitate, I am sober, I am not aggressive and so on....

CYCLE-2

2	5	8	5	2					

Keep On Observing (KOO):

I like to find out solution of problems, I always remain content, I am always enterprising, I am good at communication, I am courageous, I always speak economically, I never hesitate, I am sober, I am not aggressive and so on....

CYCLE-3

2	5	8	11	8	5	2			

Keep On Observing (KOO):

I like to find out solution of problems, I always remain content, I am always enterprising, I am good at communication, I am courageous, I always speak economically, I never hesitate, I am sober, I am not aggressive and so on....

CYCLE-4

2	5	8	11	14	11	8	5	2	

Keep On Observing (KOO):

I like to find out solution of problems, I always remain content, I am always enterprising, I am good at communication, I am courageous, I always speak economically, I never hesitate, I am sober, I am not aggressive and so on....

CYCLE-5

2	5	8	11	14	17	14	11	8	5
2									

Keep On Observing (KOO):

I like to find out solution of problems, I always remain content, I am always enterprising, I am good at communication, I am courageous, I always speak economically, I never hesitate, I am sober, I am not aggressive and so on....

CYCLE-6

2	5	8	11	14	17	20	17	14	11
8	5	2							

Keep On Observing (KOO):

I like to find out solution of problems, I always remain content, I am always enterprising, I am good at communication, I am courageous, I always speak economically, I never hesitate, I am sober, I am not aggressive and so on....

CYCLE-7

2	5	8	11	14	17	20	23	20	17
14	11	8	5	2					

Keep On Observing (KOO):

I like to find out solution of problems, I always remain content, I am always enterprising, I am good at communication, I am courageous, I always speak economically, I never hesitate, I am sober, I am not aggressive and so on....

CYCLE-8

2	5	8	11	14	17	20	23	26	23
20	17	14	11	8	5	2			

Keep On Observing (KOO):

I like to find out solution of problems, I always remain content, I am always enterprising, I am good at communication, I am courageous, I always speak economically, I never hesitate, I am sober, I am not aggressive and so on....

CYCLE-9

2	5	8	11	14	17	20	23	26	29
26	23	20	17	14	11	8	5	2	

Keep On Observing (KOO):

I like to find out solution of problems, I always remain content, I am always enterprising, I am good at communication, I am courageous, I always speak economically, I never hesitate, I am sober, I am not aggressive and so on....

CYCLE-10

2	5	8	11	14	17	20	23	26	29
32	29	26	23	20	17	14	11	8	5
2									

Keep On Observing (KOO):

I like to find out solution of problems, I always remain content, I am always enterprising, I am good at communication, I am courageous, I always speak economically, I never hesitate, I am sober, I am not aggressive and so on....

CYCLE-11

2	5	8	11	14	17	20	23	26	29
32	35	32	29	26	23	20	17	14	11
8	5	2							

Keep On Observing (KOO):

I like to find out solution of problems, I always remain content, I am always enterprising, I am good at communication, I am courageous, I always speak economically, I never hesitate, I am sober, I am not aggressive and so on....

CYCLE-12

2	5	8	11	14	17	20	23	26	29
32	35	38	35	32	29	26	23	20	17
14	11	8	5	2					

Keep On Observing (KOO):

I like to find out solution of problems, I always remain content, I am always enterprising, I am good at communication, I am courageous, I always speak economically, I never hesitate, I am sober, I am not aggressive and so on....

CYCLE-13

2	5	8	11	14	17	20	23	26	29
32	35	38	41	38	35	32	29	26	23
20	17	14	11	8	5	2			

Keep On Observing (KOO):

I like to find out solution of problems, I always remain content, I am always enterprising, I am good at communication, I am courageous, I always speak economically, I never hesitate, I am sober, I am not aggressive and so on....

CYCLE-14

2	5	8	11	14	17	20	23	26	29
32	35	38	41	44	41	38	35	32	29
26	23	20	17	14	11	8	5	2	

Keep On Observing (KOO):

I like to find out solution of problems, I always remain content, I am always enterprising, I am good at communication, I am courageous, I always speak economically, I never hesitate, I am sober, I am not aggressive and so on........

CYCLE-15

2	5	8	11	14	17	20	23	26	29
32	35	38	41	44	47	44	41	38	35
32	29	26	23	20	17	14	11	8	5
2									

Keep On Observing (KOO):

I like to find out solution of problems, I always remain content, I am always enterprising, I am good at communication, I am courageous, I always speak economically, I never hesitate, I am sober, I am not aggressive and so on....

CYCLE-16

2	5	8	11	14	17	20	23	26	29
32	35	38	41	44	47	50	47	44	41
38	35	32	29	26	23	20	17	14	11
8	5	2							

Keep On Observing (KOO):

I like to find out solution of problems, I always remain content, I am always enterprising, I am good at communication, I am courageous, I always speak economically, I never hesitate, I am sober, I am not aggressive and so on....

CYCLE-17

2	5	8	11	14	17	20	23	26	29
32	35	38	41	44	47	50	53	50	47
44	41	38	35	32	29	26	23	20	17
14	11	8	5	2					

Keep On Observing (KOO):

I like to find out solution of problems, I always remain content, I am always enterprising, I am good at communication, I am courageous, I always speak economically, I never hesitate, I am sober, I am not aggressive and so on....

CYCLE-18

2	5	8	11	14	17	20	23	26	29
32	35	38	41	44	47	50	53	56	53
50	47	44	41	38	35	32	29	26	23
20	17	14	11	8	5	2			

Keep On Observing (KOO):

I like to find out solution of problems, I always remain content, I am always enterprising, I am good at communication, I am courageous, I always speak economically, I never hesitate, I am sober, I am not aggressive and so on....

CYCLE-19

2	5	8	11	14	17	20	23	26	29
32	35	38	41	44	47	50	53	56	59
56	53	50	47	44	41	38	35	32	29
26	23	20	17	14	11	8	5	2	

Keep On Observing (KOO):

I like to find out solution of problems, I always remain content, I am always enterprising, I am good at communication, I am courageous, I always speak economically, I never hesitate, I am sober, I am not aggressive and so on....

CYCLE-20

2	5	8	11	14	17	20	23	26	29
32	35	38	41	44	47	50	53	56	59
62	59	56	53	50	47	44	41	38	35
32	29	26	23	20	17	14	11	8	5
2									

Keep On Observing (KOO):

I like to find out solution of problems, I always remain content, I am always enterprising, I am good at communication, I am courageous, I always speak economically, I never hesitate, I am sober, I am not aggressive and so on....

CYCLE-21

2	5	8	11	14	17	20	23	26	29
32	35	38	41	44	47	50	53	56	59
62	65	62	59	56	53	50	47	44	41
38	35	32	29	26	23	20	17	14	11
8	5	2							

Keep On Observing (KOO):

I like to find out solution of problems, I always remain content, I am always enterprising, I am good at communication, I am courageous, I always speak economically, I never hesitate, I am sober, I am not aggressive and so on....

CYCLE-22

2	5	8	11	14	17	20	23	26	29
32	35	38	41	44	47	50	53	56	59
62	65	68	65	62	59	56	53	50	47
44	41	38	35	32	29	26	23	20	17
14	11	8	5	2					

Keep On Observing (KOO):

I like to find out solution of problems, I always remain content, I am always enterprising, I am good at communication, I am courageous, I always speak economically, I never hesitate, I am sober, I am not aggressive and so on....

CYCLE-23

2	5	8	11	14	17	20	23	26	29
32	35	38	41	44	47	50	53	56	59
62	65	68	71	68	65	62	59	56	53
50	47	44	41	38	35	32	29	26	23
20	17	14	11	8	5	2			

Keep On Observing (KOO):

I like to find out solution of problems, I always remain content, I am always enterprising, I am good at communication, I am courageous, I always speak economically, I never hesitate, I am sober, I am not aggressive and so on....

CYCLE-24

2	5	8	11	14	17	20	23	26	29
32	35	38	41	44	47	50	53	56	59
62	65	68	71	74	71	68	65	62	59
56	53	50	47	44	41	38	35	32	29
26	23	20	17	14	11	8	5	2	

Keep On Observing (KOO):

I like to find out solution of problems, I always remain content, I am always enterprising, I am good at communication, I am courageous, I always speak economically, I never hesitate, I am sober, I am not aggressive and so on....

CYCLE-25

2	5	8	11	14	17	20	23	26	29
32	35	38	41	44	47	50	53	56	59
62	65	68	71	74	77	74	71	68	65
62	59	56	53	50	47	44	41	38	35
32	29	26	23	20	17	14	11	8	5
2									

Keep On Observing (KOO):

I like to find out solution of problems, I always remain content, I am always enterprising, I am good at communication, I am courageous, I always speak economically, I never hesitate, I am sober, I am not aggressive and so on....

CYCLE-26

2	5	8	11	14	17	20	23	26	29
32	35	38	41	44	47	50	53	56	59
62	65	68	71	74	77	80	77	74	71
68	65	62	59	56	53	50	47	44	41
38	35	32	29	26	23	20	17	14	11
8	5	2							

Keep On Observing (KOO):

I like to find out solution of problems, I always remain content, I am always enterprising, I am good at communication, I am courageous, I always speak economically, I never hesitate, I am sober, I am not aggressive and so on....

CYCLE-27

2	5	8	11	14	17	20	23	26	29
32	35	38	41	44	47	50	53	56	59
62	65	68	71	74	77	80	83	80	77
74	71	68	65	62	59	56	53	50	47
44	41	38	35	32	29	26	23	20	17
14	11	8	5	2					

Keep On Observing (KOO):

I like to find out solution of problems, I always remain content, I am always enterprising, I am good at communication, I am courageous, I always speak economically, I never hesitate, I am sober, I am not aggressive and so on....

CYCLE-28

2	5	8	11	14	17	20	23	26	29
32	35	38	41	44	47	50	53	56	59
62	65	68	71	74	77	80	83	86	83
80	77	74	71	68	65	62	59	56	53
50	47	44	41	38	35	32	29	26	23
20	17	14	11	8	5	2			

Keep On Observing (KOO):

I like to find out solution of problems, I always remain content, I am always enterprising, I am good at communication, I am courageous, I always speak economically, I never hesitate, I am sober, I am not aggressive and so on....

CYCLE-29

2	5	8	11	14	17	20	23	26	29
32	35	38	41	44	47	50	53	56	59
62	65	68	71	74	77	80	83	86	89
86	83	80	77	74	71	68	65	62	59
56	53	50	47	44	41	38	35	32	29
26	23	20	17	14	11	8	5	2	

Keep On Observing (KOO):

I like to find out solution of problems, I always remain content, I am always enterprising, I am good at communication, I am courageous, I always speak economically, I never hesitate, I am sober, I am not aggressive and so on....

CYCLE-30

2	5	8	11	14	17	20	23	26	29
32	35	38	41	44	47	50	53	56	59
62	65	68	71	74	77	80	83	86	89
92	89	86	83	80	77	74	71	68	65
62	59	56	53	50	47	44	41	38	35
32	29	26	23	20	17	14	11	8	5
2									

Keep On Observing (KOO):

I like to find out solution of problems, I always remain content, I am always enterprising, I am good at communication, I am courageous, I always speak economically, I never hesitate, I am sober, I am not aggressive and so on....

CYCLE-31

2	5	8	11	14	17	20	23	26	29
32	35	38	41	44	47	50	53	56	59
62	65	68	71	74	77	80	83	86	89
92	95	92	89	86	83	80	77	74	71
68	65	62	59	56	53	50	47	44	41
38	35	32	29	26	23	20	17	14	11
8	5	2							

Keep On Observing (KOO):

I like to find out solution of problems, I always remain content, I am always enterprising, I am good at communication, I am courageous, I always speak economically, I never hesitate, I am sober, I am not aggressive and so on....

CYCLE-32

2	5	8	11	14	17	20	23	26	29
32	35	38	41	44	47	50	53	56	59
62	65	68	71	74	77	80	83	86	89
92	95	98	95	92	89	86	83	80	77
74	71	68	65	62	59	56	53	50	47
44	41	38	35	32	29	26	23	20	17
14	11	8	5	2					

Keep On Observing (KOO):

I like to find out solution of problems, I always remain content, I am always enterprising, I am good at communication, I am courageous, I always speak economically, I never hesitate, I am sober, I am not aggressive and so on....

Let's do an introspective exercise:

Please check what you achieved and able to exercise now in your life

Sr. No.	Qualities/ characteristics	Posses by a mathematised mind	Posses by a successfull mind	Posses by a happy mind	Posses by a pattern	Posses by you		
						Beginning	Consolidating	Exercising
1	like to find out solution of problems	yes	yes	Yes	yes			
2	remain content	yes	yes	Yes	yes			
3	enterprising	yes	yes	Yes	yes			
4	good at communication	yes	yes	Yes	yes			
5	courageous	yes	yes	Yes	yes			
6	speak economically	yes	yes	Yes	yes			
7	never hesitate	yes	yes	Yes	yes			
8	Sober	yes	yes	Yes	yes			
9	aggressive	no	no	No	no			
10	straight forward	yes	Yes	Yes	yes			
11	daring	yes	yes	Yes	Yes			
12	enthusiastic	yes	yes	Yes	yes			
13	risk taking	yes	calculated	calculated	calculated			
14	bold	yes	yes	Yes	Yes			
15	can take stress	yes	Yes	Yes	yes			
16	dominant	yes	no	No	No			
17	influenced by facts than by feeling	yes	Yes	Yes	yes			
18	Hard working	yes	yes	yes	Yes			
19	easy going never in hurry	yes	yes	Yes	yes			
20	quick decision	yes	yes	yes	Yes			
21	communicative	yes	yes	Yes	yes			
22	free from guilt	yes	yes	yes	yes			
23	never hesitate	yes	yes	yes	yes			
24	Secure	yes	yes	Yes	yes			
25	never act according to others	yes	yes	yes	yes			
26	capable of getting things done	yes	yes	Yes	yes			
27	assertive behaviour	yes	yes	yes	yes			

28	develop their own sets of rules	yes	If required	If required	If required			
29	self disciplined	yes	yes	yes	Yes			
30	abstract thinking	yes	yes	Yes	yes			
31	reliable behaviour	yes	yes	yes	yes			
32	experementive	yes	yes	yes	yes			
33	impulsive	yes	no	no	no			
34	self destructive	no	no	no	no			
35	social	yes	yes	yes	yes			
36	cope with routine life		yes	yes	yes			
37	highly self motivated	yes	yes	Yes	yes			
38	practical	yes	yes	yes	yes			
39	mindful	yes	yes	yes	yes			
40	lost in the world of dreams	no	no	no	no			
41	participating	yes	yes	yes	yes			
42	Cautious	yes	yes	Yes	yes			
43	likes people	yes	yes	yes	yes			
44	open minded	yes	yes	yes	yes			
45	resolve conflicts	yes	yes	Yes	yes			
46	emotionally mature	yes	yes	Yes	yes			
47	realistic	yes	yes	yes	yes			
48	Cheerful	yes	yes	Yes	yes			
49	Intuitive	yes	yes	yes	yes			
50	keep things under control	yes	yes	yes	yes			
51	Competitor of self	yes	yes	Yes	yes			
52	self confident	yes	yes	Yes	yes			
53	Assertive	yes	yes	Yes	yes			
54	Mature	yes	yes	Yes	yes			
55	Relax	yes	yes	Yes	yes			
56	Adaptive	yes	yes	Yes	yes			
57	Flexible	yes	yes	Yes	yes			
58	open to change	yes	yes	Yes	yes			
59	accommodative	yes	yes	Yes	yes			
60	socially active	yes	yes	Yes	yes			
61	cultural interests	yes	yes	Yes	yes			
62	down to earth	yes	yes	Yes	yes			
63	friendly nature	yes	yes	Yes	yes			
64	Sociable	yes	yes	Yes	yes			
65	good reasoning	yes	yes	Yes	yes			
66	intelligent	yes	yes	Yes	yes			
67	hard to fool	yes	yes	Yes	yes			

Express your feeling about your accomplishments through mathyogs9211:

....

....

....

....

....

....

....

....

....

....

....

....

....

....

....

....

....

....

....

....

....

....

....

....

....

....

....

....

CHAPTER-VIII

COUNTING BY FOUR'S

Group 4: Counting by four's

Sr. No.	GROUP IV			
Term	PATTERN-1	PATTERN-2	PATTERN-3	PATTERN-4
1	1	2	3	4
2	5	6	7	8
3	9	10	11	12
4	13	14	15	16
5	17	18	19	20
6	21	22	23	24
7	25	26	27	28
8	29	30	31	32
9	33	34	35	36
10	37	38	39	40
11	41	42	43	44
12	45	46	47	48
13	49	50	51	52
14	53	54	55	56
15	57	58	59	60
16	61	62	63	64

17	65	66	67	68
18	69	70	71	72
19	73	74	75	76
20	77	78	79	80
21	81	82	83	84
22	85	86	87	88
23	89	90	91	92
24	93	94	95	96
25	97	98	99	100

PATTERN 1

CYCLE-1

1	5	1							

Keep On Observing (KOO):

I like to find out solution of problems, I always remain content, I am always enterprising, I am good at communication, I am courageous, I always speak economically, I never hesitate, I am sober, I am not aggressive and so on....

CYCLE-2

1	5	9	5	1					

Keep On Observing (KOO):

I like to find out solution of problems, I always remain content, I am always enterprising, I am good at communication, I am courageous, I always speak economically, I never hesitate, I am sober, I am not aggressive and so on.....

CYCLE-3

1	5	9	13	9	5	1			

Keep On Observing (KOO):

I like to find out solution of problems, I always remain content, I am always enterprising, I am good at communication, I am courageous, I always speak economically, I never hesitate, I am sober, I am not aggressive and so on....

CYCLE-4

1	5	9	13	17	13	9	5	1	

Keep On Observing (KOO):

I like to find out solution of problems, I always remain content, I am always enterprising, I am good at communication, I am courageous, I always speak economically, I never hesitate, I am sober, I am not aggressive and so on....

CYCLE-5

1	5	9	13	17	21	17	13	9	5
1									

Keep On Observing (KOO):

I like to find out solution of problems, I always remain content, I am always enterprising, I am good at communication, I am courageous, I always speak economically, I never hesitate, I am sober, I am not aggressive and so on....

CYCLE-6

1	5	9	13	17	21	25	21	17	13
9	5	1							

Keep On Observing (KOO):

I like to find out solution of problems, I always remain content, I am always enterprising, I am good at communication, I am courageous, I always speak economically, I never hesitate, I am sober, I am not aggressive and so on....

CYCLE-7

1	5	9	13	17	21	25	29	25	21
17	13	9	5	1					

Keep On Observing (KOO):

I like to find out solution of problems, I always remain content, I am always enterprising, I am good at communication, I am courageous, I always speak economically, I never hesitate, I am sober, I am not aggressive and so on....

CYCLE-8

1	5	9	13	17	21	25	29	33	29
25	21	17	13	9	5	1			

Keep On Observing (KOO):

I like to find out solution of problems, I always remain content, I am always enterprising, I am good at communication, I am courageous, I always speak economically, I never hesitate, I am sober, I am not aggressive and so on....

CYCLE-9

1	5	9	13	17	21	25	29	33	37
33	29	25	21	17	13	9	5	1	

Keep On Observing (KOO):

I like to find out solution of problems, I always remain content, I am always enterprising, I am good at communication, I am courageous, I always speak economically, I never hesitate, I am sober, I am not aggressive and so on....

CYCLE-10

1	5	9	13	17	21	25	29	33	37
41	37	33	29	25	21	17	13	9	5
1									

Keep On Observing (KOO):

I like to find out solution of problems, I always remain content, I am always enterprising, I am good at communication, I am courageous, I always speak economically, I never hesitate, I am sober, I am not aggressive and so on....

CYCLE-11

1	5	9	13	17	21	25	29	33	37
41	45	41	37	33	29	25	21	17	13
9	5	1							

Keep On Observing (KOO):

I like to find out solution of problems, I always remain content, I am always enterprising, I am good at communication, I am courageous, I always speak economically, I never hesitate, I am sober, I am not aggressive and so on....

CYCLE-12

1	5	9	13	17	21	25	29	33	37
41	45	49	45	41	37	33	29	25	21
17	13	9	5	1					

Keep On Observing (KOO):

I like to find out solution of problems, I always remain content, I am always enterprising, I am good at communication, I am courageous, I always speak economically, I never hesitate, I am sober, I am not aggressive and so on....

CYCLE-13

1	5	9	13	17	21	25	29	33	37
41	45	49	53	49	45	41	37	33	29
25	21	17	13	9	5	1			

Keep On Observing (KOO):

I like to find out solution of problems, I always remain content, I am always enterprising, I am good at communication, I am courageous, I always speak economically, I never hesitate, I am sober, I am not aggressive and so on....

CYCLE-14

1	5	9	13	17	21	25	29	33	37
41	45	49	53	57	53	49	45	41	37
33	29	25	21	17	13	9	5	1	

Keep On Observing (KOO):

I like to find out solution of problems, I always remain content, I am always enterprising, I am good at communication, I am courageous, I always speak economically, I never hesitate, I am sober, I am not aggressive and so on....

CYCLE-15

1	5	9	13	17	21	25	29	33	37
41	45	49	53	57	61	57	53	49	45
41	37	33	29	25	21	17	13	9	5
1									

Keep On Observing (KOO):

I like to find out solution of problems, I always remain content, I am always enterprising, I am good at communication, I am courageous, I always speak economically, I never hesitate, I am sober, I am not aggressive and so on....

CYCLE-16

1	5	9	13	17	21	25	29	33	37
41	45	49	53	57	61	65	61	57	53
49	45	41	37	33	29	25	21	17	13
9	5	1							

Keep On Observing (KOO):

I like to find out solution of problems, I always remain content, I am always enterprising, I am good at communication, I am courageous, I always speak economically, I never hesitate, I am sober, I am not aggressive and so on.....

CYCLE-17

1	5	9	13	17	21	25	29	33	37
41	45	49	53	57	61	65	69	65	61
57	53	49	45	41	37	33	29	25	21
17	13	9	5	1					

Keep On Observing (KOO):

I like to find out solution of problems, I always remain content, I am always enterprising, I am good at communication, I am courageous, I always speak economically, I never hesitate, I am sober, I am not aggressive and so on....

CYCLE-18

1	5	9	13	17	21	25	29	33	37
41	45	49	53	57	61	65	69	73	69
65	61	57	53	49	45	41	37	33	29
25	21	17	13	9	5	1			

Keep On Observing (KOO):

I like to find out solution of problems, I always remain content, I am always enterprising, I am good at communication, I am courageous, I always speak economically, I never hesitate, I am sober, I am not aggressive and so on....

CYCLE-19

1	5	9	13	17	21	25	29	33	37
41	45	49	53	57	61	65	69	73	77
73	69	65	61	57	53	49	45	41	37
33	29	25	21	17	13	9	5	1	

Keep On Observing (KOO):

I like to find out solution of problems, I always remain content, I am always enterprising, I am good at communication, I am courageous, I always speak economically, I never hesitate, I am sober, I am not aggressive and so on....

CYCLE-20

1	5	9	13	17	21	25	29	33	37
41	45	49	53	57	61	65	69	73	77
81	77	73	69	65	61	57	53	49	45
41	37	33	29	25	21	17	13	9	5
1									

Keep On Observing (KOO):

I like to find out solution of problems, I always remain content, I am always enterprising, I am good at communication, I am courageous, I always speak economically, I never hesitate, I am sober, I am not aggressive and so on....

CYCLE-21

1	5	9	13	17	21	25	29	33	37
41	45	49	53	57	61	65	69	73	77
81	85	81	77	73	69	65	61	57	53
49	45	41	37	33	29	25	21	17	13
9	5	1							

Keep On Observing (KOO):

I like to find out solution of problems, I always remain content, I am always enterprising, I am good at communication, I am courageous, I always speak economically, I never hesitate, I am sober, I am not aggressive and so on....

CYCLE-22

1	5	9	13	17	21	25	29	33	37
41	45	49	53	57	61	65	69	73	77
81	85	89	85	81	77	73	69	65	61
57	53	49	45	41	37	33	29	25	21
17	13	9	5	1					

Keep On Observing (KOO):

I like to find out solution of problems, I always remain content, I am always enterprising, I am good at communication, I am courageous, I always speak economically, I never hesitate, I am sober, I am not aggressive and so on....

CYCLE-23

1	5	9	13	17	21	25	29	33	37
41	45	49	53	57	61	65	69	73	77
81	85	89	93	89	85	81	77	73	69
65	61	57	53	49	45	41	37	33	29
25	21	17	13	9	5	1			

Keep On Observing (KOO):

I like to find out solution of problems, I always remain content, I am always enterprising, I am good at communication, I am courageous, I always speak economically, I never hesitate, I am sober, I am not aggressive and so on....

CYCLE-24

1	5	9	13	17	21	25	29	33	37
41	45	49	53	57	61	65	69	73	77
81	85	89	93	97	93	89	85	81	77
73	69	65	61	57	53	49	45	41	37
33	29	25	21	17	13	9	5	1	

Keep On Observing (KOO):

I like to find out solution of problems, I always remain content, I am always enterprising, I am good at communication, I am courageous, I always speak economically, I never hesitate, I am sober, I am not aggressive and so on....

PATTERN: 2

CYCLE-1

2	6	2							

Keep On Observing (KOO):

I like to find out solution of problems, I always remain content, I am always enterprising, I am good at communication, I am courageous, I always speak economically, I never hesitate, I am sober, I am not aggressive and so on....

CYCLE-2

2	6	10	6	2					

Keep On Observing (KOO):

I like to find out solution of problems, I always remain content, I am always enterprising, I am good at communication, I am courageous, I always speak economically, I never hesitate, I am sober, I am not aggressive and so on....

CYCLE-3

2	6	10	14	10	6	2			

Keep On Observing (KOO):

I like to find out solution of problems, I always remain content, I am always enterprising, I am good at communication, I am courageous, I always speak economically, I never hesitate, I am sober, I am not aggressive and so on....

CYCLE-4

2	6	10	14	18	14	10	6	2	

Keep On Observing (KOO):

I like to find out solution of problems, I always remain content, I am always enterprising, I am good at communication, I am courageous, I always speak economically, I never hesitate, I am sober, I am not aggressive and so on....

CYCLE-5

2	6	10	14	18	22	18	14	10	6
2									

Keep On Observing (KOO):

I like to find out solution of problems, I always remain content, I am always enterprising, I am good at communication, I am courageous, I always speak economically, I never hesitate, I am sober, I am not aggressive and so on....

CYCLE-6

2	6	10	14	18	22	26	22	18	14
10	6	2							

Keep On Observing (KOO):

I like to find out solution of problems, I always remain content, I am always enterprising, I am good at communication, I am courageous, I always speak economically, I never hesitate, I am sober, I am not aggressive and so on....

CYCLE-7

2	6	10	14	18	22	26	30	26	22
18	14	10	6	2					

Keep On Observing (KOO):

I like to find out solution of problems, I always remain content, I am always enterprising, I am good at communication, I am courageous, I always speak economically, I never hesitate, I am sober, I am not aggressive and so on....

CYCLE-8

2	6	10	14	18	22	26	30	34	30
26	22	18	14	10	6	2			

Keep On Observing (KOO):

I like to find out solution of problems, I always remain content, I am always enterprising, I am good at communication, I am courageous, I always speak economically, I never hesitate, I am sober, I am not aggressive and so on........

CYCLE-9

2	6	10	14	18	22	26	30	34	38
34	30	26	22	18	14	10	6	2	

Keep On Observing (KOO):

I like to find out solution of problems, I always remain content, I am always enterprising, I am good at communication, I am courageous, I always speak economically, I never hesitate, I am sober, I am not aggressive and so on....

CYCLE-10

2	6	10	14	18	22	26	30	34	38
42	38	34	30	26	22	18	14	10	6
2									

Keep On Observing (KOO):

I like to find out solution of problems, I always remain content, I am always enterprising, I am good at communication, I am courageous, I always speak economically, I never hesitate, I am sober, I am not aggressive and so on....

CYCLE-11

2	6	10	14	18	22	26	30	34	38
42	46	42	38	34	30	26	22	18	14
10	6	2							

Keep On Observing (KOO):

I like to find out solution of problems, I always remain content, I am always enterprising, I am good at communication, I am courageous, I always speak economically, I never hesitate, I am sober, I am not aggressive and so on....

CYCLE-12

2	6	10	14	18	22	26	30	34	38
42	46	50	46	42	38	34	30	26	22
18	14	10	6	2					

Keep On Observing (KOO):

I like to find out solution of problems, I always remain content, I am always enterprising, I am good at communication, I am courageous, I always speak economically, I never hesitate, I am sober, I am not aggressive and so on....

CYCLE-13

2	6	10	14	18	22	26	30	34	38
42	46	50	54	50	46	42	38	34	30
26	22	18	14	10	6	2			

Keep On Observing (KOO):

I like to find out solution of problems, I always remain content, I am always enterprising, I am good at communication, I am courageous, I always speak economically, I never hesitate, I am sober, I am not aggressive and so on....

CYCLE-14

2	6	10	14	18	22	26	30	34	38
42	46	50	54	58	54	50	46	42	38
34	30	26	22	18	14	10	6	2	

Keep On Observing (KOO):

I like to find out solution of problems, I always remain content, I am always enterprising, I am good at communication, I am courageous, I always speak economically, I never hesitate, I am sober, I am not aggressive and so on....

CYCLE-15

2	6	10	14	18	22	26	30	34	38
42	46	50	54	58	62	58	54	50	46
42	38	34	30	26	22	18	14	10	6
2									

Keep On Observing (KOO):

I like to find out solution of problems, I always remain content, I am always enterprising, I am good at communication, I am courageous, I always speak economically, I never hesitate, I am sober, I am not aggressive and so on....

CYCLE-16

2	6	10	14	18	22	26	30	34	38
42	46	50	54	58	62	66	62	58	54
50	46	42	38	34	30	26	22	18	14
10	6	2							

Keep On Observing (KOO):

I like to find out solution of problems, I always remain content, I am always enterprising, I am good at communication, I am courageous, I always speak economically, I never hesitate, I am sober, I am not aggressive and so on....

CYCLE-17

2	6	10	14	18	22	26	30	34	38
42	46	50	54	58	62	66	70	66	62
58	54	50	46	42	38	34	30	26	22
18	14	10	6	2					

Keep On Observing (KOO):

I like to find out solution of problems, I always remain content, I am always enterprising, I am good at communication, I am courageous, I always speak economically, I never hesitate, I am sober, I am not aggressive and so on....

CYCLE-18

2	6	10	14	18	22	26	30	34	38
42	46	50	54	58	62	66	70	74	70
66	62	58	54	50	46	42	38	34	30
26	22	18	14	10	6	2			

Keep On Observing (KOO):

I like to find out solution of problems, I always remain content, I am always enterprising, I am good at communication, I am courageous, I always speak economically, I never hesitate, I am sober, I am not aggressive and so on....

CYCLE-19

2	6	10	14	18	22	26	30	34	38
42	46	50	54	58	62	66	70	74	78
74	70	66	62	58	54	50	46	42	38
34	30	26	22	18	14	10	6	2	

Keep On Observing (KOO):

I like to find out solution of problems, I always remain content, I am always enterprising, I am good at communication, I am courageous, I always speak economically, I never hesitate, I am sober, I am not aggressive and so on....

CYCLE-20

2	6	10	14	18	22	26	30	34	38
42	46	50	54	58	62	66	70	74	78
82	78	74	70	66	62	58	54	50	46
42	38	34	30	26	22	18	14	10	6
2									

Keep On Observing (KOO):

I like to find out solution of problems, I always remain content, I am always enterprising, I am good at communication, I am courageous, I always speak economically, I never hesitate, I am sober, I am not aggressive and so on........

CYCLE-21

2	6	10	14	18	22	26	30	34	38
42	46	50	54	58	62	66	70	74	78
82	86	82	78	74	70	66	62	58	54
50	46	42	38	34	30	26	22	18	14
10	6	2							

Keep On Observing (KOO):

I like to find out solution of problems, I always remain content, I am always enterprising, I am good at communication, I am courageous, I always speak economically, I never hesitate, I am sober, I am not aggressive and so on....

CYCLE-22

2	6	10	14	18	22	26	30	34	38
42	46	50	54	58	62	66	70	74	78
82	86	90	86	82	78	74	70	66	62
58	54	50	46	42	38	34	30	26	22
18	14	10	6	2					

Keep On Observing (KOO):

I like to find out solution of problems, I always remain content, I am always enterprising, I am good at communication, I am courageous, I always speak economically, I never hesitate, I am sober, I am not aggressive and so on....

CYCLE-23

2	6	10	14	18	22	26	30	34	38
42	46	50	54	58	62	66	70	74	78
82	86	90	94	90	86	82	78	74	70
66	62	58	54	50	46	42	38	34	30
26	22	18	14	10	6	2			

Keep On Observing (KOO):

I like to find out solution of problems, I always remain content, I am always enterprising, I am good at communication, I am courageous, I always speak economically, I never hesitate, I am sober, I am not aggressive and so on....

CYCLE-24

2	6	10	14	18	22	26	30	34	38
42	46	50	54	58	62	66	70	74	78
82	86	90	94	98	94	90	86	82	78
74	70	66	62	58	54	50	46	42	38
34	30	26	22	18	14	10	6	2	

Keep On Observing (KOO):

I like to find out solution of problems, I always remain content, I am always enterprising, I am good at communication, I am courageous, I always speak economically, I never hesitate, I am sober, I am not aggressive and so on....

PATTERNS: 3

CYCLE-1

3	7	3							

Keep On Observing (KOO):

I like to find out solution of problems, I always remain content, I am always enterprising, I am good at communication, I am courageous, I always speak economically, I never hesitate, I am sober, I am not aggressive and so on....

CYCLE-2

3	7	11	7	3					

Keep On Observing (KOO):

I like to find out solution of problems, I always remain content, I am always enterprising, I am good at communication, I am courageous, I always speak economically, I never hesitate, I am sober, I am not aggressive and so on....

CYCLE-3

3	7	11	15	11	7	3			

Keep On Observing (KOO):

I like to find out solution of problems, I always remain content, I am always enterprising, I am good at communication, I am courageous, I always speak economically, I never hesitate, I am sober, I am not aggressive and so on....

CYCLE-4

3	7	11	15	19	15	11	7	3	

Keep On Observing (KOO):

I like to find out solution of problems, I always remain content, I am always enterprising, I am good at communication, I am courageous, I always speak economically, I never hesitate, I am sober, I am not aggressive and so on....

CYCLE-5

3	7	11	15	19	23	19	15	11	7
3									

Keep On Observing (KOO):

I like to find out solution of problems, I always remain content, I am always enterprising, I am good at communication, I am courageous, I always speak economically, I never hesitate, I am sober, I am not aggressive and so on....

CYCLE-6

3	7	11	15	19	23	27	23	19	15
11	7	3							

Keep On Observing (KOO):

I like to find out solution of problems, I always remain content, I am always enterprising, I am good at communication, I am courageous, I always speak economically, I never hesitate, I am sober, I am not aggressive and so on....

CYCLE-7

3	7	11	15	19	23	27	31	27	23
19	15	11	7	3					

Keep On Observing (KOO):

I like to find out solution of problems, I always remain content, I am always enterprising, I am good at communication, I am courageous, I always speak economically, I never hesitate, I am sober, I am not aggressive and so on....

CYCLE-8

3	7	11	15	19	23	27	31	35	31
27	23	19	15	11	7	3			

Keep On Observing (KOO):

I like to find out solution of problems, I always remain content, I am always enterprising, I am good at communication, I am courageous, I always speak economically, I never hesitate, I am sober, I am not aggressive and so on....

CYCLE-9

3	7	11	15	19	23	27	31	35	39
35	31	27	23	19	15	11	7	3	

Keep On Observing (KOO):

I like to find out solution of problems, I always remain content, I am always enterprising, I am good at communication, I am courageous, I always speak economically, I never hesitate, I am sober, I am not aggressive and so on....

CYCLE-10

3	7	11	15	19	23	27	31	35	39
43	39	35	31	27	23	19	15	11	7
3									

Keep On Observing (KOO):

I like to find out solution of problems, I always remain content, I am always enterprising, I am good at communication, I am courageous, I always speak economically, I never hesitate, I am sober, I am not aggressive and so on....

CYCLE-11

3	7	11	15	19	23	27	31	35	39
43	47	43	39	35	31	27	23	19	15
11	7	3							

Keep On Observing (KOO):

I like to find out solution of problems, I always remain content, I am always enterprising, I am good at communication, I am courageous, I always speak economically, I never hesitate, I am sober, I am not aggressive and so on....

CYCLE-12

3	7	11	15	19	23	27	31	35	39
43	47		51	47	43	39	35	31	27
23	19	15	11	7	3				

Keep On Observing (KOO):

I like to find out solution of problems, I always remain content, I am always enterprising, I am good at communication, I am courageous, I always speak economically, I never hesitate, I am sober, I am not aggressive and so on....

CYCLE-13

3	7	11	15	19	23	27	31	35	39
43	47	51	55	51	47	43	39	35	31
27	23	19	15	11	7	3			

Keep On Observing (KOO):

I like to find out solution of problems, I always remain content, I am always enterprising, I am good at communication, I am courageous, I always speak economically, I never hesitate, I am sober, I am not aggressive and so on....

CYCLE-14

3	7	11	15	19	23	27	31	35	39
43	47	51	55	59	55	51	47	43	39
35	31	27	23	19	15	11	7	3	

Keep On Observing (KOO):

I like to find out solution of problems, I always remain content, I am always enterprising, I am good at communication, I am courageous, I always speak economically, I never hesitate, I am sober, I am not aggressive and so on....

CYCLE-15

3	7	11	15	19	23	27	31	35	39
43	47	51	55	59	63	59	55	51	47
43	39	35	31	27	23	19	15	11	7
3									

Keep On Observing (KOO):

I like to find out solution of problems, I always remain content, I am always enterprising, I am good at communication, I am courageous, I always speak economically, I never hesitate, I am sober, I am not aggressive and so on....

CYCLE-16

3	7	11	15	19	23	27	31	35	39
43	47	51	55	59	63	67	63	59	55
51	47	43	39	35	31	27	23	19	15
11	7	3							

Keep On Observing (KOO):

I like to find out solution of problems, I always remain content, I am always enterprising, I am good at communication, I am courageous, I always speak economically, I never hesitate, I am sober, I am not aggressive and so on....

CYCLE-17

3	7	11	15	19	23	27	31	35	39
43	47	51	55	59	63	67	71	67	63
59	55	51	47	43	39	35	31	27	23
19	15	11	7	3					

Keep On Observing (KOO):

I like to find out solution of problems, I always remain content, I am always enterprising, I am good at communication, I am courageous, I always speak economically, I never hesitate, I am sober, I am not aggressive and so on....

CYCLE-18

3	7	11	15	19	23	27	31	35	39
43	47	51	55	59	63	67	71	75	71
67	63	59	55	51	47	43	39	35	31
27	23	19	15	11	7	3			

Keep On Observing (KOO):

I like to find out solution of problems, I always remain content, I am always enterprising, I am good at communication, I am courageous, I always speak economically, I never hesitate, I am sober, I am not aggressive and so on....

CYCLE-19

3	7	11	15	19	23	27	31	35	39
43	47	51	55	59	63	67	71	75	79
75	71	67	63	59	55	51	47	43	39
35	31	27	23	19	15	11	7	3	

Keep On Observing (KOO):

I like to find out solution of problems, I always remain content, I am always enterprising, I am good at communication, I am courageous, I always speak economically, I never hesitate, I am sober, I am not aggressive and so on....

CYCLE-20

3	7	11	15	19	23	27	31	35	39
43	47	51	55	59	63	67	71	75	79
83	79	75	71	67	63	59	55	51	47
43	39	35	31	27	23	19	15	11	7
3									

Keep On Observing (KOO):

I like to find out solution of problems, I always remain content, I am always enterprising, I am good at communication, I am courageous, I always speak economically, I never hesitate, I am sober, I am not aggressive and so on....

CYCLE-21

3	7	11	15	19	23	27	31	35	39
43	47	51	55	59	63	67	71	75	79
83	87	83	79	75	71	67	63	59	55
51	47	43	39	35	31	27	23	19	15
11	7	3							

Keep On Observing (KOO):

I like to find out solution of problems, I always remain content, I am always enterprising, I am good at communication, I am courageous, I always speak economically, I never hesitate, I am sober, I am not aggressive and so on....

CYCLE-22

3	7	11	15	19	23	27	31	35	39
43	47	51	55	59	63	67	71	75	79
83	87	91	87	83	79	75	71	67	63
59	55	51	47	43	39	35	31	27	23
19	15	11	7	3					

Keep On Observing (KOO):

I like to find out solution of problems, I always remain content, I am always enterprising, I am good at communication, I am courageous, I always speak economically, I never hesitate, I am sober, I am not aggressive and so on....

CYCLE-23

3	7	11	15	19	23	27	31	35	39
43	47	51	55	59	63	67	71	75	79
83	87	91	95	91	87	83	79	75	71
67	63	59	55	51	47	43	39	35	31
27	23	19	15	11	7	3			

Keep On Observing (KOO):

I like to find out solution of problems, I always remain content, I am always enterprising, I am good at communication, I am courageous, I always speak economically, I never hesitate, I am sober, I am not aggressive and so on....

CYCLE-24

3	7	11	15	19	23	27	31	35	39
43	47	51	55	59	63	67	71	75	79
83	87	91	95	99	95	91	87	83	79
75	71	67	63	59	55	51	47	43	39
35	31	27	23	19	15	11	7	3	

Keep On Observing (KOO):

I like to find out solution of problems, I always remain content, I am always enterprising, I am good at communication, I am courageous, I always speak economically, I never hesitate, I am sober, I am not aggressive and so on....

PATTERNS: 4

Keep On Observing (KOO):

I like to find out solution of problems, I always remain content, I am always enterprising, I am good at communication, I am courageous, I always speak economically, I never hesitate, I am sober, I am not aggressive and so on....

CYCLE-1

4	8	4							

Keep On Observing (KOO):

I like to find out solution of problems, I always remain content, I am always enterprising, I am good at communication, I am courageous, I always speak economically, I never hesitate, I am sober, I am not aggressive and so on....

CYCLE-2

4	8	12	8	4					

Keep On Observing (KOO):

I like to find out solution of problems, I always remain content, I am always enterprising, I am good at communication, I am courageous, I always speak economically, I never hesitate, I am sober, I am not aggressive and so on....

CYCLE-3

4	8	12	16	12	8	4			

Keep On Observing (KOO):

I like to find out solution of problems, I always remain content, I am always enterprising, I am good at communication, I am courageous, I always speak economically, I never hesitate, I am sober, I am not aggressive and so on....

CYCLE-4

4	8	12	16	20	16	12	8	4	

Keep On Observing (KOO):

I like to find out solution of problems, I always remain content, I am always enterprising, I am good at communication, I am courageous, I always speak economically, I never hesitate, I am sober, I am not aggressive and so on........

CYCLE-5

4	8	12	16	20	24	20	16	12	8
4									

Keep On Observing (KOO):

I like to find out solution of problems, I always remain content, I am always enterprising, I am good at communication, I am courageous, I always speak economically, I never hesitate, I am sober, I am not aggressive and so on....

CYCLE-6

4	8	12	16	20	24	28	24	20	16
12	8	4							

Keep On Observing (KOO):

I like to find out solution of problems, I always remain content, I am always enterprising, I am good at communication, I am courageous, I always speak economically, I never hesitate, I am sober, I am not aggressive and so on....

CYCLE-7

4	8	12	16	20	24	28	32	28	24
20	16	12	8	4					

Keep On Observing (KOO):

I like to find out solution of problems, I always remain content, I am always enterprising, I am good at communication, I am courageous, I always speak economically, I never hesitate, I am sober, I am not aggressive and so on........

CYCLE-8

4	8	12	16	20	24	28	32	36	32
28	24	20	16	12	8	4			

Keep On Observing (KOO):

I like to find out solution of problems, I always remain content, I am always enterprising, I am good at communication, I am courageous, I always speak economically, I never hesitate, I am sober, I am not aggressive and so on....

CYCLE-9

4	8	12	16	20	24	28	32	36	40
36	32	28	24	20	16	12	8	4	

Keep On Observing (KOO):

I like to find out solution of problems, I always remain content, I am always enterprising, I am good at communication, I am courageous, I always speak economically, I never hesitate, I am sober, I am not aggressive and so on....

CYCLE-10

4	8	12	16	20	24	28	32	36	40
44	40	36	32	28	24	20	16	12	8
4									

Keep On Observing (KOO):

I like to find out solution of problems, I always remain content, I am always enterprising, I am good at communication, I am courageous, I always speak economically, I never hesitate, I am sober, I am not aggressive and so on....

CYCLE-11

4	8	12	16	20	24	28	32	36	40
44	48	44	40	36	32	28	24	20	16
12	8	4							

Keep On Observing (KOO):

I like to find out solution of problems, I always remain content, I am always enterprising, I am good at communication, I am courageous, I always speak economically, I never hesitate, I am sober, I am not aggressive and so on....

CYCLE-12

4	8	12	16	20	24	28	32	36	40
44	48	52	48	44	40	36	32	28	24
20	16	12	8	4					

Keep On Observing (KOO):

I like to find out solution of problems, I always remain content, I am always enterprising, I am good at communication, I am courageous, I always speak economically, I never hesitate, I am sober, I am not aggressive and so on....

CYCLE-13

4	8	12	16	20	24	28	32	36	40
44	48	52	56	52	48	44	40	36	32
28	24	20	16	12	8	4			

Keep On Observing (KOO):

I like to find out solution of problems, I always remain content, I am always enterprising, I am good at communication, I am courageous, I always speak economically, I never hesitate, I am sober, I am not aggressive and so on....

CYCLE-14

4	8	12	16	20	24	28	32	36	40
44	48	52	56	60	56	52	48	44	40
36	32	28	24	20	16	12	8	4	

Keep On Observing (KOO):

I like to find out solution of problems, I always remain content, I am always enterprising, I am good at communication, I am courageous, I always speak economically, I never hesitate, I am sober, I am not aggressive and so on....

CYCLE-15

4	8	12	16	20	24	28	32	36	40
44	48	52	56	60	64	60	56	52	48
44	40	36	32	28	24	20	16	12	8
4									

Keep On Observing (KOO):

I like to find out solution of problems, I always remain content, I am always enterprising, I am good at communication, I am courageous, I always speak economically, I never hesitate, I am sober, I am not aggressive and so on....

CYCLE-16

4	8	12	16	20	24	28	32	36	40
44	48	52	56	60	64	68	64	60	56
52	48	44	40	36	32	28	24	20	16
12	8	4							

Keep On Observing (KOO):

I like to find out solution of problems, I always remain content, I am always enterprising, I am good at communication, I am courageous, I always speak economically, I never hesitate, I am sober, I am not aggressive and so on....

CYCLE-17

4	8	12	16	20	24	28	32	36	40
44	48	52	56	60	64	68	72	68	64
60	56	52	48	44	40	36	32	28	24
20	16	12	8	4					

Keep On Observing (KOO):

I like to find out solution of problems, I always remain content, I am always enterprising, I am good at communication, I am courageous, I always speak economically, I never hesitate, I am sober, I am not aggressive and so on....

CYCLE-18

4	8	12	16	20	24	28	32	36	40
44	48	52	56	60	64	68	72	76	72
68	64	60	56	52	48	44	40	36	32
28	24	20	16	12	8	4			

Keep On Observing (KOO):

I like to find out solution of problems, I always remain content, I am always enterprising, I am good at communication, I am courageous, I always speak economically, I never hesitate, I am sober, I am not aggressive and so on....

CYCLE-19

4	8	12	16	20	24	28	32	36	40
44	48	52	56	60	64	68	72	76	80
76	72	68	64	60	56	52	48	44	40
36	32	28	24	20	16	12	8	4	

Keep On Observing (KOO):

I like to find out solution of problems, I always remain content, I am always enterprising, I am good at communication, I am courageous, I always speak economically, I never hesitate, I am sober, I am not aggressive and so on....

CYCLE-20

4	8	12	16	20	24	28	32	36	40
44	48	52	56	60	64	68	72	76	80
84	80	76	72	68	64	60	56	52	48
44	40	36	32	28	24	20	16	12	8
4									

Keep On Observing (KOO):

I like to find out solution of problems, I always remain content, I am always enterprising, I am good at communication, I am courageous, I always speak economically, I never hesitate, I am sober, I am not aggressive and so on....

CYCLE-21

4	8	12	16	20	24	28	32	36	40
44	48	52	56	60	64	68	72	76	80
84	88	84	80	76	72	68	64	60	56
52	48	44	40	36	32	28	24	20	16
12	8	4							

Keep On Observing (KOO):

I like to find out solution of problems, I always remain content, I am always enterprising, I am good at communication, I am courageous, I always speak economically, I never hesitate, I am sober, I am not aggressive and so on....

CYCLE-22

4	8	12	16	20	24	28	32	36	40
44	48	52	56	60	64	68	72	76	80
84	88	92	88	84	80	76	72	68	64
60	56	52	48	44	40	36	32	28	24
20	16	12	8	4					

Keep On Observing (KOO):

I like to find out solution of problems, I always remain content, I am always enterprising, I am good at communication, I am courageous, I always speak economically, I never hesitate, I am sober, I am not aggressive and so on....

CYCLE-23

4	8	12	16	20	24	28	32	36	40
44	48	52	56	60	64	68	72	76	80
84	88	92	96	92	88	84	80	76	72
68	64	60	56	52	48	44	40	36	32
28	24	20	16	12	8	4			

Keep On Observing (KOO):

I like to find out solution of problems, I always remain content, I am always enterprising, I am good at communication, I am courageous, I always speak economically, I never hesitate, I am sober, I am not aggressive and so on....

CYCLE-24

4	8	12	16	20	24	28	32	36	40
44	48	52	56	60	64	68	72	76	80
84	88	92	96	100	96	92	88	84	80
76	72	68	64	60	56	52	48	44	40
36	32	28	24	20	16	12	8	4	

Keep On Observing (KOO):

I like to find out solution of problems, I always remain content, I am always enterprising, I am good at communication, I am courageous, I always speak economically, I never hesitate, I am sober, I am not aggressive and so on....

Let's do an introspective exercise:

Please check what you achieved and able to exercise now in your life

Sr. No.	Qualities/ characteristics	Posses by a mathe-matised mind	Posses by a success full mind	Posses by a happy mind	Posses by a pat-tern	Posses by you		
						Begin-ning	Con-soli-dating	Exer-cising
1	like to find out solution of problems	yes	yes	Yes	yes			
2	remain content	yes	yes	Yes	yes			
3	enterprising	yes	yes	Yes	yes			
4	good at communication	yes	yes	Yes	yes			
5	courageous	yes	yes	Yes	yes			
6	speak economically	yes	yes	Yes	yes			
7	never hesitate	yes	yes	Yes	yes			
8	Sober	yes	yes	Yes	yes			
9	aggressive	no	no	No	no			
10	straight forward	yes	Yes	Yes	yes			
11	daring	yes	yes	Yes	Yes			
12	enthusiastic	yes	yes	Yes	yes			
13	risk taking	yes	calcu-lated	calcu-lated	calcu-lated			
14	bold	yes	yes	Yes	Yes			
15	can take stress	yes	Yes	Yes	yes			
16	dominant	yes	no	No	No			
17	influenced by facts than by feeling	yes	Yes	Yes	yes			
18	Hard working	yes	yes	yes	Yes			
19	easy going never in hurry	yes	yes	Yes	yes			
20	quick decision	yes	yes	yes	Yes			
21	communicative	yes	yes	Yes	yes			
22	free from guilt	yes	yes	yes	yes			
23	never hesitate	yes	yes	yes	yes			
24	Secure	yes	yes	Yes	yes			
25	never act according to others	yes	yes	yes	yes			
26	capable of getting things done	yes	yes	Yes	yes			

27	assertive behaviour	yes	yes	yes	yes			
28	develop their own sets of rules	yes	If required	If required	If required			
29	self disciplined	yes	yes	yes	Yes			
30	abstract thinking	yes	yes	Yes	yes			
31	reliable behaviour	yes	yes	yes	yes			
32	experimentive	yes	yes	yes	yes			
33	impulsive	yes	no	no	no			
34	self destructive	no	no	no	no			
35	social	yes	yes	yes	yes			
36	cope with routine life		yes	yes	yes			
37	highly self motivated	yes	yes	Yes	yes			
38	practical	yes	yes	yes	yes			
39	mindful	yes	yes	yes	yes			
40	lost in the world of dreams	no	no	no	no			
41	participating	yes	yes	yes	yes			
42	Cautious	yes	yes	Yes	yes			
43	likes people	yes	yes	yes	yes			
44	open minded	yes	yes	yes	yes			
45	resolve conflicts	yes	yes	Yes	yes			
46	emotionally mature	yes	yes	Yes	yes			
47	realistic	yes	yes	yes	yes			
48	Cheerful	yes	yes	Yes	yes			
49	Intuitive	yes	yes	yes	yes			
50	keep things under control	yes	yes	yes	yes			
51	Competitor of self	yes	yes	Yes	yes			
52	self confident	yes	yes	Yes	yes			
53	Assertive	yes	yes	Yes	yes			
54	Mature	yes	yes	Yes	yes			
55	Relax	yes	yes	Yes	yes			
56	Adaptive	yes	yes	Yes	yes			
57	Flexible	yes	yes	Yes	yes			
58	open to change	yes	yes	Yes	yes			
59	accommodative	yes	yes	Yes	yes			
60	socially active	yes	yes	Yes	yes			
61	cultural interests	yes	yes	Yes	yes			
62	down to earth	yes	yes	Yes	yes			
63	friendly nature	yes	yes	Yes	yes			
64	Sociable	yes	yes	Yes	yes			
65	good reasoning	yes	yes	Yes	yes			
66	intelligent	yes	yes	Yes	yes			
67	hard to fool	yes	yes	Yes	yes			

Express your feeling about your accomplishments through mathyogs9211:

....
....
....
....
....
....
....
....
....
....
....
....
....
....
....
....
....
....
....
....
....
....
....
....
....
....
....
....
....
....
....

CHAPTER-IX

COUNTING BY FIVE'S

Group 5: Counting by five's

Sr. No.	GROUP V				
Term	PATTERN-1	PATTERN-2	PATTERN-3	PATTERN-4	PATTERN-5
1	1	2	3	4	5
2	6	7	8	9	10
3	11	12	13	14	15
4	16	17	18	19	20
5	21	22	23	24	25
6	26	27	28	29	30
7	31	32	33	34	35
8	36	37	38	39	40
9	41	42	43	44	45
10	46	47	48	49	50
11	51	52	53	54	55
12	56	57	58	59	60
13	61	62	63	64	65
14	66	67	68	69	70
15	71	72	73	74	75
16	76	77	78	79	80
17	81	82	83	84	85
18	86	87	88	89	90
19	91	92	93	94	95
20	96	97	98	99	100

PATTERN: 1

CYCLE-1

1	6	1							

Keep On Observing (KOO):

I like to find out solution of problems, I always remain content, I am always enterprising, I am good at communication, I am courageous, I always speak economically, I never hesitate, I am sober, I am not aggressive and so on....

CYCLE-2

1	6	11	6	1					

Keep On Observing (KOO):

I like to find out solution of problems, I always remain content, I am always enterprising, I am good at communication, I am courageous, I always speak economically, I never hesitate, I am sober, I am not aggressive and so on....

CYCLE-3

1	6	11	16	11	6	1			

Keep On Observing (KOO):

I like to find out solution of problems, I always remain content, I am always enterprising, I am good at communication, I am courageous, I always speak economically, I never hesitate, I am sober, I am not aggressive and so on....

CYCLE-4

1	6	11	16	21	16	11	6	1	

Keep On Observing (KOO):

I like to find out solution of problems, I always remain content, I am always enterprising, I am good at communication, I am courageous, I always speak economically, I never hesitate, I am sober, I am not aggressive and so on....

CYCLE-5

1	6	11	16	21	26	21	16	11	6
1									

Keep On Observing (KOO):

I like to find out solution of problems, I always remain content, I am always enterprising, I am good at communication, I am courageous, I always speak economically, I never hesitate, I am sober, I am not aggressive and so on....

CYCLE-6

1	6	11	16	21	26	31	26	21	16
11	6	1							

Keep On Observing (KOO):

I like to find out solution of problems, I always remain content, I am always enterprising, I am good at communication, I am courageous, I always speak economically, I never hesitate, I am sober, I am not aggressive and so on....

CYCLE-7

1	6	11	16	21	26	31	36	31	26
21	16	11	6	1					

Keep On Observing (KOO):

I like to find out solution of problems, I always remain content, I am always enterprising, I am good at communication, I am courageous, I always speak economically, I never hesitate, I am sober, I am not aggressive and so on....

CYCLE-8

1	6	11	16	21	26	31	36	41	36
31	26	21	16	11	6	1			

Keep On Observing (KOO):

I like to find out solution of problems, I always remain content, I am always enterprising, I am good at communication, I am courageous, I always speak economically, I never hesitate, I am sober, I am not aggressive and so on....

CYCLE-9

1	6	11	16	21	26	31	36	41	46
41	36	31	26	21	16	11	6	1	

Keep On Observing (KOO):

I like to find out solution of problems, I always remain content, I am always enterprising, I am good at communication, I am courageous, I always speak economically, I never hesitate, I am sober, I am not aggressive and so on....

CYCLE-10

1	6	11	16	21	26	31	36	41	46
51	46	41	36	31	26	21	16	11	6
1									

Keep On Observing (KOO):

I like to find out solution of problems, I always remain content, I am always enterprising, I am good at communication, I am courageous, I always speak economically, I never hesitate, I am sober, I am not aggressive and so on....

CYCLE-11

1	6	11	16	21	26	31	36	41	46
51	56	51	46	41	36	31	26	21	16
11	6	1							

Keep On Observing (KOO):

I like to find out solution of problems, I always remain content, I am always enterprising, I am good at communication, I am courageous, I always speak economically, I never hesitate, I am sober, I am not aggressive and so on....

CYCLE-12

1	6	11	16	21	26	31	36	41	46
51	56	61	56	51	46	41	36	31	26
21	16	11	6	1					

Keep On Observing (KOO):

I like to find out solution of problems, I always remain content, I am always enterprising, I am good at communication, I am courageous, I always speak economically, I never hesitate, I am sober, I am not aggressive and so on....

CYCLE-13

1	6	11	16	21	26	31	36	41	46
51	56	61	66	61	56	51	46	41	36
31	26	21	16	11	6	1			

Keep On Observing (KOO):

I like to find out solution of problems, I always remain content, I am always enterprising, I am good at communication, I am courageous, I always speak economically, I never hesitate, I am sober, I am not aggressive and so on....

CYCLE-14

1	6	11	16	21	26	31	36	41	46
51	56	61	66	71	66	61	56	51	46
41	36	31	26	21	16	11	6	1	

Keep On Observing (KOO):

I like to find out solution of problems, I always remain content, I am always enterprising, I am good at communication, I am courageous, I always speak economically, I never hesitate, I am sober, I am not aggressive and so on....

CYCLE-15

1	6	11	16	21	26	31	36	41	46
51	56	61	66	71	76	71	66	61	56
51	46	41	36	31	26	21	16	11	6
1									

Keep On Observing (KOO):

I like to find out solution of problems, I always remain content, I am always enterprising, I am good at communication, I am courageous, I always speak economically, I never hesitate, I am sober, I am not aggressive and so on....

CYCLE-16

1	6	11	16	21	26	31	36	41	46
51	56	61	66	71	76	81	76	71	66
61	56	51	46	41	36	31	26	21	16
11	6	1							

Keep On Observing (KOO):

I like to find out solution of problems, I always remain content, I am always enterprising, I am good at communication, I am courageous, I always speak economically, I never hesitate, I am sober, I am not aggressive and so on....

CYCLE-17

1	6	11	16	21	26	31	36	41	46
51	56	61	66	71	76	81	86	81	76
71	66	61	56	51	46	41	36	31	26
21	16	11	6	1					

Keep On Observing (KOO):

I like to find out solution of problems, I always remain content, I am always enterprising, I am good at communication, I am courageous, I always speak economically, I never hesitate, I am sober, I am not aggressive and so on....

CYCLE-18

1	6	11	16	21	26	31	36	41	46
51	56	61	66	71	76	81	86	91	86
81	76	71	66	61	56	51	46	41	36
31	26	21	16	11	6	1			

Keep On Observing (KOO):

I like to find out solution of problems, I always remain content, I am always enterprising, I am good at communication, I am courageous, I always speak economically, I never hesitate, I am sober, I am not aggressive and so on....

CYCLE-19

1	6	11	16	21	26	31	36	41	46
51	56	61	66	71	76	81	86	91	96
91	86	81	76	71	66	61	56	51	46
41	36	31	26	21	16	11	6	1	

Keep On Observing (KOO):

I like to find out solution of problems, I always remain content, I am always enterprising, I am good at communication, I am courageous, I always speak economically, I never hesitate, I am sober, I am not aggressive and so on....

PATTERN: 2

CYCLE-1

2	7	2							

Keep On Observing (KOO):

I like to find out solution of problems, I always remain content, I am always enterprising, I am good at communication, I am courageous, I always speak economically, I never hesitate, I am sober, I am not aggressive and so on....

CYCLE-2

2	7	12	7	2					

Keep On Observing (KOO):

I like to find out solution of problems, I always remain content, I am always enterprising, I am good at communication, I am courageous, I always speak economically, I never hesitate, I am sober, I am not aggressive and so on....

CYCLE-3

2	7	12	17	12	7	2			

Keep On Observing (KOO):

I like to find out solution of problems, I always remain content, I am always enterprising, I am good at communication, I am courageous, I always speak economically, I never hesitate, I am sober, I am not aggressive and so on....

CYCLE-4

2	7	12	17	22	17	12	7	2	

Keep On Observing (KOO):

I like to find out solution of problems, I always remain content, I am always enterprising, I am good at communication, I am courageous, I always speak economically, I never hesitate, I am sober, I am not aggressive and so on....

CYCLE-5

2	7	12	17	22	27	22	17	12	7
2									

Keep On Observing (KOO):

I like to find out solution of problems, I always remain content, I am always enterprising, I am good at communication, I am courageous, I always speak economically, I never hesitate, I am sober, I am not aggressive and so on....

CYCLE-6

2	7	12	17	22	27	32	27	22	17
12	7	2							

Keep On Observing (KOO):

I like to find out solution of problems, I always remain content, I am always enterprising, I am good at communication, I am courageous, I always speak economically, I never hesitate, I am sober, I am not aggressive and so on....

CYCLE-7

2	7	12	17	22	27	32	37	32	27
22	17	12	7	2					

Keep On Observing (KOO):

I like to find out solution of problems, I always remain content, I am always enterprising, I am good at communication, I am courageous, I always speak economically, I never hesitate, I am sober, I am not aggressive and so on....

CYCLE-8

2	7	12	17	22	27	32	37	42	37
32	27	22	17	12	7	2			

Keep On Observing (KOO):

I like to find out solution of problems, I always remain content, I am always enterprising, I am good at communication, I am courageous, I always speak economically, I never hesitate, I am sober, I am not aggressive and so on....

CYCLE-9

2	7	12	17	22	27	32	37	42	47
42	37	32	27	22	17	12	7	2	

Keep On Observing (KOO):

I like to find out solution of problems, I always remain content, I am always enterprising, I am good at communication, I am courageous, I always speak economically, I never hesitate, I am sober, I am not aggressive and so on....

CYCLE-10

2	7	12	17	22	27	32	37	42	47
52	47	42	37	32	27	22	17	12	7
2									

Keep On Observing (KOO):

I like to find out solution of problems, I always remain content, I am always enterprising, I am good at communication, I am courageous, I always speak economically, I never hesitate, I am sober, I am not aggressive and so on....

CYCLE-11

2	7	12	17	22	27	32	37	42	47
52	57	52	47	42	37	32	27	22	17
12	7	2							

Keep On Observing (KOO):

I like to find out solution of problems, I always remain content, I am always enterprising, I am good at communication, I am courageous, I always speak economically, I never hesitate, I am sober, I am not aggressive and so on....

CYCLE-12

2	7	12	17	22	27	32	37	42	47
52	57		62	57	52	47	42	37	32
27	22	17	12	7	2				

Keep On Observing (KOO):

I like to find out solution of problems, I always remain content, I am always enterprising, I am good at communication, I am courageous, I always speak economically, I never hesitate, I am sober, I am not aggressive and so on....

CYCLE-13

2	7	12	17	22	27	32	37	42	47
52	57	62	67	62	57	52	47	42	37
32	27	22	17	12	7	2			

Keep On Observing (KOO):

I like to find out solution of problems, I always remain content, I am always enterprising, I am good at communication, I am courageous, I always speak economically, I never hesitate, I am sober, I am not aggressive and so on....

CYCLE-14

2	7	12	17	22	27	32	37	42	47
52	57	62	67	72	67	62	57	52	47
42	37	32	27	22	17	12	7	2	

Keep On Observing (KOO):

I like to find out solution of problems, I always remain content, I am always enterprising, I am good at communication, I am courageous, I always speak economically, I never hesitate, I am sober, I am not aggressive and so on....

CYCLE-15

2	7	12	17	22	27	32	37	42	47
52	5	62	67	72	77	72	67	62	57
52	47	42	37	32	27	22	17	12	7
2									

Keep On Observing (KOO):

I like to find out solution of problems, I always remain content, I am always enterprising, I am good at communication, I am courageous, I always speak economically, I never hesitate, I am sober, I am not aggressive and so on....

CYCLE-16

2	7	12	17	22	27	32	37	42	47
52	57	62	67	72	77	82	77	72	67
62	57	52	47	42	37	32	27	22	17
12	7	2							

Keep On Observing (KOO):

I like to find out solution of problems, I always remain content, I am always enterprising, I am good at communication, I am courageous, I always speak economically, I never hesitate, I am sober, I am not aggressive and so on....

CYCLE-17

2	7	12	17	22	27	32	37	42	47
52	57	62	67	72	77	82	87	82	77
72	67	62	57	52	47	42	37	32	27
22	17	12	7	2					

Keep On Observing (KOO):

I like to find out solution of problems, I always remain content, I am always enterprising, I am good at communication, I am courageous, I always speak economically, I never hesitate, I am sober, I am not aggressive and so on....

CYCLE-18

2	7	12	17	22	27	32	37	42	47
52	57	62	67	72	77	82	87	92	87
82	77	72	67	62	57	52	47	42	37
32	27	22	17	12	7	2			

Keep On Observing (KOO):

I like to find out solution of problems, I always remain content, I am always enterprising, I am good at communication, I am courageous, I always speak economically, I never hesitate, I am sober, I am not aggressive and so on....

CYCLE-19

2	7	12	17	22	27	32	37	42	47
52	57	62	67	72	77	82	87	92	97
92	87	82	77	72	67	62	57	52	47
42	37	32	27	22	17	12	7	2	

Keep On Observing (KOO):

I like to find out solution of problems, I always remain content, I am always enterprising, I am good at communication, I am courageous, I always speak economically, I never hesitate, I am sober, I am not aggressive and so on....

PATTERN: 3

CYCLE-1

3	8	3							

Keep On Observing (KOO):

I like to find out solution of problems, I always remain content, I am always enterprising, I am good at communication, I am courageous, I always speak economically, I never hesitate, I am sober, I am not aggressive and so on....

CYCLE-2

3	8	13	8	3					

Keep On Observing (KOO):

I like to find out solution of problems, I always remain content, I am always enterprising, I am good at communication, I am courageous, I always speak economically, I never hesitate, I am sober, I am not aggressive and so on....

CYCLE-3

3	8	13	18	13	8	3			

Keep On Observing (KOO):

I like to find out solution of problems, I always remain content, I am always enterprising, I am good at communication, I am courageous, I always speak economically, I never hesitate, I am sober, I am not aggressive and so on....

CYCLE-4

3	8	13	18	23	18	13	8	3	

Keep On Observing (KOO):

I like to find out solution of problems, I always remain content, I am always enterprising, I am good at communication, I am courageous, I always speak economically, I never hesitate, I am sober, I am not aggressive and so on....

CYCLE-5

3	8	13	18	23	28	23	18	13	8
3									

Keep On Observing (KOO):

I like to find out solution of problems, I always remain content, I am always enterprising, I am good at communication, I am courageous, I always speak economically, I never hesitate, I am sober, I am not aggressive and so on....

CYCLE-6

3	8	13	18	23	28	33	28	23	18
13	8	3							

Keep On Observing (KOO):

I like to find out solution of problems, I always remain content, I am always enterprising, I am good at communication, I am courageous, I always speak economically, I never hesitate, I am sober, I am not aggressive and so on....

CYCLE-7

3	8	13	18	23	28	33	38	33	28
23	18	13	8	3					

Keep On Observing (KOO):

I like to find out solution of problems, I always remain content, I am always enterprising, I am good at communication, I am courageous, I always speak economically, I never hesitate, I am sober, I am not aggressive and so on....

CYCLE-8

3	8	13	18	23	28	33	38	43	38
33	28	23	18	13	8	3			

Keep On Observing (KOO):

I like to find out solution of problems, I always remain content, I am always enterprising, I am good at communication, I am courageous, I always speak economically, I never hesitate, I am sober, I am not aggressive and so on....

CYCLE-9

3	8	13	18	23	28	33	38	43	48
43	38	33	28	23	13	8	3		

Keep On Observing (KOO):

I like to find out solution of problems, I always remain content, I am always enterprising, I am good at communication, I am courageous, I always speak economically, I never hesitate, I am sober, I am not aggressive and so on....

CYCLE-10

3	8	13	18	23	28	33	38	43	48
53	48	43	38	33	28	23	18	13	8
3									

Keep On Observing (KOO):

I like to find out solution of problems, I always remain content, I am always enterprising, I am good at communication, I am courageous, I always speak economically, I never hesitate, I am sober, I am not aggressive and so on....

CYCLE-11

3	8	13	18	23	28	33	38	43	48
53	58	53	48	43	37	33	27	23	18
13	8	3							

Keep On Observing (KOO):

I like to find out solution of problems, I always remain content, I am always enterprising, I am good at communication, I am courageous, I always speak economically, I never hesitate, I am sober, I am not aggressive and so on....

CYCLE-12

3	8	13	18	23	28	33	38	43	48
53	58	63	58	53	48	43	38	33	28
23	18	13	8	3					

Keep On Observing (KOO):

I like to find out solution of problems, I always remain content, I am always enterprising, I am good at communication, I am courageous, I always speak economically, I never hesitate, I am sober, I am not aggressive and so on....

CYCLE-13

3	8	13	18	23	28	33	38	43	48
53	58	63	68	63	58	53	48	43	38
33	28	23	13	8	3				

Keep On Observing (KOO):

I like to find out solution of problems, I always remain content, I am always enterprising, I am good at communication, I am courageous, I always speak economically, I never hesitate, I am sober, I am not aggressive and so on....

CYCLE-14

3	8	13	18	23	28	33	38	43	48
53	58	63	68	73	68	63	58	53	48
43	38	33	28	23	13	8	3		

Keep On Observing (KOO):

I like to find out solution of problems, I always remain content, I am always enterprising, I am good at communication, I am courageous, I always speak economically, I never hesitate, I am sober, I am not aggressive and so on....

CYCLE-15

3	8	13	23	28	33	38	43	48	53
58	63	68	73	78	73	68	63	58	53
48	43	38	33	28	23	13	8	3	

Keep On Observing (KOO):

I like to find out solution of problems, I always remain content, I am always enterprising, I am good at communication, I am courageous, I always speak economically, I never hesitate, I am sober, I am not aggressive and so on....

CYCLE-16

3	8	13	23	28	33	38	43	48	53
58	63	68	73	78	83	78	73	68	63
58	53	48	43	38	33	28	23	13	8
3									

Keep On Observing (KOO):

I like to find out solution of problems, I always remain content, I am always enterprising, I am good at communication, I am courageous, I always speak economically, I never hesitate, I am sober, I am not aggressive and so on....

CYCLE-17

3	8	13	23	28	33	38	43	48	53
58	63	68	73	78	83	88	83	78	73
68	63	58	53	48	43	38	33	28	23
13	8	3							

Keep On Observing (KOO):

I like to find out solution of problems, I always remain content, I am always enterprising, I am good at communication, I am courageous, I always speak economically, I never hesitate, I am sober, I am not aggressive and so on....

CYCLE-18

3	8	13	23	28	33	38	43	48	53
58	63	68	73	78	83	88	93	88	83
78	73	68	63	58	53	48	43	38	33
28	23	13	8	3					

Keep On Observing (KOO):

I like to find out solution of problems, I always remain content, I am always enterprising, I am good at communication, I am courageous, I always speak economically, I never hesitate, I am sober, I am not aggressive and so on....

CYCLE-19

3	8	13	23	28	33	38	43	48	53
58	63	68	73	78	83	88	93	98	93
88	83	78	73	68	63	58	53	48	43
38	33	28	23	13	8	3			

Keep On Observing (KOO):

I like to find out solution of problems, I always remain content, I am always enterprising, I am good at communication, I am courageous, I always speak economically, I never hesitate, I am sober, I am not aggressive and so on....

PATTERN: 4

Keep On Observing (KOO):

I like to find out solution of problems, I always remain content, I am always enterprising, I am good at communication, I am courageous, I always speak economically, I never hesitate, I am sober, I am not aggressive and so on....

CYCLE-1

4	9	4							

Keep On Observing (KOO):

I like to find out solution of problems, I always remain content, I am always enterprising, I am good at communication, I am courageous, I always speak economically, I never hesitate, I am sober, I am not aggressive and so on....

CYCLE-2

4	9	14	9	4					

Keep On Observing (KOO):

I like to find out solution of problems, I always remain content, I am always enterprising, I am good at communication, I am courageous, I always speak economically, I never hesitate, I am sober, I am not aggressive and so on....

CYCLE-3

4	9	14	19	14	9	4			

Keep On Observing (KOO):

I like to find out solution of problems, I always remain content, I am always enterprising, I am good at communication, I am courageous, I always speak economically, I never hesitate, I am sober, I am not aggressive and so on....

CYCLE-4

4	9	14	19	24	19	14	9	4	

Keep On Observing (KOO):

I like to find out solution of problems, I always remain content, I am always enterprising, I am good at communication, I am courageous, I always speak economically, I never hesitate, I am sober, I am not aggressive and so on....

CYCLE-5

4	9	14	19	24	29	24	19	14	9
4									

Keep On Observing (KOO):

I like to find out solution of problems, I always remain content, I am always enterprising, I am good at communication, I am courageous, I always speak economically, I never hesitate, I am sober, I am not aggressive and so on....

CYCLE-6

4	9	14	19	24	29	34	29	24	19
14	9	4							

Keep On Observing (KOO):

I like to find out solution of problems, I always remain content, I am always enterprising, I am good at communication, I am courageous, I always speak economically, I never hesitate, I am sober, I am not aggressive and so on....

CYCLE-7

4	9	14	19	24	29	34	39	34	29
24	19	14	9	4					

Keep On Observing (KOO):

I like to find out solution of problems, I always remain content, I am always enterprising, I am good at communication, I am courageous, I always speak economically, I never hesitate, I am sober, I am not aggressive and so on....

CYCLE-8

4	9	14	19	24	29	34	39	44	39
34	29	24	19	14	9	4			

Keep On Observing (KOO):

I like to find out solution of problems, I always remain content, I am always enterprising, I am good at communication, I am courageous, I always speak economically, I never hesitate, I am sober, I am not aggressive and so on....

CYCLE-9

4	9	14	19	24	29	34	39	44	49
44	39	34	29	24	19	14	9	4	

Keep On Observing (KOO):

I like to find out solution of problems, I always remain content, I am always enterprising, I am good at communication, I am courageous, I always speak economically, I never hesitate, I am sober, I am not aggressive and so on....

CYCLE-10

4	9	14	19	24	29	34	39	44	49
54	49	44	39	34	29	24	19	14	9
4									

Keep On Observing (KOO):

I like to find out solution of problems, I always remain content, I am always enterprising, I am good at communication, I am courageous, I always speak economically, I never hesitate, I am sober, I am not aggressive and so on....

CYCLE-11

4	9	14	19	24	29	34	39	44	49
54	59	54	49	44	39	34	29	24	19
14	9	4							

Keep On Observing (KOO):

I like to find out solution of problems, I always remain content, I am always enterprising, I am good at communication, I am courageous, I always speak economically, I never hesitate, I am sober, I am not aggressive and so on....

CYCLE-12

4	9	14	19	24	29	34	39	44	49
54	59	64	59	54	49	44	39	34	29
24	19	14	9	4					

Keep On Observing (KOO):

I like to find out solution of problems, I always remain content, I am always enterprising, I am good at communication, I am courageous, I always speak economically, I never hesitate, I am sober, I am not aggressive and so on....

CYCLE-13

4	9	14	19	24	29	34	39	44	49	54	59	64
69	64	59	54	49	44	39	34	29	24	19	14	9
4												

Keep On Observing (KOO):

I like to find out solution of problems, I always remain content, I am always enterprising, I am good at communication, I am courageous, I always speak economically, I never hesitate, I am sober, I am not aggressive and so on....

CYCLE-14

4	9	14	19	24	29	34	39	44	49
54	59	64	69	74	69	64	59	54	49
44	39	34	29	24	19	14	9	4	

Keep On Observing (KOO):

I like to find out solution of problems, I always remain content, I am always enterprising, I am good at communication, I am courageous, I always speak economically, I never hesitate, I am sober, I am not aggressive and so on....

CYCLE-15

4	9	14	19	24	29	34	39	44	49
54	59	64	69	74	79	74	69	64	59
54	49	44	39	34	29	24	19	14	9
4									

Keep On Observing (KOO):

I like to find out solution of problems, I always remain content, I am always enterprising, I am good at communication, I am courageous, I always speak economically, I never hesitate, I am sober, I am not aggressive and so on....

CYCLE-16

4	9	14	19	24	29	34	39	44	49
54	59	64	69	74	79	84	79	74	69
64	59	54	49	44	39	34	29	24	19
14	9	4							

Keep On Observing (KOO):

I like to find out solution of problems, I always remain content, I am always enterprising, I am good at communication, I am courageous, I always speak economically, I never hesitate, I am sober, I am not aggressive and so on....

CYCLE-17

4	9	14	19	24	29	34	39	44	49
54	59	64	69	74	79	84	89	84	79
74	69	64	59	54	49	44	39	34	29
24	19	14	9	4					

Keep On Observing (KOO):

I like to find out solution of problems, I always remain content, I am always enterprising, I am good at communication, I am courageous, I always speak economically, I never hesitate, I am sober, I am not aggressive and so on....

CYCLE-18

4	9	14	19	24	29	34	39	44	49
54	59	64	69	74	79	84	89	94	89
84	79	74	69	64	59	54	49	44	39
34	29	24	19	14	9	4			

Keep On Observing (KOO):

I like to find out solution of problems, I always remain content, I am always enterprising, I am good at communication, I am courageous, I always speak economically, I never hesitate, I am sober, I am not aggressive and so on....

CYCLE-19

4	9	14	19	24	29	34	39	44	49
54	59	64	69	74	79	84	89	94	99
94	89	84	79	74	69	64	59	54	49
44	39	34	29	24	19	14	9	4	

Keep On Observing (KOO):

I like to find out solution of problems, I always remain content, I am always enterprising, I am good at communication, I am courageous, I always speak economically, I never hesitate, I am sober, I am not aggressive and so on....

PATTERN: 5

CYCLE-1

5	10	5							

Keep On Observing (KOO):

I like to find out solution of problems, I always remain content, I am always enterprising, I am good at communication, I am courageous, I always speak economically, I never hesitate, I am sober, I am not aggressive and so on....

CYCLE-2

5	10	15	10	5					

Keep On Observing (KOO):

I like to find out solution of problems, I always remain content, I am always enterprising, I am good at communication, I am courageous, I always speak economically, I never hesitate, I am sober, I am not aggressive and so on....

CYCLE-3

5	10	15	20	15	10	5			

Keep On Observing (KOO):

I like to find out solution of problems, I always remain content, I am always enterprising, I am good at communication, I am courageous, I always speak economically, I never hesitate, I am sober, I am not aggressive and so on....

CYCLE-4

5	10	15	20	25	20	15	10	5	

Keep On Observing (KOO):

I like to find out solution of problems, I always remain content, I am always enterprising, I am good at communication, I am courageous, I always speak economically, I never hesitate, I am sober, I am not aggressive and so on....

CYCLE-5

5	10	15	20	25	30	25	20	15	10
5									

Keep On Observing (KOO):

I like to find out solution of problems, I always remain content, I am always enterprising, I am good at communication, I am courageous, I always speak economically, I never hesitate, I am sober, I am not aggressive and so on....

CYCLE-6

5	10	15	20	25	30	35	30	25	20
15	10	5							

Keep On Observing (KOO):

I like to find out solution of problems, I always remain content, I am always enterprising, I am good at communication, I am courageous, I always speak economically, I never hesitate, I am sober, I am not aggressive and so on....

CYCLE-7

5	10	15	20	25	30	35	40	35	30
25	20	15	10	5					

Keep On Observing (KOO):

I like to find out solution of problems, I always remain content, I am always enterprising, I am good at communication, I am courageous, I always speak economically, I never hesitate, I am sober, I am not aggressive and so on....

CYCLE-8

5	10	15	20	25	30	35	40	45	40
35	30	25	20	15	10	5			

Keep On Observing (KOO):

I like to find out solution of problems, I always remain content, I am always enterprising, I am good at communication, I am courageous, I always speak economically, I never hesitate, I am sober, I am not aggressive and so on....

CYCLE-9

5	10	15	20	25	30	35	40	45	50
45	40	35	30	25	20	15	10	5	

Keep On Observing (KOO):

I like to find out solution of problems, I always remain content, I am always enterprising, I am good at communication, I am courageous, I always speak economically, I never hesitate, I am sober, I am not aggressive and so on....

CYCLE-10

5	10	15	20	25	30	35	40	45	50
55	50	45	40	35	30	25	20	15	10
5									

Keep On Observing (KOO):

I like to find out solution of problems, I always remain content, I am always enterprising, I am good at communication, I am courageous, I always speak economically, I never hesitate, I am sober, I am not aggressive and so on....

CYCLE-11

5	10	15	20	25	30	35	40	45	50
55		60	55	50	45	40	35	30	25
20	15	10	5						

Keep On Observing (KOO):

I like to find out solution of problems, I always remain content, I am always enterprising, I am good at communication, I am courageous, I always speak economically, I never hesitate, I am sober, I am not aggressive and so on....

CYCLE-12

5	10	15	20	25	30	35	40	45	50
55	60	65	60	55	50	45	40	35	30
25	20	15	10	5					

Keep On Observing (KOO):

I like to find out solution of problems, I always remain content, I am always enterprising, I am good at communication, I am courageous, I always speak economically, I never hesitate, I am sober, I am not aggressive and so on....

CYCLE-13

5	10	15	20	25	30	35	40	45	50
55	60	65	70	65	60	55	50	45	40
35	30	25	20	15	10	5			

Keep On Observing (KOO):

I like to find out solution of problems, I always remain content, I am always enterprising, I am good at communication, I am courageous, I always speak economically, I never hesitate, I am sober, I am not aggressive and so on....

CYCLE-14

5	10	15	20	25	30	35	40	45	50
55	60	65	70	75	70	65	60	55	50
45	40	35	30	25	20	15	10	5	

Keep On Observing (KOO):

I like to find out solution of problems, I always remain content, I am always enterprising, I am good at communication, I am courageous, I always speak economically, I never hesitate, I am sober, I am not aggressive and so on....

CYCLE-15

5	10	15	20	25	30	35	40	45	50
55	60	65	70	75	80	75	70	65	60
55	50	45	40	35	30	25	20	15	10
5									

Keep On Observing (KOO):

I like to find out solution of problems, I always remain content, I am always enterprising, I am good at communication, I am courageous, I always speak economically, I never hesitate, I am sober, I am not aggressive and so on....

CYCLE-16

5	10	15	20	25	30	35	40	45	50
55	60	65	70	75	80	85	80	75	70
65	60	55	50	45	40	35	30	25	20
15	10	5							

Keep On Observing (KOO):

I like to find out solution of problems, I always remain content, I am always enterprising, I am good at communication, I am courageous, I always speak economically, I never hesitate, I am sober, I am not aggressive and so on....

CYCLE-17

5	10	15	20	25	30	35	40	45	50
55	60	65	70	75	80	85	90	85	80
75	70	65	60	55	50	45	40	35	30
25	20	15	10	5					

Keep On Observing (KOO):

I like to find out solution of problems, I always remain content, I am always enterprising, I am good at communication, I am courageous, I always speak economically, I never hesitate, I am sober, I am not aggressive and so on....

CYCLE-18

5	10	15	20	25	30	35	40	45	50
55	60	65	70	75	80	85	90	95	90
85	80	75	70	65	60	55	50	45	40
35	30	25	20	15	10	5			

Keep On Observing (KOO):

I like to find out solution of problems, I always remain content, I am always enterprising, I am good at communication, I am courageous, I always speak economically, I never hesitate, I am sober, I am not aggressive and so on....

CYCLE-19

5	10	15	20	25	30	35	40	45	50
55	60	65	70	75	80	85	90	95	100
95	90	85	80	75	70	65	60	55	50
45	40	35	30	25	20	15	10	5	

Keep On Observing (KOO):

I like to find out solution of problems, I always remain content, I am always enterprising, I am good at communication, I am courageous, I always speak economically, I never hesitate, I am sober, I am not aggressive and so on....

Let's do an introspective exercise:

Please check what you achieved and able to exercise now in your life

Sr. No.	Qualities/ characteristics	Posses by a mathe-matised mind	Posses by a success full mind	Posses by a happy mind	Posses by a pat-tern	Posses by you		
						Begin-ning	Con-soli-dating	Exer-cising
1	like to find out solution of problems	yes	yes	Yes	yes			
2	remain content	yes	yes	Yes	yes			
3	enterprising	yes	yes	Yes	yes			
4	good at communication	yes	yes	Yes	yes			
5	courageous	yes	yes	Yes	yes			
6	speak economically	yes	yes	Yes	yes			
7	never hesitate	yes	yes	Yes	yes			
8	Sober	yes	yes	Yes	yes			
9	aggressive	no	no	No	no			
10	straight forward	yes	Yes	Yes	yes			
11	daring	yes	yes	Yes	Yes			
12	enthusiastic	yes	yes	Yes	yes			
13	risk taking	yes	calcu-lated	calcu-lated	calcu-lated			
14	bold	yes	yes	Yes	Yes			
15	can take stress	yes	Yes	Yes	yes			
16	dominant	yes	no	No	No			
17	influenced by facts than by feeling	yes	Yes	Yes	yes			
18	Hard working	yes	yes	yes	Yes			
19	easy going never in hurry	yes	yes	Yes	yes			
20	quick decision	yes	yes	yes	Yes			
21	communicative	yes	yes	Yes	yes			
22	free from guilt	yes	yes	yes	yes			
23	never hesitate	yes	yes	yes	yes			
24	Secure	yes	yes	Yes	yes			
25	never act according to others	yes	yes	yes	yes			
26	capable of getting things done	yes	yes	Yes	yes			
27	assertive behaviour	yes	yes	yes	yes			

28	develop their own sets of rules	yes	If required	If required	If required			
29	self disciplined	yes	yes	yes	Yes			
30	abstract thinking	yes	yes	Yes	yes			
31	reliable behaviour	yes	yes	yes	yes			
32	experimentive	yes	yes	yes	yes			
33	impulsive	yes	no	no	no			
34	self destructive	no	no	no	no			
35	social	yes	yes	yes	yes			
36	cope with routine life		yes	yes	yes			
37	highly self motivated	yes	yes	Yes	yes			
38	practical	yes	yes	yes	yes			
39	mindful	yes	yes	yes	yes			
40	lost in the world of dreams	no	no	no	no			
41	participating	yes	yes	yes	yes			
42	Cautious	yes	yes	Yes	yes			
43	likes people	yes	yes	yes	yes			
44	open minded	yes	yes	yes	yes			
45	resolve conflicts	yes	yes	Yes	yes			
46	emotionally mature	yes	yes	Yes	yes			
47	realistic	yes	yes	yes	yes			
48	Cheerful	yes	yes	Yes	yes			
49	Intuitive	yes	yes	yes	yes			
50	keep things under control	yes	yes	yes	yes			
51	Competitor of self	yes	yes	Yes	yes			
52	self confident	yes	yes	Yes	yes			
53	Assertive	yes	yes	Yes	yes			
54	Mature	yes	yes	Yes	yes			
55	Relax	yes	yes	Yes	yes			
56	Adaptive	yes	yes	Yes	yes			
57	Flexible	yes	yes	Yes	yes			
58	open to change	yes	yes	Yes	yes			
59	accommodative	yes	yes	Yes	yes			
60	socially active	yes	yes	Yes	yes			
61	cultural interests	yes	yes	Yes	yes			
62	down to earth	yes	yes	Yes	yes			
63	friendly nature	yes	yes	Yes	yes			
64	Sociable	yes	yes	Yes	yes			
65	good reasoning	yes	yes	Yes	yes			
66	intelligent	yes	yes	Yes	yes			
67	hard to fool	yes	yes	Yes	yes			

Express your feeling about your accomplishments through mathyogs9211:

....
....
....
....
....
....
....
....
....
....
....
....
....
....
....
....
....
....
....
....
....
....
....
....
....
....
....
....
....

CHAPTER-X

COUNTING BY SIX'S

Group 6: Counting by six's

Sr. No.	GROUP VI					
Term	PATTERN-1	PATTERN-2	PATTERN-3	PATTERN-4	PATTERN-5	PATTERN-6
1	1	2	3	4	5	6
2	7	8	9	10	11	12
3	13	14	15	16	17	18
4	19	20	21	22	23	24
5	25	26	27	28	29	30
6	31	32	33	34	35	36
7	37	38	39	40	41	42
8	43	44	45	46	47	48
9	49	50	51	52	53	54
10	55	56	57	58	59	60
11	61	62	63	64	65	66
12	67	68	69	70	71	72
13	73	74	75	76	77	78
14	79	80	81	82	83	84
15	85	86	87	88	89	90
16	91	92	93	94	95	96
17	97	98	99	100	101	102

PATTERN: 1

CYCLE-1

1	7	1							

Keep On Observing (KOO):

I like to find out solution of problems, I always remain content, I am always enterprising, I am good at communication, I am courageous, I always speak economically, I never hesitate, I am sober, I am not aggressive and so on....

CYCLE-2

1	7	13	7	1					

Keep On Observing (KOO):

I like to find out solution of problems, I always remain content, I am always enterprising, I am good at communication, I am courageous, I always speak economically, I never hesitate, I am sober, I am not aggressive and so on....

CYCLE-3

1	7	13	19	13	7	1			

Keep On Observing (KOO):

I like to find out solution of problems, I always remain content, I am always enterprising, I am good at communication, I am courageous, I always speak economically, I never hesitate, I am sober, I am not aggressive and so on....

CYCLE-4

1	7	13	19	25	19	13	7	1	

Keep On Observing (KOO):

I like to find out solution of problems, I always remain content, I am always enterprising, I am good at communication, I am courageous, I always speak economically, I never hesitate, I am sober, I am not aggressive and so on....

CYCLE-5

1	7	13	19	25	31	25	19	13	7
1									

Keep On Observing (KOO):

I like to find out solution of problems, I always remain content, I am always enterprising, I am good at communication, I am courageous, I always speak economically, I never hesitate, I am sober, I am not aggressive and so on....

CYCLE-6

1	7	13	19	25	31	37	31	25	19
13	7	1							

Keep On Observing (KOO):

I like to find out solution of problems, I always remain content, I am always enterprising, I am good at communication, I am courageous, I always speak economically, I never hesitate, I am sober, I am not aggressive and so on....

CYCLE-7

1	7	13	19	25	31	37	43	37	31
25	19	13	7	1					

Keep On Observing (KOO):

I like to find out solution of problems, I always remain content, I am always enterprising, I am good at communication, I am courageous, I always speak economically, I never hesitate, I am sober, I am not aggressive and so on....

CYCLE-8

1	7	13	19	25	31	37	43	49	43
37	31	25	19	13	7	1			

Keep On Observing (KOO):

I like to find out solution of problems, I always remain content, I am always enterprising, I am good at communication, I am courageous, I always speak economically, I never hesitate, I am sober, I am not aggressive and so on....

CYCLE-9

1	7	13	19	25	31	37	43	49	55
49	43	37	31	25	19	13	7	1	

Keep On Observing (KOO):

I like to find out solution of problems, I always remain content, I am always enterprising, I am good at communication, I am courageous, I always speak economically, I never hesitate, I am sober, I am not aggressive and so on....

CYCLE-10

1	7	13	19	25	31	37	43	49	55
61	55	49	43	37	31	25	19	13	7
1									

Keep On Observing (KOO):

I like to find out solution of problems, I always remain content, I am always enterprising, I am good at communication, I am courageous, I always speak economically, I never hesitate, I am sober, I am not aggressive and so on....

CYCLE-11

1	7	13	19	25	31	37	43	49	55
61	67	61	55	49	43	37	31	25	19
13	7	1							

Keep On Observing (KOO):

I like to find out solution of problems, I always remain content, I am always enterprising, I am good at communication, I am courageous, I always speak economically, I never hesitate, I am sober, I am not aggressive and so on....

CYCLE-12

1	7	13	19	25	31	37	43	49	55
61	67	73	67	61	55	49	43	37	31
25	19	13	7	1					

Keep On Observing (KOO):

I like to find out solution of problems, I always remain content, I am always enterprising, I am good at communication, I am courageous, I always speak economically, I never hesitate, I am sober, I am not aggressive and so on....

CYCLE-13

1	7	13	19	25	31	37	43	49	55
61	67	73	79	73	67	61	55	49	43
37	31	25	19	13	7	1			

Keep On Observing (KOO):

I like to find out solution of problems, I always remain content, I am always enterprising, I am good at communication, I am courageous, I always speak economically, I never hesitate, I am sober, I am not aggressive and so on....

CYCLE-14

1	7	13	19	25	31	37	43	49	55
61	67	73	79	85	79	73	67	61	55
49	43	37	31	25	19	13	7	1	

Keep On Observing (KOO):

I like to find out solution of problems, I always remain content, I am always enterprising, I am good at communication, I am courageous, I always speak economically, I never hesitate, I am sober, I am not aggressive and so on....

CYCLE-15

1	7	13	19	25	31	37	43	49	55
61	67	73	79	85	91	85	79	73	67
61	55	49	43	37	31	25	19	13	7
1									

Keep On Observing (KOO):

I like to find out solution of problems, I always remain content, I am always enterprising, I am good at communication, I am courageous, I always speak economically, I never hesitate, I am sober, I am not aggressive and so on....

CYCLE-16

1	7	13	19	25	31	37	43	49	55
61	67	73	79	85	91	97	91	85	79
73	67	61	55	49	43	37	31	25	19
13	7	1							

Keep On Observing (KOO):

I like to find out solution of problems, I always remain content, I am always enterprising, I am good at communication, I am courageous, I always speak economically, I never hesitate, I am sober, I am not aggressive and so on....

PATTERN-2

CYCLE-1

2	8	2							

Keep On Observing (KOO):

I like to find out solution of problems, I always remain content, I am always enterprising, I am good at communication, I am courageous, I always speak economically, I never hesitate, I am sober, I am not aggressive and so on....

CYCLE-2

2	8	14	8	2					

Keep On Observing (KOO):

I like to find out solution of problems, I always remain content, I am always enterprising, I am good at communication, I am courageous, I always speak economically, I never hesitate, I am sober, I am not aggressive and so on....

CYCLE-3

2	8	14	20	14	8	2			

Keep On Observing (KOO):

I like to find out solution of problems, I always remain content, I am always enterprising, I am good at communication, I am courageous, I always speak economically, I never hesitate, I am sober, I am not aggressive and so on....

CYCLE-4

2	8	14	20	26	20	14	8	2	

Keep On Observing (KOO):

I like to find out solution of problems, I always remain content, I am always enterprising, I am good at communication, I am courageous, I always speak economically, I never hesitate, I am sober, I am not aggressive and so on....

CYCLE-5

2	8	14	20	26	32	26	20	14	8
2									

Keep On Observing (KOO):

I like to find out solution of problems, I always remain content, I am always enterprising, I am good at communication, I am courageous, I always speak economically, I never hesitate, I am sober, I am not aggressive and so on....

CYCLE-6

2	8	14	20	26	32	38	32	26	20
14	8	2							

Keep On Observing (KOO):

I like to find out solution of problems, I always remain content, I am always enterprising, I am good at communication, I am courageous, I always speak economically, I never hesitate, I am sober, I am not aggressive and so on....

CYCLE-7

2	8	14	20	26	32	38	44	38	32
26	20	14	8	2					

Keep On Observing (KOO):

I like to find out solution of problems, I always remain content, I am always enterprising, I am good at communication, I am courageous, I always speak economically, I never hesitate, I am sober, I am not aggressive and so on....

CYCLE-8

2	8	14	20	26	32	38	44	50	44
38	32	26	20	14	8	2			

Keep On Observing (KOO):

I like to find out solution of problems, I always remain content, I am always enterprising, I am good at communication, I am courageous, I always speak economically, I never hesitate, I am sober, I am not aggressive and so on....

CYCLE-9

2	8	14	20	26	32	38	44	50	56
50	44	38	32	26	20	14	8	2	

Keep On Observing (KOO):

I like to find out solution of problems, I always remain content, I am always enterprising, I am good at communication, I am courageous, I always speak economically, I never hesitate, I am sober, I am not aggressive and so on....

CYCLE-10

2	8	14	20	26	32	38	44	50	56
62	56	50	44	38	32	26	20	14	8
2									

Keep On Observing (KOO):

I like to find out solution of problems, I always remain content, I am always enterprising, I am good at communication, I am courageous, I always speak economically, I never hesitate, I am sober, I am not aggressive and so on....

CYCLE-11

2	8	14	20	26	32	38	44	50	56
62	68	62	56	50	44	38	32	26	20
14	8	2							

Keep On Observing (KOO):

I like to find out solution of problems, I always remain content, I am always enterprising, I am good at communication, I am courageous, I always speak economically, I never hesitate, I am sober, I am not aggressive and so on....

CYCLE-12

2	8	14	20	26	32	38	44	50	56
62	68	74	68	62	56	50	44	38	32
26	20	14	8	2					

Keep On Observing (KOO):

I like to find out solution of problems, I always remain content, I am always enterprising, I am good at communication, I am courageous, I always speak economically, I never hesitate, I am sober, I am not aggressive and so on....

CYCLE-13

2	8	14	20	26	32	38	44	50	56
62	68	74	80	74	68	62	56	50	44
38	32	26	20	14	8	2			

Keep On Observing (KOO):

I like to find out solution of problems, I always remain content, I am always enterprising, I am good at communication, I am courageous, I always speak economically, I never hesitate, I am sober, I am not aggressive and so on....

CYCLE-14

2	8	14	20	26	32	38	44	50	56
62	68	74	80	86	80	74	68	62	56
50	44	38	32	26	20	14	8	2	

Keep On Observing (KOO):

I like to find out solution of problems, I always remain content, I am always enterprising, I am good at communication, I am courageous, I always speak economically, I never hesitate, I am sober, I am not aggressive and so on....

CYCLE-15

2	8	14	20	26	32	38	44	50	56
62	68	74	80	86	92	86	80	74	68
62	56	50	44	38	32	26	20	14	8
2									

Keep On Observing (KOO):

I like to find out solution of problems, I always remain content, I am always enterprising, I am good at communication, I am courageous, I always speak economically, I never hesitate, I am sober, I am not aggressive and so on....

CYCLE-16

2	8	14	20	26	32	38	44	50	56
62	68	74	80	86	92	98	92	86	80
74	68	62	56	50	44	38	32	26	20
14	8	2							

Keep On Observing (KOO):

I like to find out solution of problems, I always remain content, I am always enterprising, I am good at communication, I am courageous, I always speak economically, I never hesitate, I am sober, I am not aggressive and so on....

PATTERN: 3

CYCLE-1

3	9	3							

Keep On Observing (KOO):

I like to find out solution of problems, I always remain content, I am always enterprising, I am good at communication, I am courageous, I always speak economically, I never hesitate, I am sober, I am not aggressive and so on....

CYCLE-2

3	9	15	9	3					

Keep On Observing (KOO):

I like to find out solution of problems, I always remain content, I am always enterprising, I am good at communication, I am courageous, I always speak economically, I never hesitate, I am sober, I am not aggressive and so on....

CYCLE-3

3	9	15	21	15	9	3			

Keep On Observing (KOO):

I like to find out solution of problems, I always remain content, I am always enterprising, I am good at communication, I am courageous, I always speak economically, I never hesitate, I am sober, I am not aggressive and so on....

CYCLE-4

3	9	15	21	27	21	15	9	3	

Keep On Observing (KOO):

I like to find out solution of problems, I always remain content, I am always enterprising, I am good at communication, I am courageous, I always speak economically, I never hesitate, I am sober, I am not aggressive and so on....

CYCLE-5

3	9	15	21	27	33	27	21	15	9
3									

Keep On Observing (KOO):

I like to find out solution of problems, I always remain content, I am always enterprising, I am good at communication, I am courageous, I always speak economically, I never hesitate, I am sober, I am not aggressive and so on....

CYCLE-6

3	9	15	21	27	33	39	33	27	21
15	9	3							

Keep On Observing (KOO):

I like to find out solution of problems, I always remain content, I am always enterprising, I am good at communication, I am courageous, I always speak economically, I never hesitate, I am sober, I am not aggressive and so on....

CYCLE-7

3	9	15	21	27	33	39	45	39	33
27	21	15	9	3					

Keep On Observing (KOO):

I like to find out solution of problems, I always remain content, I am always enterprising, I am good at communication, I am courageous, I always speak economically, I never hesitate, I am sober, I am not aggressive and so on....

CYCLE-8

3	9	15	21	27	33	39	45	51	45
39	33	27	21	15	9	3			

Keep On Observing (KOO):

I like to find out solution of problems, I always remain content, I am always enterprising, I am good at communication, I am courageous, I always speak economically, I never hesitate, I am sober, I am not aggressive and so on....

CYCLE-9

3	9	15	21	27	33	39	45	51	57
51	45	39	33	27	21	15	9	3	

Keep On Observing (KOO):

I like to find out solution of problems, I always remain content, I am always enterprising, I am good at communication, I am courageous, I always speak economically, I never hesitate, I am sober, I am not aggressive and so on....

CYCLE-10

3	9	15	21	27	33	39	45	51	57
63	57	51	45	39	33	27	21	15	9
3									

Keep On Observing (KOO):

I like to find out solution of problems, I always remain content, I am always enterprising, I am good at communication, I am courageous, I always speak economically, I never hesitate, I am sober, I am not aggressive and so on....

CYCLE-11

3	9	15	21	27	33	39	45	51	57
63	69	63	57	51	45	39	33	27	21
15	9	3							

Keep On Observing (KOO):

I like to find out solution of problems, I always remain content, I am always enterprising, I am good at communication, I am courageous, I always speak economically, I never hesitate, I am sober, I am not aggressive and so on....

CYCLE-12

3	9	15	21	27	33	39	45	51	57
63	69	75	69	63	57	51	45	39	33
27	21	15	9	3					

Keep On Observing (KOO):

I like to find out solution of problems, I always remain content, I am always enterprising, I am good at communication, I am courageous, I always speak economically, I never hesitate, I am sober, I am not aggressive and so on....

CYCLE-13

3	9	15	21	27	33	39	45	51	57
63	69	75	81	75	69	63	57	51	45
39	33	27	21	15	9	3			

Keep On Observing (KOO):

I like to find out solution of problems, I always remain content, I am always enterprising, I am good at communication, I am courageous, I always speak economically, I never hesitate, I am sober, I am not aggressive and so on....

CYCLE-14

3	9	15	21	27	33	39	45	51	57
63	69	75	81	87	81	75	69	63	57
51	45	39	33	27	21	15	9	3	

Keep On Observing (KOO):

I like to find out solution of problems, I always remain content, I am always enterprising, I am good at communication, I am courageous, I always speak economically, I never hesitate, I am sober, I am not aggressive and so on....

CYCLE-15

3	9	15	21	27	33	39	45	51	57
63	69	75	81	87	93	87	81	75	69
63	57	51	45	39	33	27	21	15	9
3									

Keep On Observing (KOO):

I like to find out solution of problems, I always remain content, I am always enterprising, I am good at communication, I am courageous, I always speak economically, I never hesitate, I am sober, I am not aggressive and so on....

CYCLE-16

3	9	15	21	27	33	39	45	51	57
63	69	75	81	87	93	99	93	87	81
75	69	63	57	51	45	39	33	27	21
15	9	3							

Keep On Observing (KOO):

I like to find out solution of problems, I always remain content, I am always enterprising, I am good at communication, I am courageous, I always speak economically, I never hesitate, I am sober, I am not aggressive and so on....

PATTERN: 4

CYCLE-1

4	10	4							

Keep On Observing (KOO):

I like to find out solution of problems, I always remain content, I am always enterprising, I am good at communication, I am courageous, I always speak economically, I never hesitate, I am sober, I am not aggressive and so on....

CYCLE-2

4	10	16	10	4					

Keep On Observing (KOO):

I like to find out solution of problems, I always remain content, I am always enterprising, I am good at communication, I am courageous, I always speak economically, I never hesitate, I am sober, I am not aggressive and so on....

CYCLE-2

4	10	16	10	4					

Keep On Observing (KOO):

I like to find out solution of problems, I always remain content, I am always enterprising, I am good at communication, I am courageous, I always speak economically, I never hesitate, I am sober, I am not aggressive and so on....

CYCLE-3

4	10	16	22	16	10	4			

Keep On Observing (KOO):

I like to find out solution of problems, I always remain content, I am always enterprising, I am good at communication, I am courageous, I always speak economically, I never hesitate, I am sober, I am not aggressive and so on....

CYCLE-4

4	10	16	22	28	22	16	10	4	

Keep On Observing (KOO):

I like to find out solution of problems, I always remain content, I am always enterprising, I am good at communication, I am courageous, I always speak economically, I never hesitate, I am sober, I am not aggressive and so on....

CYCLE-5

4	10	16	22	28	34	28	22	16	10
4									

Keep On Observing (KOO):

I like to find out solution of problems, I always remain content, I am always enterprising, I am good at communication, I am courageous, I always speak economically, I never hesitate, I am sober, I am not aggressive and so on....

CYCLE-6

4	10	16	22	28	34	40	34	28	22
16	10	4							

Keep On Observing (KOO):

I like to find out solution of problems, I always remain content, I am always enterprising, I am good at communication, I am courageous, I always speak economically, I never hesitate, I am sober, I am not aggressive and so on....

CYCLE-7

4	10	16	22	28	34	40	46	40	34
28	22	16	10	4					

Keep On Observing (KOO):

I like to find out solution of problems, I always remain content, I am always enterprising, I am good at communication, I am courageous, I always speak economically, I never hesitate, I am sober, I am not aggressive and so on....

CYCLE-8

4	10	16	22	28	34	40	46	52	46
40	34	28	22	16	10	4			

Keep On Observing (KOO):

I like to find out solution of problems, I always remain content, I am always enterprising, I am good at communication, I am courageous, I always speak economically, I never hesitate, I am sober, I am not aggressive and so on....

CYCLE-9

4	10	16	22	28	34	40	46	52	58
52	46	40	34	28	22	16	10	4	

Keep On Observing (KOO):

I like to find out solution of problems, I always remain content, I am always enterprising, I am good at communication, I am courageous, I always speak economically, I never hesitate, I am sober, I am not aggressive and so on....

CYCLE-10

4	10	16	22	28	34	40	46	52	58
64	58	52	46	40	34	28	22	16	10
4									

Keep On Observing (KOO):

I like to find out solution of problems, I always remain content, I am always enterprising, I am good at communication, I am courageous, I always speak economically, I never hesitate, I am sober, I am not aggressive and so on....

CYCLE-11

4	10	16	22	28	34	40	46	52	58
64		70	64	58	52	46	40	34	28
22	16	10	4						

Keep On Observing (KOO):

I like to find out solution of problems, I always remain content, I am always enterprising, I am good at communication, I am courageous, I always speak economically, I never hesitate, I am sober, I am not aggressive and so on....

CYCLE-12

4	10	16	22	28	34	40	46	52	58
64	70	76	70	64	58	52	46	40	34
28	22	16	10	4					

Keep On Observing (KOO):

I like to find out solution of problems, I always remain content, I am always enterprising, I am good at communication, I am courageous, I always speak economically, I never hesitate, I am sober, I am not aggressive and so on....

CYCLE-13

4	10	16	22	28	34	40	46	52	58
64	70	76	82	76	70	64	58	52	46
40	34	28	22	16	10	4			

Keep On Observing (KOO):

I like to find out solution of problems, I always remain content, I am always enterprising, I am good at communication, I am courageous, I always speak economically, I never hesitate, I am sober, I am not aggressive and so on....

CYCLE-14

4	10	16	22	28	34	40	46	52	58
64	70	76	82	88	82	76	70	64	58
52	46	40	34	28	22	16	10	4	

Keep On Observing (KOO):

I like to find out solution of problems, I always remain content, I am always enterprising, I am good at communication, I am courageous, I always speak economically, I never hesitate, I am sober, I am not aggressive and so on....

CYCLE-15

4	10	16	22	28	34	40	46	52	58
64	70	76	82	88	94	88	82	76	70
64	58	52	46	40	34	28	22	16	10
4									

Keep On Observing (KOO):

I like to find out solution of problems, I always remain content, I am always enterprising, I am good at communication, I am courageous, I always speak economically, I never hesitate, I am sober, I am not aggressive and so on....

CYCLE-16

4	10	16	22	28	34	40	46	52	58
64	70	76	82	88	94	100	94	88	82
76	70	64	58	52	46	40	34	28	22
16	10	4							

Keep On Observing (KOO):

I like to find out solution of problems, I always remain content, I am always enterprising, I am good at communication, I am courageous, I always speak economically, I never hesitate, I am sober, I am not aggressive and so on....

PATTERN: 5

CYCLE-1

5	11	5							

Keep On Observing (KOO):

I like to find out solution of problems, I always remain content, I am always enterprising, I am good at communication, I am courageous, I always speak economically, I never hesitate, I am sober, I am not aggressive and so on....

CYCLE-2

5	11	17	11	5					

Keep On Observing (KOO):

I like to find out solution of problems, I always remain content, I am always enterprising, I am good at communication, I am courageous, I always speak economically, I never hesitate, I am sober, I am not aggressive and so on....

CYCLE-3

5	11	17	23	17	11	5			

Keep On Observing (KOO):

I like to find out solution of problems, I always remain content, I am always enterprising, I am good at communication, I am courageous, I always speak economically, I never hesitate, I am sober, I am not aggressive and so on....

CYCLE-4

5	11	17	23	29	23	17	11	5	

Keep On Observing (KOO):

I like to find out solution of problems, I always remain content, I am always enterprising, I am good at communication, I am courageous, I always speak economically, I never hesitate, I am sober, I am not aggressive and so on....

CYCLE-5

5	11	17	23	29	35	29	23	17	11
5									

Keep On Observing (KOO):

I like to find out solution of problems, I always remain content, I am always enterprising, I am good at communication, I am courageous, I always speak economically, I never hesitate, I am sober, I am not aggressive and so on....

CYCLE-6

5	11	17	23	29	35	41	35	29	23
17	11	5							

Keep On Observing (KOO):

I like to find out solution of problems, I always remain content, I am always enterprising, I am good at communication, I am courageous, I always speak economically, I never hesitate, I am sober, I am not aggressive and so on....

CYCLE-7

5	11	17	23	29	35	41	47	41	35
29	23	17	11	5					

Keep On Observing (KOO):

I like to find out solution of problems, I always remain content, I am always enterprising, I am good at communication, I am courageous, I always speak economically, I never hesitate, I am sober, I am not aggressive and so on....

CYCLE-8

5	11	17	23	29	35	41	47	53	47
41	35	29	23	17	11	5			

Keep On Observing (KOO):

I like to find out solution of problems, I always remain content, I am always enterprising, I am good at communication, I am courageous, I always speak economically, I never hesitate, I am sober, I am not aggressive and so on....

CYCLE-9

5	11	17	23	29	35	41	47	53	59
53	47	41	35	29	23	17	11	5	

Keep On Observing (KOO):

I like to find out solution of problems, I always remain content, I am always enterprising, I am good at communication, I am courageous, I always speak economically, I never hesitate, I am sober, I am not aggressive and so on....

CYCL-10

5	11	17	23	29	35	41	47	53	59
65	59	53	47	41	35	29	23	17	11
5									

Keep On Observing (KOO):

I like to find out solution of problems, I always remain content, I am always enterprising, I am good at communication, I am courageous, I always speak economically, I never hesitate, I am sober, I am not aggressive and so on....

CYCL-11

5	11	17	23	29	35	41	47	53	59
65		71	65	59	53	47	41	35	29
23	17	11	5						

Keep On Observing (KOO):

I like to find out solution of problems, I always remain content, I am always enterprising, I am good at communication, I am courageous, I always speak economically, I never hesitate, I am sober, I am not aggressive and so on....

CYCLE-12

5	11	17	23	29	35	41	47	53	59
65	71	77	71	65	59	53	47	41	35
29	23	17	11	5					

Keep On Observing (KOO):

I like to find out solution of problems, I always remain content, I am always enterprising, I am good at communication, I am courageous, I always speak economically, I never hesitate, I am sober, I am not aggressive and so on....

CYCL-13

5	11	17	23	29	35	41	47	53	59
65	71	77	83	77	71	65	59	53	47
41	35	29	23	17	11	5			

Keep On Observing (KOO):

I like to find out solution of problems, I always remain content, I am always enterprising, I am good at communication, I am courageous, I always speak economically, I never hesitate, I am sober, I am not aggressive and so on....

CYCLE-14

5	11	17	23	29	35	41	47	53	59
65	71	77	83	89	83	77	71	65	59
53	47	41	35	29	23	17	11	5	

Keep On Observing (KOO):

I like to find out solution of problems, I always remain content, I am always enterprising, I am good at communication, I am courageous, I always speak economically, I never hesitate, I am sober, I am not aggressive and so on....

CYCLE-15

5	11	17	23	29	35	41	47	53	59
65	71	77	83	89	95	89	83	77	71
65	59	53	47	41	35	29	23	17	11
5									

Keep On Observing (KOO):

I like to find out solution of problems, I always remain content, I am always enterprising, I am good at communication, I am courageous, I always speak economically, I never hesitate, I am sober, I am not aggressive and so on....

CYCLE-16

5	11	17	23	29	35	41	47	53	59
65	71	77	83	89	95	101	95	89	83
77	71	65	59	53	47	41	35	29	23
17	11	5							

Keep On Observing (KOO):

I like to find out solution of problems, I always remain content, I am always enterprising, I am good at communication, I am courageous, I always speak economically, I never hesitate, I am sober, I am not aggressive and so on....

PATTERN: 6

CYCLE-1

6	12	6							

Keep On Observing (KOO):

I like to find out solution of problems, I always remain content, I am always enterprising, I am good at communication, I am courageous, I always speak economically, I never hesitate, I am sober, I am not aggressive and so on....

CYCLE-2

6	12	18	12	6					

Keep On Observing (KOO):

I like to find out solution of problems, I always remain content, I am always enterprising, I am good at communication, I am courageous, I always speak economically, I never hesitate, I am sober, I am not aggressive and so on....

CYCLE-3

6	12	18	24	18	12	6			

Keep On Observing (KOO):

I like to find out solution of problems, I always remain content, I am always enterprising, I am good at communication, I am courageous, I always speak economically, I never hesitate, I am sober, I am not aggressive and so on....

CYCLE-4

6	12	18	24	30	24	18	12	6	

Keep On Observing (KOO):

I like to find out solution of problems, I always remain content, I am always enterprising, I am good at communication, I am courageous, I always speak economically, I never hesitate, I am sober, I am not aggressive and so on....

CYCLE-5

6	12	18	24	30	36	30	24	18	12
6									

Keep On Observing (KOO):

I like to find out solution of problems, I always remain content, I am always enterprising, I am good at communication, I am courageous, I always speak economically, I never hesitate, I am sober, I am not aggressive and so on....

CYCLE-6

6	12	18	24	30	36	42	36	30	24
18	12	6							

Keep On Observing (KOO):

I like to find out solution of problems, I always remain content, I am always enterprising, I am good at communication, I am courageous, I always speak economically, I never hesitate, I am sober, I am not aggressive and so on....

CYCLE-7

6	12	18	24	30	36	42	48	42	36
30	24	18	12	6					

Keep On Observing (KOO:

I like to find out solution of problems, I always remain content, I am always enterprising, I am good at communication, I am courageous, I always speak economically, I never hesitate, I am sober, I am not aggressive and so on....

CYCLE-8

6	12	18	24	30	36	42	48	54	48
42	36	30	24	18	12	6			

Keep On Observing (KOO):

I like to find out solution of problems, I always remain content, I am always enterprising, I am good at communication, I am courageous, I always speak economically, I never hesitate, I am sober, I am not aggressive and so on....

CYCLE-9

6	12	18	24	30	36	42	48	54	60
54	48	42	36	30	24	18	12	6	

Keep On Observing (KOO):

I like to find out solution of problems, I always remain content, I am always enterprising, I am good at communication, I am courageous, I always speak economically, I never hesitate, I am sober, I am not aggressive and so on....

CYCLE-10

6	12	18	24	30	36	42	48	54	60
66	60	54	48	42	36	30	24	18	12
6									

Keep On Observing (KOO):

I like to find out solution of problems, I always remain content, I am always enterprising, I am good at communication, I am courageous, I always speak economically, I never hesitate, I am sober, I am not aggressive and so on....

CYCLE-11

6	12	18	24	30	36	42	48	54	60
66	72	66	60	54	48	42	36	30	24
18	12	6							

Keep On Observing (KOO):

I like to find out solution of problems, I always remain content, I am always enterprising, I am good at communication, I am courageous, I always speak economically, I never hesitate, I am sober, I am not aggressive and so on....

CYCLE-12

6	12	18	24	30	36	42	48	54	60
66	72	78	72	66	60	54	48	42	36
30	24	18	12	6					

Keep On Observing (KOO):

I like to find out solution of problems, I always remain content, I am always enterprising, I am good at communication, I am courageous, I always speak economically, I never hesitate, I am sober, I am not aggressive and so on....

CYCLE-13

6	12	18	24	30	36	42	48	54	60
66	72	78	84	78	72	66	60	54	48
42	36	30	24	18	12	6			

Keep On Observing (KOO):

I like to find out solution of problems, I always remain content, I am always enterprising, I am good at communication, I am courageous, I always speak economically, I never hesitate, I am sober, I am not aggressive and so on....

CYCLE-14

6	12	18	24	30	36	42	48	54	60
66	72	78	84	90	84	78	72	66	60
54	48	42	36	30	24	18	12	6	

Keep On Observing (KOO):

I like to find out solution of problems, I always remain content, I am always enterprising, I am good at communication, I am courageous, I always speak economically, I never hesitate, I am sober, I am not aggressive and so on....

CYCLE-15

6	12	18	24	30	36	42	48	54	60
66	72	78	84	90	96	90	84	78	72
66	60	54	48	42	36	30	24	18	12
6									

Keep On Observing (KOO):

I like to find out solution of problems, I always remain content, I am always enterprising, I am good at communication, I am courageous, I always speak economically, I never hesitate, I am sober, I am not aggressive and so on....

CYCLE-16

6	12	18	24	30	36	42	48	54	60
66	72	78	84	90	96	102	96	90	84
78	72	66	60	54	48	42	36	30	24
18	12	6							

Keep On Observing (KOO):

I like to find out solution of problems, I always remain content, I am always enterprising, I am good at communication, I am courageous, I always speak economically, I never hesitate, I am sober, I am not aggressive and so on....

Let's do an introspective exercise:

Please check what you achieved and able to exercise now in your life

Sr. No.	Qualities/ characteristics	Posses by a mathe-matised mind	Posses by a success full mind	Posses by a happy mind	Posses by a pat-tern	Posses by you		
						Begin-ning	Con-soli-dating	Exer-cising
1	like to find out solution of problems	yes	yes	Yes	yes			
2	remain content	yes	yes	Yes	yes			
3	enterprising	yes	yes	Yes	yes			
4	good at communication	yes	yes	Yes	yes			
5	courageous	yes	yes	Yes	yes			
6	speak economically	yes	yes	Yes	yes			
7	never hesitate	yes	yes	Yes	yes			
8	Sober	yes	yes	Yes	yes			
9	aggressive	no	no	No	no			
10	straight forward	yes	Yes	Yes	yes			
11	daring	yes	yes	Yes	Yes			
12	enthusiastic	yes	yes	Yes	yes			
13	risk taking	yes	calcu-lated	calcu-lated	calcu-lated			
14	bold	yes	yes	Yes	Yes			
15	can take stress	yes	Yes	Yes	yes			
16	dominant	yes	no	No	No			
17	influenced by facts than by feeling	yes	Yes	Yes	yes			
18	Hard working	yes	yes	yes	Yes			
19	easy going never in hurry	yes	yes	Yes	yes			
20	quick decision	yes	yes	yes	Yes			
21	communicative	yes	yes	Yes	yes			
22	free from guilt	yes	yes	yes	yes			
23	never hesitate	yes	yes	yes	yes			
24	Secure	yes	yes	Yes	yes			
25	never act according to others	yes	yes	yes	yes			
26	capable of getting things done	yes	yes	Yes	yes			
27	assertive behaviour	yes	yes	yes	yes			

28	develop their own sets of rules	yes	If required	If required	If required			
29	self disciplined	yes	yes	yes	Yes			
30	abstract thinking	yes	yes	Yes	yes			
31	reliable behaviour	yes	yes	yes	yes			
32	experementive	yes	yes	yes	yes			
33	impulsive	yes	no	no	no			
34	self destructive	no	no	no	no			
35	social	yes	yes	yes	yes			
36	cope with routine life		yes	yes	yes			
37	highly self motivated	yes	yes	Yes	yes			
38	practical	yes	yes	yes	yes			
39	mindful	yes	yes	yes	yes			
40	lost in the world of dreams	no	no	no	no			
41	participating	yes	yes	yes	yes			
42	Cautious	yes	yes	Yes	yes			
43	likes people	yes	yes	yes	yes			
44	open minded	yes	yes	yes	yes			
45	resolve conflicts	yes	yes	Yes	yes			
46	emotionally mature	yes	yes	Yes	yes			
47	realistic	yes	yes	yes	yes			
48	Cheerful	yes	yes	Yes	yes			
49	Intuitive	yes	yes	yes	yes			
50	keep things under control	yes	yes	yes	yes			
51	Competitor of self	yes	yes	Yes	yes			
52	self confident	yes	yes	Yes	yes			
53	Assertive	yes	yes	Yes	yes			
54	Mature	yes	yes	Yes	yes			
55	Relax	yes	yes	Yes	yes			
56	Adaptive	yes	yes	Yes	yes			
57	Flexible	yes	yes	Yes	yes			
58	open to change	yes	yes	Yes	yes			
59	accommodative	yes	yes	Yes	yes			
60	socially active	yes	yes	Yes	yes			
61	cultural interests	yes	yes	Yes	yes			
62	down to earth	yes	yes	Yes	yes			
63	friendly nature	yes	yes	Yes	yes			
64	Sociable	yes	yes	Yes	yes			
65	good reasoning	yes	yes	Yes	yes			
66	intelligent	yes	yes	Yes	yes			
67	hard to fool	yes	yes	Yes	yes			

Express your feeling about your accomplishments through mathyogs9211:

....
....
....
....
....
....
....
....
....
....
....
....
....
....
....
....
....
....
....
....
....
....
....
....
....
....
....
....
....

CHAPTER-XI

COUNTING BY SEVEN'S

Group 7: Counting by seven's

Sr. No.	GROUP VII						
Term	PATTERN-1	PATTERN-2	PATTERN-3	PATTERN-4	PATTERN-5	PATTERN-6	PATTERN-7
1	1	2	3	4	5	6	7
2	8	9	10	11	12	13	14
3	15	16	17	18	19	20	21
4	22	23	24	25	26	27	28
5	29	30	31	32	33	34	35
6	36	37	38	39	40	41	42
7	43	44	45	46	47	48	49
8	50	51	52	53	54	55	56
9	57	58	59	60	61	62	63
10	64	65	66	67	68	69	70
11	71	72	73	74	75	76	77
12	78	79	80	81	82	83	84
13	85	86	87	88	89	90	91
14	92	93	94	95	96	97	98
15	99	100	101	102	103	104	105

PATTERN 1:

CYCLE-1

1	8	1							

Keep On Observing (KOO):

I like to find out solution of problems, I always remain content, I am always enterprising, I am good at communication, I am courageous, I always speak economically, I never hesitate, I am sober, I am not aggressive and so on....

CYCLE-2

1	8	15	8	1					

Keep On Observing (KOO):

I like to find out solution of problems, I always remain content, I am always enterprising, I am good at communication, I am courageous, I always speak economically, I never hesitate, I am sober, I am not aggressive and so on....

CYCLE-3

1	8	15	22	15	8	1			

Keep On Observing (KOO):

I like to find out solution of problems, I always remain content, I am always enterprising, I am good at communication, I am courageous, I always speak economically, I never hesitate, I am sober, I am not aggressive and so on....

CYCLE-4

1	8	15	22	29	22	15	8	1	

Keep On Observing (KOO):

I like to find out solution of problems, I always remain content, I am always enterprising, I am good at communication, I am courageous, I always speak economically, I never hesitate, I am sober, I am not aggressive and so on....

CYCLE-5

1	8	15	22	29	36	29	22	15	8
1									

Keep On Observing (KOO):

I like to find out solution of problems, I always remain content, I am always enterprising, I am good at communication, I am courageous, I always speak economically, I never hesitate, I am sober, I am not aggressive and so on....

CYCLE-6

1	8	15	22	29	36	43	36	29	22
15	8	1							

Keep On Observing (KOO):

I like to find out solution of problems, I always remain content, I am always enterprising, I am good at communication, I am courageous, I always speak economically, I never hesitate, I am sober, I am not aggressive and so on....

CYCLE-7

1	8	15	22	29	36	43	50	43	36
29	22	15	8	1					

Keep On Observing (KOO):

I like to find out solution of problems, I always remain content, I am always enterprising, I am good at communication, I am courageous, I always speak economically, I never hesitate, I am sober, I am not aggressive and so on....

CYCLE-8

1	8	15	22	29	36	43	50	57	50
43	36	29	22	15	8	1			

Keep On Observing (KOO):

I like to find out solution of problems, I always remain content, I am always enterprising, I am good at communication, I am courageous, I always speak economically, I never hesitate, I am sober, I am not aggressive and so on....

CYCLE-9

1	8	15	22	29	36	43	50	57	64
57	50	43	36	29	22	15	8	1	

Keep On Observing (KOO):

I like to find out solution of problems, I always remain content, I am always enterprising, I am good at communication, I am courageous, I always speak economically, I never hesitate, I am sober, I am not aggressive and so on....

CYCLE-10

1	8	15	22	29	36	43	50	57	64
71	64	57	50	43	36	29	22	15	8
1									

Keep On Observing (KOO):

I like to find out solution of problems, I always remain content, I am always enterprising, I am good at communication, I am courageous, I always speak economically, I never hesitate, I am sober, I am not aggressive and so on....

CYCLE-11

1	8	15	22	29	36	43	50	57	64
71	78	71	64	57	50	43	36	29	22
15	8	1							

Keep On Observing (KOO):

I like to find out solution of problems, I always remain content, I am always enterprising, I am good at communication, I am courageous, I always speak economically, I never hesitate, I am sober, I am not aggressive and so on....

CYCLE-12

1	8	15	22	29	36	43	50	57	64
71	78	85	78	71	64	57	50	43	36
29	22	15	8	1					

Keep On Observing (KOO):

I like to find out solution of problems, I always remain content, I am always enterprising, I am good at communication, I am courageous, I always speak economically, I never hesitate, I am sober, I am not aggressive and so on....

CYCLE-13

1	8	15	22	29	36	43	50	57	64
71	78	85	92	85	78	71	64	57	50
43	36	29	22	15	8	1			

Keep On Observing (KOO):

I like to find out solution of problems, I always remain content, I am always enterprising, I am good at communication, I am courageous, I always speak economically, I never hesitate, I am sober, I am not aggressive and so on....

CYCLE-14

1	8	15	22	29	36	43	50	57	64
71	78	85	92	99	92	85	78	71	64
57	50	43	36	29	22	15	8	1	

Keep On Observing (KOO):

I like to find out solution of problems, I always remain content, I am always enterprising, I am good at communication, I am courageous, I always speak economically, I never hesitate, I am sober, I am not aggressive and so on....

PATTERN: 2

CYCLE-1

2	9	2							

Keep On Observing (KOO):

I like to find out solution of problems, I always remain content, I am always enterprising, I am good at communication, I am courageous, I always speak economically, I never hesitate, I am sober, I am not aggressive and so on....

CYCLE-2

2	9	16	9	2					

Keep On Observing (KOO):

I like to find out solution of problems, I always remain content, I am always enterprising, I am good at communication, I am courageous, I always speak economically, I never hesitate, I am sober, I am not aggressive and so on....

CYCLE-3

2	9	16	23	16	9	2			

Keep On Observing (KOO):

I like to find out solution of problems, I always remain content, I am always enterprising, I am good at communication, I am courageous, I always speak economically, I never hesitate, I am sober, I am not aggressive and so on....

CYCLE-4

2	9	16	23	30	23	16	9	2	

Keep On Observing (KOO):

I like to find out solution of problems, I always remain content, I am always enterprising, I am good at communication, I am courageous, I always speak economically, I never hesitate, I am sober, I am not aggressive and so on....

CYCLE-5

2	9	16	23	30	37	30	23	16	9
2									

Keep On Observing (KOO):

I like to find out solution of problems, I always remain content, I am always enterprising, I am good at communication, I am courageous, I always speak economically, I never hesitate, I am sober, I am not aggressive and so on....

CYCLE-6

2	9	16	23	30	37	44	37	30	23
16	9	2							

Keep On Observing (KOO):

I like to find out solution of problems, I always remain content, I am always enterprising, I am good at communication, I am courageous, I always speak economically, I never hesitate, I am sober, I am not aggressive and so on....

CYCLE-7

2	9	16	23	30	37	44	51	44	37
30	23	16	9	2					

Keep On Observing (KOO):

I like to find out solution of problems, I always remain content, I am always enterprising, I am good at communication, I am courageous, I always speak economically, I never hesitate, I am sober, I am not aggressive and so on....

CYCLE-8

2	9	16	23	30	37	44	51	58	51
44	37	30	23	16	9	2			

Keep On Observing (KOO):

I like to find out solution of problems, I always remain content, I am always enterprising, I am good at communication, I am courageous, I always speak economically, I never hesitate, I am sober, I am not aggressive and so on....

CYCLE-9

2	9	16	23	30	37	44	51	58	65
58	51	44	37	30	23	16	9	2	

Keep On Observing (KOO):

I like to find out solution of problems, I always remain content, I am always enterprising, I am good at communication, I am courageous, I always speak economically, I never hesitate, I am sober, I am not aggressive and so on....

CYCLE-10

2	9	16	23	30	37	44	51	58	65
72	65	58	51	44	37	30	23	16	9
2									

Keep On Observing (KOO):

I like to find out solution of problems, I always remain content, I am always enterprising, I am good at communication, I am courageous, I always speak economically, I never hesitate, I am sober, I am not aggressive and so on....

CYCLE-11

2	9	16	23	30	37	44	51	58	65
72	79	72	65	58	51	44	37	30	23
16	9	2							

Keep On Observing (KOO):

I like to find out solution of problems, I always remain content, I am always enterprising, I am good at communication, I am courageous, I always speak economically, I never hesitate, I am sober, I am not aggressive and so on....

CYCLE-12

2	9	16	23	30	37	44	51	58	65
72	79	86	79	72	65	58	51	44	37
30	23	16	9	2					

Keep On Observing (KOO):

I like to find out solution of problems, I always remain content, I am always enterprising, I am good at communication, I am courageous, I always speak economically, I never hesitate, I am sober, I am not aggressive and so on....

CYCLE-13

2	9	16	23	30	37	44	51	58	65
72	79	86	93	86	79	72	65	58	51
44	37	30	23	16	9	2			

Keep On Observing (KOO):

I like to find out solution of problems, I always remain content, I am always enterprising, I am good at communication, I am courageous, I always speak economically, I never hesitate, I am sober, I am not aggressive and so on....

CYCLE-14

2	9	16	23	30	37	44	51	58	65
72	79	86	93	100	93	86	79	72	65
58	51	44	37	30	23	16	9	2	

Keep On Observing (KOO):

I like to find out solution of problems, I always remain content, I am always enterprising, I am good at communication, I am courageous, I always speak economically, I never hesitate, I am sober, I am not aggressive and so on....

PATTERN: 3

CYCLE-1

3	10	3							

Keep On Observing (KOO):

I like to find out solution of problems, I always remain content, I am always enterprising, I am good at communication, I am courageous, I always speak economically, I never hesitate, I am sober, I am not aggressive and so on....

CYCLE-2

3	10	17	10	3					

Keep On Observing (KOO):

I like to find out solution of problems, I always remain content, I am always enterprising, I am good at communication, I am courageous, I always speak economically, I never hesitate, I am sober, I am not aggressive and so on....

CYCLE-3

3	10	17	24	17	10	3			

Keep On Observing (KOO):

I like to find out solution of problems, I always remain content, I am always enterprising, I am good at communication, I am courageous, I always speak economically, I never hesitate, I am sober, I am not aggressive and so on....

CYCLE-4

3	10	17	24	31	24	17	10	3	

Keep On Observing (KOO):

I like to find out solution of problems, I always remain content, I am always enterprising, I am good at communication, I am courageous, I always speak economically, I never hesitate, I am sober, I am not aggressive and so on....

CYCLE-5

3	10	17	24	31	38	31	24	17	10
3									

Keep On Observing (KOO):

I like to find out solution of problems, I always remain content, I am always enterprising, I am good at communication, I am courageous, I always speak economically, I never hesitate, I am sober, I am not aggressive and so on....

CYCLE-6

3	10	17	24	31	38	45	38	31	24
17	10	3							

Keep On Observing (KOO):

I like to find out solution of problems, I always remain content, I am always enterprising, I am good at communication, I am courageous, I always speak economically, I never hesitate, I am sober, I am not aggressive and so on....

CYCLE-7

3	10	17	24	31	38	45	52	45	38
31	24	17	10	3					

Keep On Observing (KOO):

I like to find out solution of problems, I always remain content, I am always enterprising, I am good at communication, I am courageous, I always speak economically, I never hesitate, I am sober, I am not aggressive and so on....

CYCLE-8

3	10	17	24	31	38	45	52	59	52
45	38	31	24	17	10	3			

Keep On Observing (KOO):

I like to find out solution of problems, I always remain content, I am always enterprising, I am good at communication, I am courageous, I always speak economically, I never hesitate, I am sober, I am not aggressive and so on....

CYCLE-9

3	10	17	24	31	38	45	52	59	66
59	52	45	38	31	24	17	10	3	

Keep On Observing (KOO):

I like to find out solution of problems, I always remain content, I am always enterprising, I am good at communication, I am courageous, I always speak economically, I never hesitate, I am sober, I am not aggressive and so on....

CYCLE-10

3	10	17	24	31	38	45	52	59	66
73	66	59	52	45	38	31	24	17	10
3									

Keep On Observing (KOO):

I like to find out solution of problems, I always remain content, I am always enterprising, I am good at communication, I am courageous, I always speak economically, I never hesitate, I am sober, I am not aggressive and so on....

CYCLE-11

3	10	17	24	31	38	45	52	59	66
73	80	73	66	59	52	45	38	31	24
17	10	3							

Keep On Observing (KOO):

I like to find out solution of problems, I always remain content, I am always enterprising, I am good at communication, I am courageous, I always speak economically, I never hesitate, I am sober, I am not aggressive and so on....

CYCLE-12

3	10	17	24	31	38	45	52	59	66
73	80	87	80	73	66	59	52	45	38
31	24	17	10	3					

Keep On Observing (KOO):

I like to find out solution of problems, I always remain content, I am always enterprising, I am good at communication, I am courageous, I always speak economically, I never hesitate, I am sober, I am not aggressive and so on....

CYCLE-13

3	10	17	24	31	38	45	52	59	66
73	80	87	94	87	80	73	66	59	52
45	38	31	24	17	10	3			

Keep On Observing (KOO):

I like to find out solution of problems, I always remain content, I am always enterprising, I am good at communication, I am courageous, I always speak economically, I never hesitate, I am sober, I am not aggressive and so on....

CYCLE-14

3	10	17	24	31	38	45	52	59	66
73	80	87	94	101	94	87	80	73	66
59	52	45	38	31	24	17	10	3	

Keep On Observing (KOO):

I like to find out solution of problems, I always remain content, I am always enterprising, I am good at communication, I am courageous, I always speak economically, I never hesitate, I am sober, I am not aggressive and so on....

PATTERN: 4

CYCLE-1

4	11	4							

Keep On Observing (KOO):

I like to find out solution of problems, I always remain content, I am always enterprising, I am good at communication, I am courageous, I always speak economically, I never hesitate, I am sober, I am not aggressive and so on....

CYCLE-2

4	11	18	11	4					

Keep On Observing (KOO):

I like to find out solution of problems, I always remain content, I am always enterprising, I am good at communication, I am courageous, I always speak economically, I never hesitate, I am sober, I am not aggressive and so on....

CYCLE-3

4	11	18	25	18	11	4			

Keep On Observing (KOO):

I like to find out solution of problems, I always remain content, I am always enterprising, I am good at communication, I am courageous, I always speak economically, I never hesitate, I am sober, I am not aggressive and so on....

CYCLE-5

4	11	18	25	32	25	18	11	4	

Keep On Observing (KOO):

I like to find out solution of problems, I always remain content, I am always enterprising, I am good at communication, I am courageous, I always speak economically, I never hesitate, I am sober, I am not aggressive and so on....

CYCLE-5

4	11	18	25	32	39	32	25	18	11
4									

Keep On Observing (KOO):

I like to find out solution of problems, I always remain content, I am always enterprising, I am good at communication, I am courageous, I always speak economically, I never hesitate, I am sober, I am not aggressive and so on....

CYCLE-6

4	11	18	25	32	39	46	39	32	25
18	11	4							

Keep On Observing (KOO):

I like to find out solution of problems, I always remain content, I am always enterprising, I am good at communication, I am courageous, I always speak economically, I never hesitate, I am sober, I am not aggressive and so on....

CYCLE-7

4	11	18	25	32	39	46	53	46	39
32	25	18	11	4					

Keep On Observing (KOO):

I like to find out solution of problems, I always remain content, I am always enterprising, I am good at communication, I am courageous, I always speak economically, I never hesitate, I am sober, I am not aggressive and so on....

CYCLE-8

4	11	18	25	32	39	46	53	60	53
46	39	32	25	18	11	4			

Keep On Observing (KOO):

I like to find out solution of problems, I always remain content, I am always enterprising, I am good at communication, I am courageous, I always speak economically, I never hesitate, I am sober, I am not aggressive and so on....

CYCLE-9

4	11	18	25	32	39	46	53	60	67
60	53	46	39	32	25	18	11	4	

Keep On Observing (KOO):

I like to find out solution of problems, I always remain content, I am always enterprising, I am good at communication, I am courageous, I always speak economically, I never hesitate, I am sober, I am not aggressive and so on....

CYCLE-10

4	11	18	25	32	39	46	53	60	67
74	67	60	53	46	39	32	25	18	11
4									

Keep On Observing (KOO):

I like to find out solution of problems, I always remain content, I am always enterprising, I am good at communication, I am courageous, I always speak economically, I never hesitate, I am sober, I am not aggressive and so on....

CYCLE-11

4	11	18	25	32	39	46	53	60	67
74	81	74	67	60	53	46	39	32	25
18	11	4							

Keep On Observing (KOO):

I like to find out solution of problems, I always remain content, I am always enterprising, I am good at communication, I am courageous, I always speak economically, I never hesitate, I am sober, I am not aggressive and so on....

CYCLE-12

4	11	18	25	32	39	46	53	60	67
74	81	88	81	74	67	60	53	46	39
32	25	18	11	4					

Keep On Observing (KOO):

I like to find out solution of problems, I always remain content, I am always enterprising, I am good at communication, I am courageous, I always speak economically, I never hesitate, I am sober, I am not aggressive and so on....

CYCLE-13

4	11	18	25	32	39	46	53	60	67
74	81	88	95	88	81	74	67	60	53
46	39	32	25	18	11	4			

Keep On Observing (KOO):

I like to find out solution of problems, I always remain content, I am always enterprising, I am good at communication, I am courageous, I always speak economically, I never hesitate, I am sober, I am not aggressive and so on....

CYCLE-14

4	11	18	25	32	39	46	53	60	67
74	81	88	95	102	95	88	81	74	67
60	53	46	39	32	25	18	11	4	

Keep On Observing (KOO):

I like to find out solution of problems, I always remain content, I am always enterprising, I am good at communication, I am courageous, I always speak economically, I never hesitate, I am sober, I am not aggressive and so on....

PATTERN: 5

CYCLE-1

5	12	5							

Keep On Observing (KOO):

I like to find out solution of problems, I always remain content, I am always enterprising, I am good at communication, I am courageous, I always speak economically, I never hesitate, I am sober, I am not aggressive and so on....

CYCLE-2

5	12	19	12	5					

Keep On Observing (KOO):

I like to find out solution of problems, I always remain content, I am always enterprising, I am good at communication, I am courageous, I always speak economically, I never hesitate, I am sober, I am not aggressive and so on....

CYCLE-3

5	12	19	26	19	12	5			

Keep On Observing (KOO):

I like to find out solution of problems, I always remain content, I am always enterprising, I am good at communication, I am courageous, I always speak economically, I never hesitate, I am sober, I am not aggressive and so on....

CYCLE-4

5	12	19	26	33	26	19	12	5	

Keep On Observing (KOO):

I like to find out solution of problems, I always remain content, I am always enterprising, I am good at communication, I am courageous, I always speak economically, I never hesitate, I am sober, I am not aggressive and so on....

CYCLE-5

5	12	19	26	33	40	33	26	19	12
5									

Keep On Observing (KOO):

I like to find out solution of problems, I always remain content, I am always enterprising, I am good at communication, I am courageous, I always speak economically, I never hesitate, I am sober, I am not aggressive and so on....

CYCLE-6

5	12	19	26	33	40	47	40	33	26
19	12	5							

Keep On Observing (KOO):

I like to find out solution of problems, I always remain content, I am always enterprising, I am good at communication, I am courageous, I always speak economically, I never hesitate, I am sober, I am not aggressive and so on....

CYCLE-7

5	12	19	26	33	40	47	54	47	40
33	26	19	12	5					

Keep On Observing (KOO):

I like to find out solution of problems, I always remain content, I am always enterprising, I am good at communication, I am courageous, I always speak economically, I never hesitate, I am sober, I am not aggressive and so on....

CYCLE-8

5	12	19	26	33	40	47	54	61	54
47	40	33	26	19	12	5			

Keep On Observing (KOO):

I like to find out solution of problems, I always remain content, I am always enterprising, I am good at communication, I am courageous, I always speak economically, I never hesitate, I am sober, I am not aggressive and so on....

CYCLE-9

5	12	19	26	33	40	47	54	61	68
61	54	47	40	33	26	19	12	5	

Keep On Observing (KOO):

I like to find out solution of problems, I always remain content, I am always enterprising, I am good at communication, I am courageous, I always speak economically, I never hesitate, I am sober, I am not aggressive and so on....

CYCLE-10

5	12	19	26	33	40	47	54	61	68
75	68	61	54	47	40	33	26	19	12
5									

Keep On Observing (KOO):

I like to find out solution of problems, I always remain content, I am always enterprising, I am good at communication, I am courageous, I always speak economically, I never hesitate, I am sober, I am not aggressive and so on....

CYCLE-11

5	12	19	26	33	40	47	54	61	68
75		82	75	68	61	54	47	40	33
26	19	12	5						

Keep On Observing (KOO):

I like to find out solution of problems, I always remain content, I am always enterprising, I am good at communication, I am courageous, I always speak economically, I never hesitate, I am sober, I am not aggressive and so on....

CYCLE-12

5	12	19	26	33	40	47	54	61	68
75	82	89	82	75	68	61	54	47	40
33	26	19	12	5					

Keep On Observing (KOO):

I like to find out solution of problems, I always remain content, I am always enterprising, I am good at communication, I am courageous, I always speak economically, I never hesitate, I am sober, I am not aggressive and so on....

CYCLE-13

5	12	19	26	33	40	47	54	61	68
75	82	89	96	89	82	75	68	61	54
47	40	33	26	19	12	5			

Keep On Observing (KOO):

I like to find out solution of problems, I always remain content, I am always enterprising, I am good at communication, I am courageous, I always speak economically, I never hesitate, I am sober, I am not aggressive and so on....

CYCLE-14

5	12	19	26	33	40	47	54	61	68
75	82	89	96	103	96	89	82	75	68
61	54	47	40	33	26	19	12	5	

Keep On Observing (KOO):

I like to find out solution of problems, I always remain content, I am always enterprising, I am good at communication, I am courageous, I always speak economically, I never hesitate, I am sober, I am not aggressive and so on....

PATTERN: 6

CYCLE-1

6	13	6							

Keep On Observing (KOO):

I like to find out solution of problems, I always remain content, I am always enterprising, I am good at communication, I am courageous, I always speak economically, I never hesitate, I am sober, I am not aggressive and so on....

CYCLE-2

6	13	20	13	6					

Keep On Observing (KOO):

I like to find out solution of problems, I always remain content, I am always enterprising, I am good at communication, I am courageous, I always speak economically, I never hesitate, I am sober, I am not aggressive and so on....

CYCLE-3

6	13	20	27	20	13	6			

Keep On Observing (KOO):

I like to find out solution of problems, I always remain content, I am always enterprising, I am good at communication, I am courageous, I always speak economically, I never hesitate, I am sober, I am not aggressive and so on....

CYCLE-4

6	13	20	27	34	27	20	13	6	

Keep On Observing (KOO):

I like to find out solution of problems, I always remain content, I am always enterprising, I am good at communication, I am courageous, I always speak economically, I never hesitate, I am sober, I am not aggressive and so on....

CYCLE-5

6	13	20	27	34	41	34	27	20	13
6									

Keep On Observing (KOO):

I like to find out solution of problems, I always remain content, I am always enterprising, I am good at communication, I am courageous, I always speak economically, I never hesitate, I am sober, I am not aggressive and so on....

CYCLE-6

6	13	20	27	34	41	48	41	34	27
20	13	6							

Keep On Observing (KOO):

I like to find out solution of problems, I always remain content, I am always enterprising, I am good at communication, I am courageous, I always speak economically, I never hesitate, I am sober, I am not aggressive and so on....

CYCLE-7

6	13	20	27	34	41	48	55	48	41
34	27	20	13	6					

Keep On Observing (KOO):

I like to find out solution of problems, I always remain content, I am always enterprising, I am good at communication, I am courageous, I always speak economically, I never hesitate, I am sober, I am not aggressive and so on....

CYCLE-8

6	13	20	27	34	41	48	55	62	55
48	41	34	27	20	13	6			

Keep On Observing (KOO):

I like to find out solution of problems, I always remain content, I am always enterprising, I am good at communication, I am courageous, I always speak economically, I never hesitate, I am sober, I am not aggressive and so on....

CYCLE-9

6	13	20	27	34	41	48	55	62	69
62	55	48	41	34	27	20	13	6	

Keep On Observing (KOO):

I like to find out solution of problems, I always remain content, I am always enterprising, I am good at communication, I am courageous, I always speak economically, I never hesitate, I am sober, I am not aggressive and so on....

CYCLE-10

6	13	20	27	34	41	48	55	62	69
76	69	62	55	48	41	34	27	20	13
6									

Keep On Observing (KOO):

I like to find out solution of problems, I always remain content, I am always enterprising, I am good at communication, I am courageous, I always speak economically, I never hesitate, I am sober, I am not aggressive and so on....

CYCLE-11

6	13	20	27	34	41	48	55	62	69
76		83	76	69	62	55	48	41	34
27	20	13	6						

Keep On Observing (KOO):

I like to find out solution of problems, I always remain content, I am always enterprising, I am good at communication, I am courageous, I always speak economically, I never hesitate, I am sober, I am not aggressive and so on....

CYCLE-12

6	13	20	27	34	41	48	55	62	69
76	83	90	83	76	69	62	55	48	41
34	27	20	13	6					

Keep On Observing (KOO):

I like to find out solution of problems, I always remain content, I am always enterprising, I am good at communication, I am courageous, I always speak economically, I never hesitate, I am sober, I am not aggressive and so on....

CYCLE-13

6	13	20	27	34	41	48	55	62	69
76	83	90	97	90	83	76	69	62	55
48	41	34	27	20	13	6			

Keep On Observing (KOO):

I like to find out solution of problems, I always remain content, I am always enterprising, I am good at communication, I am courageous, I always speak economically, I never hesitate, I am sober, I am not aggressive and so on....

CYCLE-14

6	13	20	27	34	41	48	55	62	69
76	83	90	97	104	97	90	83	76	69
62	55	48	41	34	27	20	13	6	

Keep On Observing (KOO):

I like to find out solution of problems, I always remain content, I am always enterprising, I am good at communication, I am courageous, I always speak economically, I never hesitate, I am sober, I am not aggressive and so on....

PATTERN: 7

CYCLE-1

7	14	7							

Keep On Observing (KOO):

I like to find out solution of problems, I always remain content, I am always enterprising, I am good at communication, I am courageous, I always speak economically, I never hesitate, I am sober, I am not aggressive and so on....

CYCLE-2

7	14	21	14	7					

Keep On Observing (KOO):

I like to find out solution of problems, I always remain content, I am always enterprising, I am good at communication, I am courageous, I always speak economically, I never hesitate, I am sober, I am not aggressive and so on....

CYCLE-3

7	14	21	28	21	14	7			

Keep On Observing (KOO):

I like to find out solution of problems, I always remain content, I am always enterprising, I am good at communication, I am courageous, I always speak economically, I never hesitate, I am sober, I am not aggressive and so on....

CYCLE-4

7	14	21	28	35	28	21	14	7	

Keep On Observing (KOO):

I like to find out solution of problems, I always remain content, I am always enterprising, I am good at communication, I am courageous, I always speak economically, I never hesitate, I am sober, I am not aggressive and so on....

CYCLE-5

7	14	21	28	35	42	35	28	21	14
7									

Keep On Observing (KOO):

I like to find out solution of problems, I always remain content, I am always enterprising, I am good at communication, I am courageous, I always speak economically, I never hesitate, I am sober, I am not aggressive and so on....

CYCLE-6

7	14	21	28	35	42	49	42	35	28
21	14	7							

Keep On Observing (KOO):

I like to find out solution of problems, I always remain content, I am always enterprising, I am good at communication, I am courageous, I always speak economically, I never hesitate, I am sober, I am not aggressive and so on....

CYCLE-7

7	14	21	28	35	42	49	56	49	42
35	28	21	14	7					

Keep On Observing (KOO):

I like to find out solution of problems, I always remain content, I am always enterprising, I am good at communication, I am courageous, I always speak economically, I never hesitate, I am sober, I am not aggressive and so on....

CYCLE-8

7	14	21	28	35	42	49	56	63	56
49	42	35	28	21	14	7			

Keep On Observing (KOO):

I like to find out solution of problems, I always remain content, I am always enterprising, I am good at communication, I am courageous, I always speak economically, I never hesitate, I am sober, I am not aggressive and so on....

CYCLE-9

7	14	21	28	35	42	49	56	63	70
63	56	49	42	35	28	21	14	7	

Keep On Observing (KOO):

I like to find out solution of problems, I always remain content, I am always enterprising, I am good at communication, I am courageous, I always speak economically, I never hesitate, I am sober, I am not aggressive and so on....

CYCLE-10

7	14	21	28	35	42	49	56	63	70
77	70	63	56	49	42	35	28	21	14
7									

Keep On Observing (KOO):

I like to find out solution of problems, I always remain content, I am always enterprising, I am good at communication, I am courageous, I always speak economically, I never hesitate, I am sober, I am not aggressive and so on....

CYCLE-11

7	14	21	28	35	42	49	56	63	70
77		84	77	70	63	56	49	42	35
28	21	14	7						

Keep On Observing (KOO):

I like to find out solution of problems, I always remain content, I am always enterprising, I am good at communication, I am courageous, I always speak economically, I never hesitate, I am sober, I am not aggressive and so on....

CYCLE-12

7	14	21	28	35	42	49	56	63	70
77	84	91	84	77	70	63	56	49	42
35	28	21	14	7					

Keep On Observing (KOO):

I like to find out solution of problems, I always remain content, I am always enterprising, I am good at communication, I am courageous, I always speak economically, I never hesitate, I am sober, I am not aggressive and so on....

CYCLE-13

7	14	21	28	35	42	49	56	63	70
77	84	91	98	91	84	77	70	63	56
49	42	35	28	21	14	7			

Keep On Observing (KOO):

I like to find out solution of problems, I always remain content, I am always enterprising, I am good at communication, I am courageous, I always speak economically, I never hesitate, I am sober, I am not aggressive and so on....

CYCLE-14

7	14	21	28	35	42	49	56	63	70
77	84	91	98	105	98	91	84	77	70
63	56	49	42	35	28	21	14	7	

Keep On Observing (KOO):

I like to find out solution of problems, I always remain content, I am always enterprising, I am good at communication, I am courageous, I always speak economically, I never hesitate, I am sober, I am not aggressive and so on....

Let's do an introspective exercise:

Please check what you achieved and able to exercise now in your life

Sr. No.	Qualities/ characteristics	Posses by a mathe-matised mind	Posses by a success full mind	Posses by a happy mind	Posses by a pat-tern	Posses by you		
						Begin-ning	Con-soli-dating	Exer-cising
1	like to find out solution of problems	yes	yes	Yes	yes			
2	remain content	yes	yes	Yes	yes			
3	enterprising	yes	yes	Yes	yes			
4	good at communication	yes	yes	Yes	yes			
5	courageous	yes	yes	Yes	yes			
6	speak economically	yes	yes	Yes	yes			
7	never hesitate	yes	yes	Yes	yes			
8	Sober	yes	yes	Yes	yes			
9	aggressive	no	no	No	no			
10	straight forward	yes	Yes	Yes	yes			
11	daring	yes	yes	Yes	Yes			
12	enthusiastic	yes	yes	Yes	yes			
13	risk taking	yes	calcu-lated	calcu-lated	calcu-lated			
14	bold	yes	yes	Yes	Yes			
15	can take stress	yes	Yes	Yes	yes			
16	dominant	yes	no	No	No			
17	influenced by facts than by feeling	yes	Yes	Yes	yes			
18	Hard working	yes	yes	yes	Yes			
19	easy going never in hurry	yes	yes	Yes	yes			
20	quick decision	yes	yes	yes	Yes			
21	communicative	yes	yes	Yes	yes			
22	free from guilt	yes	yes	yes	yes			
23	never hesitate	yes	yes	yes	yes			
24	Secure	yes	yes	Yes	yes			
25	never act according to others	yes	yes	yes	yes			
26	capable of getting things done	yes	yes	Yes	yes			
27	assertive behaviour	yes	yes	yes	yes			

28	develop their own sets of rules	yes	If required	If required	If required			
29	self disciplined	yes	yes	yes	Yes			
30	abstract thinking	yes	yes	Yes	yes			
31	reliable behaviour	yes	yes	yes	yes			
32	experementive	yes	yes	yes	yes			
33	impulsive	yes	no	no	no			
34	self destructive	no	no	no	no			
35	social	yes	yes	yes	yes			
36	cope with routine life		yes	yes	yes			
37	highly self motivated	yes	yes	Yes	yes			
38	practical	yes	yes	yes	yes			
39	mindful	yes	yes	yes	yes			
40	lost in the world of dreams	no	no	no	no			
41	participating	yes	yes	yes	yes			
42	Cautious	yes	yes	Yes	yes			
43	likes people	yes	yes	yes	yes			
44	open minded	yes	yes	yes	yes			
45	resolve conflicts	yes	yes	Yes	yes			
46	emotionally mature	yes	yes	Yes	yes			
47	realistic	yes	yes	yes	yes			
48	Cheerful	yes	yes	Yes	yes			
49	Intuitive	yes	yes	yes	yes			
50	keep things under control	yes	yes	yes	yes			
51	Competitor of self	yes	yes	Yes	yes			
52	self confident	yes	yes	Yes	yes			
53	Assertive	yes	yes	Yes	yes			
54	Mature	yes	yes	Yes	yes			
55	Relax	yes	yes	Yes	yes			
56	Adaptive	yes	yes	Yes	yes			
57	Flexible	yes	yes	Yes	yes			
58	open to change	yes	yes	Yes	yes			
59	accommodative	yes	yes	Yes	yes			
60	socially active	yes	yes	Yes	yes			
61	cultural interests	yes	yes	Yes	yes			
62	down to earch	yes	yes	Yes	yes			
63	friendly nature	yes	yes	Yes	yes			
64	Sociable	yes	yes	Yes	yes			
65	good reasoning	yes	yes	Yes	yes			
66	intelligent	yes	yes	Yes	yes			
67	hard to fool	yes	yes	Yes	yes			

Express your feeling about your accomplishments through mathyogs9211:

....
....
....
....
....
....
....
....
....
....
....
....
....
....
....
....
....
....
....
....
....
....
....
....
....
....
....
....
....
....

CHAPTER-XII

COUNTING BY EIGHT'S

Group 8: Counting by eight's

Sr. No.	GROUP VIII							
Term	PATTERN-1	PATTERN-2	PATTERN-3	PATTERN-4	PATTERN-5	PATTERN-6	PATTERN-7	PATTERN-8
1	1	2	3	4	5	6	7	8
2	9	10	11	12	13	14	15	16
3	17	18	19	20	21	22	23	24
4	25	26	27	28	29	30	31	32
5	33	34	35	36	37	38	39	40
6	41	42	43	44	45	46	47	48
7	49	50	51	52	53	54	55	56
8	57	58	59	60	61	62	63	64
9	65	66	67	68	69	70	71	72
10	73	74	75	76	77	78	79	80
11	81	82	83	84	85	86	87	88
12	89	90	91	92	93	94	95	96
13	97	98	99	100	101	102	103	104

PATTERN: 1

CYCLE-1

1	9	1							

Keep On Observing (KOO):

I like to find out solution of problems, I always remain content, I am always enterprising, I am good at communication, I am courageous, I always speak economically, I never hesitate, I am sober, I am not aggressive and so on....

CYCLE-2

1	9	17	9	1					

Keep On Observing (KOO):

I like to find out solution of problems, I always remain content, I am always enterprising, I am good at communication, I am courageous, I always speak economically, I never hesitate, I am sober, I am not aggressive and so on....

CYCLE-3

1	9	17	25	17	9	1			

Keep On Observing (KOO):

I like to find out solution of problems, I always remain content, I am always enterprising, I am good at communication, I am courageous, I always speak economically, I never hesitate, I am sober, I am not aggressive and so on....

CYCLE-5

1	9	17	25	33	25	17	9	1	

Keep On Observing (KOO):

I like to find out solution of problems, I always remain content, I am always enterprising, I am good at communication, I am courageous, I always speak economically, I never hesitate, I am sober, I am not aggressive and so on....

CYCLE-5

1	9	17	25	33	41	33	25	17	9
1									

Keep On Observing (KOO):

I like to find out solution of problems, I always remain content, I am always enterprising, I am good at communication, I am courageous, I always speak economically, I never hesitate, I am sober, I am not aggressive and so on....

CYCLE-6

1	9	17	25	33	41	49	41	33	25
17	9	1							

Keep On Observing (KOO):

I like to find out solution of problems, I always remain content, I am always enterprising, I am good at communication, I am courageous, I always speak economically, I never hesitate, I am sober, I am not aggressive and so on....

CYCLE-7

1	9	17	25	33	41	49	57	49	41
33	25	17	9	1					

Keep On Observing (KOO):

I like to find out solution of problems, I always remain content, I am always enterprising, I am good at communication, I am courageous, I always speak economically, I never hesitate, I am sober, I am not aggressive and so on....

CYCLE-8

1	9	17	25	33	41	49	57	65	57
49	41	33	25	17	9	1			

Keep On Observing (KOO):

I like to find out solution of problems, I always remain content, I am always enterprising, I am good at communication, I am courageous, I always speak economically, I never hesitate, I am sober, I am not aggressive and so on....

CYCLE-9

1	9	17	25	33	41	49	57	65	73
65	57	49	41	33	25	17	9	1	

Keep On Observing (KOO):

I like to find out solution of problems, I always remain content, I am always enterprising, I am good at communication, I am courageous, I always speak economically, I never hesitate, I am sober, I am not aggressive and so on....

CYCLE-10

1	9	17	25	33	41	49	57	65	73
81	73	65	57	49	41	33	25	17	9
1									

Keep On Observing (KOO):

I like to find out solution of problems, I always remain content, I am always enterprising, I am good at communication, I am courageous, I always speak economically, I never hesitate, I am sober, I am not aggressive and so on....

CYCLE-11

1	9	17	25	33	41	49	57	65	73
81	89	81	73	65	57	49	41	33	25
17	9	1							

Keep On Observing (KOO):

I like to find out solution of problems, I always remain content, I am always enterprising, I am good at communication, I am courageous, I always speak economically, I never hesitate, I am sober, I am not aggressive and so on....

CYCLE-12

1	9	17	25	33	41	49	57	65	73
81	89	97	89	81	73	65	57	49	41
33	25	17		9	1				

PATTERN: 2

CYCLE-1

2	10	2							

Keep On Observing (KOO):

I like to find out solution of problems, I always remain content, I am always enterprising, I am good at communication, I am courageous, I always speak economically, I never hesitate, I am sober, I am not aggressive and so on....

CYCLE-2

2	10	18	10	2					

Keep On Observing (KOO):

I like to find out solution of problems, I always remain content, I am always enterprising, I am good at communication, I am courageous, I always speak economically, I never hesitate, I am sober, I am not aggressive and so on....

CYCLE-3

2	10	18	26	18	10	2			

Keep On Observing (KOO):

I like to find out solution of problems, I always remain content, I am always enterprising, I am good at communication, I am courageous, I always speak economically, I never hesitate, I am sober, I am not aggressive and so on....

CYCLE-4

2	10	18	26	34	26	18	10	2	

Keep On Observing (KOO):

I like to find out solution of problems, I always remain content, I am always enterprising, I am good at communication, I am courageous, I always speak economically, I never hesitate, I am sober, I am not aggressive and so on....

CYCLE-5

2	10	18	26	34	42	34	26	18	10
2									

Keep On Observing (KOO):

I like to find out solution of problems, I always remain content, I am always enterprising, I am good at communication, I am courageous, I always speak economically, I never hesitate, I am sober, I am not aggressive and so on....

CYCLE-6

2	10	18	26	34	42	50	42	34	26
18	10	2							

Keep On Observing (KOO):

I like to find out solution of problems, I always remain content, I am always enterprising, I am good at communication, I am courageous, I always speak economically, I never hesitate, I am sober, I am not aggressive and so on....

CYCLE-7

2	10	18	26	34	42	50	58	50	42
34	26	18	10	2					

Keep On Observing (KOO):

I like to find out solution of problems, I always remain content, I am always enterprising, I am good at communication, I am courageous, I always speak economically, I never hesitate, I am sober, I am not aggressive and so on....

CYCLE-8

2	10	18	26	34	42	50	58	66	58
50	42	34	26	18	10	2			

Keep On Observing (KOO):

I like to find out solution of problems, I always remain content, I am always enterprising, I am good at communication, I am courageous, I always speak economically, I never hesitate, I am sober, I am not aggressive and so on....

CYCLE-9

2	10	18	26	34	42	50	58	66	74
66	58	50	42	34	26	18	10	2	

Keep On Observing (KOO):

I like to find out solution of problems, I always remain content, I am always enterprising, I am good at communication, I am courageous, I always speak economically, I never hesitate, I am sober, I am not aggressive and so on....

CYCLE-10

2	10	18	26	34	42	50	58	66	74
82	74	66	58	50	42	34	26	18	10
2									

Keep On Observing (KOO):

I like to find out solution of problems, I always remain content, I am always enterprising, I am good at communication, I am courageous, I always speak economically, I never hesitate, I am sober, I am not aggressive and so on....

CYCLE-11

2	10	18	26	34	42	50	58	66	74
82	90	82	74	66	58	50	42	34	26
18	10	2							

Keep On Observing (KOO):

I like to find out solution of problems, I always remain content, I am always enterprising, I am good at communication, I am courageous, I always speak economically, I never hesitate, I am sober, I am not aggressive and so on....

CYCLE-12

2	10	18	26	34	42	50	58	66	74
82	90	98	90	82	74	66	58	50	42
34	26	18	10	2					

PATTERN: 3

CYCLE-1

3	11	3							

Keep On Observing (KOO):

I like to find out solution of problems, I always remain content, I am always enterprising, I am good at communication, I am courageous, I always speak economically, I never hesitate, I am sober, I am not aggressive and so on....

CYCLE-2

3	11	19	11	3					

Keep On Observing (KOO):

I like to find out solution of problems, I always remain content, I am always enterprising, I am good at communication, I am courageous, I always speak economically, I never hesitate, I am sober, I am not aggressive and so on....

CYCLE-3

3	11	19	27	19	11	3			

Keep On Observing (KOO):

I like to find out solution of problems, I always remain content, I am always enterprising, I am good at communication, I am courageous, I always speak economically, I never hesitate, I am sober, I am not aggressive and so on....

CYCLE-4

3	11	19	27	35	27	19	11	3	

Keep On Observing (KOO):

I like to find out solution of problems, I always remain content, I am always enterprising, I am good at communication, I am courageous, I always speak economically, I never hesitate, I am sober, I am not aggressive and so on....

CYCLE-5

3	11	19	27	35	43	35	27	19	11
3									

Keep On Observing (KOO):

I like to find out solution of problems, I always remain content, I am always enterprising, I am good at communication, I am courageous, I always speak economically, I never hesitate, I am sober, I am not aggressive and so on....

CYCLE-6

3	11	19	27	35	43	51	43	35	27
19	11	3							

Keep On Observing (KOO):

I like to find out solution of problems, I always remain content, I am always enterprising, I am good at communication, I am courageous, I always speak economically, I never hesitate, I am sober, I am not aggressive and so on....

CYCLE-7

3	11	19	27	35	43	51	59	51	43
35	27	19	11	3					

Keep On Observing (KOO):

I like to find out solution of problems, I always remain content, I am always enterprising, I am good at communication, I am courageous, I always speak economically, I never hesitate, I am sober, I am not aggressive and so on....

CYCLE-8

3	11	19	27	35	43	51	59	67	59
51	43	35	27	19	11	3			

Keep On Observing (KOO):

I like to find out solution of problems, I always remain content, I am always enterprising, I am good at communication, I am courageous, I always speak economically, I never hesitate, I am sober, I am not aggressive and so on....

CYCLE-9

3	11	19	27	35	43	51	59	67	75
67	59	51	43	35	27	19	11	3	

Keep On Observing (KOO):

I like to find out solution of problems, I always remain content, I am always enterprising, I am good at communication, I am courageous, I always speak economically, I never hesitate, I am sober, I am not aggressive and so on....

CYCLE-10

3	11	19	27	35	43	51	59	67	75
83	75	67	59	51	43	35	27	19	11
3									

Keep On Observing (KOO):

I like to find out solution of problems, I always remain content, I am always enterprising, I am good at communication, I am courageous, I always speak economically, I never hesitate, I am sober, I am not aggressive and so on....

CYCLE-11

3	11	19	27	35	43	51	59	67	75
83		91	83	75	67	59	51	43	35
27	19	11	3						

Keep On Observing (KOO):

I like to find out solution of problems, I always remain content, I am always enterprising, I am good at communication, I am courageous, I always speak economically, I never hesitate, I am sober, I am not aggressive and so on....

CYCLE-12

3	11	19	27	35	43	51	59	67	75
83	91	99	91	83	75	67	59	51	43
35	27	19	11	3					

PATTERN: 4

Keep On Observing (KOO):

I like to find out solution of problems, I always remain content, I am always enterprising, I am good at communication, I am courageous, I always speak economically, I never hesitate, I am sober, I am not aggressive and so on....

CYCLE-1

4	12	4								

Keep On Observing (KOO):

I like to find out solution of problems, I always remain content, I am always enterprising, I am good at communication, I am courageous, I always speak economically, I never hesitate, I am sober, I am not aggressive and so on....

CYCLE-2

4	12	20	12	4						

Keep On Observing (KOO):

I like to find out solution of problems, I always remain content, I am always enterprising, I am good at communication, I am courageous, I always speak economically, I never hesitate, I am sober, I am not aggressive and so on....

CYCLE-3

4	12	20	28	20	12	4			

Keep On Observing (KOO):

I like to find out solution of problems, I always remain content, I am always enterprising, I am good at communication, I am courageous, I always speak economically, I never hesitate, I am sober, I am not aggressive and so on....

CYCLE-4

4	12	20	28	36	28	20	12	4	

Keep On Observing (KOO):

I like to find out solution of problems, I always remain content, I am always enterprising, I am good at communication, I am courageous, I always speak economically, I never hesitate, I am sober, I am not aggressive and so on....

CYCLE-5

4	12	20	28	36	44	36	28	20	12
4									

Keep On Observing (KOO):

I like to find out solution of problems, I always remain content, I am always enterprising, I am good at communication, I am courageous, I always speak economically, I never hesitate, I am sober, I am not aggressive and so on....

CYCLE-6

4	12	20	28	36	44	52	44	36	28
20	12	4							

Keep On Observing (KOO):

I like to find out solution of problems, I always remain content, I am always enterprising, I am good at communication, I am courageous, I always speak economically, I never hesitate, I am sober, I am not aggressive and so on....

CYCLE-7

4	12	20	28	36	44	52	60	52	44
36	28	20	12	4					

Keep On Observing (KOO):

I like to find out solution of problems, I always remain content, I am always enterprising, I am good at communication, I am courageous, I always speak economically, I never hesitate, I am sober, I am not aggressive and so on....

CYCLE-8

4	12	20	28	36	44	52	60	68	60
52	44	36	28	20	12	4			

Keep On Observing (KOO):

I like to find out solution of problems, I always remain content, I am always enterprising, I am good at communication, I am courageous, I always speak economically, I never hesitate, I am sober, I am not aggressive and so on....

CYCLE-9

4	12	20	28	36	44	52	60	68	76
68	60	52	44	36	28	20	12	4	

Keep On Observing (KOO):

I like to find out solution of problems, I always remain content, I am always enterprising, I am good at communication, I am courageous, I always speak economically, I never hesitate, I am sober, I am not aggressive and so on....

CYCLE-10

4	12	20	28	36	44	52	60	68	76
84	76	68	60	52	44	36	28	20	12
4									

Keep On Observing (KOO):

I like to find out solution of problems, I always remain content, I am always enterprising, I am good at communication, I am courageous, I always speak economically, I never hesitate, I am sober, I am not aggressive and so on....

CYCLE-11

4	12	20	28	36	44	52	60	68	76
84	92	84	76	68	60	52	44	36	28
20	12	4							

Keep On Observing (KOO):

I like to find out solution of problems, I always remain content, I am always enterprising, I am good at communication, I am courageous, I always speak economically, I never hesitate, I am sober, I am not aggressive and so on....

CYCLE-12

4	12	20	28	36	44	52	60	68	76
84	92	100	92	84	76	68	60	52	44
36	28	20	12	4					

PATTERN: 5

Keep On Observing (KOO):

I like to find out solution of problems, I always remain content, I am always enterprising, I am good at communication, I am courageous, I always speak economically, I never hesitate, I am sober, I am not aggressive and so on....

CYCLE-1

5	13	21	13	5					

Keep On Observing (KOO):

I like to find out solution of problems, I always remain content, I am always enterprising, I am good at communication, I am courageous, I always speak economically, I never hesitate, I am sober, I am not aggressive and so on....

CYCLE-2

5	13	21	29	21	13	5			

Keep On Observing (KOO):

I like to find out solution of problems, I always remain content, I am always enterprising, I am good at communication, I am courageous, I always speak economically, I never hesitate, I am sober, I am not aggressive and so on....

CYCLE-3

5	13	21	29	37	29	21	13	5	

Keep On Observing (KOO):

I like to find out solution of problems, I always remain content, I am always enterprising, I am good at communication, I am courageous, I always speak economically, I never hesitate, I am sober, I am not aggressive and so on....

CYCLE-4

5	13	21	29	37	45	37	29	21	13
5									

Keep On Observing (KOO):

I like to find out solution of problems, I always remain content, I am always enterprising, I am good at communication, I am courageous, I always speak economically, I never hesitate, I am sober, I am not aggressive and so on....

CYCLE-5

5	13	21	29	37	45	53	45	37	29
21	13	5							

Keep On Observing (KOO):

I like to find out solution of problems, I always remain content, I am always enterprising, I am good at communication, I am courageous, I always speak economically, I never hesitate, I am sober, I am not aggressive and so on....

CYCLE-6

5	13	21	29	37	45	53	61	53	45
37	29	21	13	5					

Keep On Observing (KOO):

I like to find out solution of problems, I always remain content, I am always enterprising, I am good at communication, I am courageous, I always speak economically, I never hesitate, I am sober, I am not aggressive and so on....

CYCLE-7

5	13	21	29	37	45	53	61	69	61
53	45	37	29	21	13	5			

Keep On Observing (KOO):

I like to find out solution of problems, I always remain content, I am always enterprising, I am good at communication, I am courageous, I always speak economically, I never hesitate, I am sober, I am not aggressive and so on....

CYCLE-8

5	13	21	29	37	45	53	61	69	77
69	61	53	45	37	29	21	13	5	

Keep On Observing (KOO):

I like to find out solution of problems, I always remain content, I am always enterprising, I am good at communication, I am courageous, I always speak economically, I never hesitate, I am sober, I am not aggressive and so on....

CYCLE-9

5	13	21	29	37	45	53	61	69	77
69	61	53	45	37	29	21	13	5	

Keep On Observing (KOO):

I like to find out solution of problems, I always remain content, I am always enterprising, I am good at communication, I am courageous, I always speak economically, I never hesitate, I am sober, I am not aggressive and so on....

CYCLE-10

5	13	21	29	37	45	53	61	69	77
85	77	69	61	53	45	37	29	21	13
5									

Keep On Observing (KOO):

I like to find out solution of problems, I always remain content, I am always enterprising, I am good at communication, I am courageous, I always speak economically, I never hesitate, I am sober, I am not aggressive and so on....

CYCLE-11

5	13	21	29	37	45	53	61	69	77
85		93	85	77	69	61	53	45	37
29	21	13	5						

Keep On Observing (KOO):

I like to find out solution of problems, I always remain content, I am always enterprising, I am good at communication, I am courageous, I always speak economically, I never hesitate, I am sober, I am not aggressive and so on....

CYCLE-12

5	13	21	29	37	45	53	61	69	77
85	93	101	93	85	77	69	61	53	45
37	29	21	13	5					

PATTERN: 6

Keep On Observing (KOO):

I like to find out solution of problems, I always remain content, I am always enterprising, I am good at communication, I am courageous, I always speak economically, I never hesitate, I am sober, I am not aggressive and so on....

CYCLE-1

6	14	6							

Keep On Observing (KOO):

I like to find out solution of problems, I always remain content, I am always enterprising, I am good at communication, I am courageous, I always speak economically, I never hesitate, I am sober, I am not aggressive and so on....

CYCLE-2

6	14	22	14	6					

Keep On Observing (KOO):

I like to find out solution of problems, I always remain content, I am always enterprising, I am good at communication, I am courageous, I always speak economically, I never hesitate, I am sober, I am not aggressive and so on....

CYCLE-3

6	14	22	30	22	14	6			

Keep On Observing (KOO):

I like to find out solution of problems, I always remain content, I am always enterprising, I am good at communication, I am courageous, I always speak economically, I never hesitate, I am sober, I am not aggressive and so on....

CYCLE-4

6	14	22	30	38	30	22	14	6	

Keep On Observing (KOO):

I like to find out solution of problems, I always remain content, I am always enterprising, I am good at communication, I am courageous, I always speak economically, I never hesitate, I am sober, I am not aggressive and so on....

CYCLE-5

6	14	22	30	38	46	38	30	22	14
6									

Keep On Observing (KOO):

I like to find out solution of problems, I always remain content, I am always enterprising, I am good at communication, I am courageous, I always speak economically, I never hesitate, I am sober, I am not aggressive and so on....

CYCLE-6

6	14	22	30	38	46	54	46	38	30
22	14	6							

Keep On Observing (KOO):

I like to find out solution of problems, I always remain content, I am always enterprising, I am good at communication, I am courageous, I always speak economically, I never hesitate, I am sober, I am not aggressive and so on....

CYCLE-7

6	14	22	30	38	46	54	62	54	46
38	30	22	14	6					

Keep On Observing (KOO):

I like to find out solution of problems, I always remain content, I am always enterprising, I am good at communication, I am courageous, I always speak economically, I never hesitate, I am sober, I am not aggressive and so on....

CYCLE-8

6	14	22	30	38	46	54	62	70	62
54	46	38	30	22	14	6			

Keep On Observing (KOO):

I like to find out solution of problems, I always remain content, I am always enterprising, I am good at communication, I am courageous, I always speak economically, I never hesitate, I am sober, I am not aggressive and so on....

CYCLE-9

6	14	22	30	38	46	54	62	70	78
70	62	54	46	38	30	22	14	6	

Keep On Observing (KOO):

I like to find out solution of problems, I always remain content, I am always enterprising, I am good at communication, I am courageous, I always speak economically, I never hesitate, I am sober, I am not aggressive and so on....

CYCLE-10

6	14	22	30	38	46	54	62	70	78
86	78	70	62	54	46	38	30	22	14
6									

Keep On Observing (KOO):

I like to find out solution of problems, I always remain content, I am always enterprising, I am good at communication, I am courageous, I always speak economically, I never hesitate, I am sober, I am not aggressive and so on....

CYCLE-11

6	14	22	30	38	46	54	62	70	78
86		94	86	78	70	62	54	46	38
30	22	14	6						

Keep On Observing (KOO):

I like to find out solution of problems, I always remain content, I am always enterprising, I am good at communication, I am courageous, I always speak economically, I never hesitate, I am sober, I am not aggressive and so on....

CYCLE-12

6	14	22	30	38	46	54	62	70	78
86	94	102	94	86	78	70	62	54	46
38	30	22	14	6					

PATTERN: 7

Keep On Observing (KOO):

I like to find out solution of problems, I always remain content, I am always enterprising, I am good at communication, I am courageous, I always speak economically, I never hesitate, I am sober, I am not aggressive and so on....

CYCLE-1

7	15	7							

Keep On Observing (KOO):

I like to find out solution of problems, I always remain content, I am always enterprising, I am good at communication, I am courageous, I always speak economically, I never hesitate, I am sober, I am not aggressive and so on....

CYCLE-2

7	15	23	15	7					

Keep On Observing (KOO):

I like to find out solution of problems, I always remain content, I am always enterprising, I am good at communication, I am courageous, I always speak economically, I never hesitate, I am sober, I am not aggressive and so on....

CYCLE-3

7	15	23	31	23	15	7			

Keep On Observing (KOO):

I like to find out solution of problems, I always remain content, I am always enterprising, I am good at communication, I am courageous, I always speak economically, I never hesitate, I am sober, I am not aggressive and so on....

CYCLE-4

| 7 | 15 | 23 | 31 | 39 | 31 | 23 | 15 | 7 | |

Keep On Observing (KOO):

I like to find out solution of problems, I always remain content, I am always enterprising, I am good at communication, I am courageous, I always speak economically, I never hesitate, I am sober, I am not aggressive and so on....

CYCLE-5

| 7 | 15 | 23 | 31 | 39 | 47 | 39 | 31 | 23 | 15 |
| 7 | | | | | | | | | |

Keep On Observing (KOO):

I like to find out solution of problems, I always remain content, I am always enterprising, I am good at communication, I am courageous, I always speak economically, I never hesitate, I am sober, I am not aggressive and so on....

CYCLE-6

| 7 | 15 | 23 | 31 | 39 | 47 | 55 | 47 | 39 | 31 |
| 23 | 15 | 7 | | | | | | | |

Keep On Observing (KOO):

I like to find out solution of problems, I always remain content, I am always enterprising, I am good at communication, I am courageous, I always speak economically, I never hesitate, I am sober, I am not aggressive and so on....

CYCLE-7

7	15	23	31	39	47	55	63	55	47
39	31	23	15	7					

Keep On Observing (KOO):

I like to find out solution of problems, I always remain content, I am always enterprising, I am good at communication, I am courageous, I always speak economically, I never hesitate, I am sober, I am not aggressive and so on....

CYCLE-8

7	15	23	31	39	47	55	63	71	63
55	47	39	31	23	15	7			

Keep On Observing (KOO):

I like to find out solution of problems, I always remain content, I am always enterprising, I am good at communication, I am courageous, I always speak economically, I never hesitate, I am sober, I am not aggressive and so on....

CYCLE-9

7	15	23	31	39	47	55	63	71	79
71	63	55	47	39	31	23	15	7	

Keep On Observing (KOO):

I like to find out solution of problems, I always remain content, I am always enterprising, I am good at communication, I am courageous, I always speak economically, I never hesitate, I am sober, I am not aggressive and so on....

CYCLE-10

7	15	23	31	39	47	55	63	71	79
87	79	71	63	55	47	39	31	23	15
7									

Keep On Observing (KOO):

I like to find out solution of problems, I always remain content, I am always enterprising, I am good at communication, I am courageous, I always speak economically, I never hesitate, I am sober, I am not aggressive and so on....

CYCLE-11

7	15	23	31	39	47	55	63	71	79
87		95	87	79	71	63	55	47	39
31	23	15	7						

Keep On Observing (KOO):

I like to find out solution of problems, I always remain content, I am always enterprising, I am good at communication, I am courageous, I always speak economically, I never hesitate, I am sober, I am not aggressive and so on....

CYCLE-12

7	15	23	31	39	47	55	63	71	79
87	95	103	95	87	79	71	63	55	47
39	31	23	15	7					

PATTERN: 8

CYCLE-1

8	16	8							

Keep On Observing (KOO):

I like to find out solution of problems, I always remain content, I am always enterprising, I am good at communication, I am courageous, I always speak economically, I never hesitate, I am sober, I am not aggressive and so on....

CYCLE-2

8	16	24	16	8					

Keep On Observing (KOO):

I like to find out solution of problems, I always remain content, I am always enterprising, I am good at communication, I am courageous, I always speak economically, I never hesitate, I am sober, I am not aggressive and so on....

CYCLE-3

8	16	24	32	24	16	8			

Keep On Observing (KOO):

I like to find out solution of problems, I always remain content, I am always enterprising, I am good at communication, I am courageous, I always speak economically, I never hesitate, I am sober, I am not aggressive and so on....

CYCLE-5

8	16	24	32	40	32	24	16	8	

Keep On Observing (KOO):

I like to find out solution of problems, I always remain content, I am always enterprising, I am good at communication, I am courageous, I always speak economically, I never hesitate, I am sober, I am not aggressive and so on....

CYCLE-5

8	16	24	32	40	48	40	32	24	16
8									

Keep On Observing (KOO):

I like to find out solution of problems, I always remain content, I am always enterprising, I am good at communication, I am courageous, I always speak economically, I never hesitate, I am sober, I am not aggressive and so on....

CYCLE-6

8	16	24	32	40	48	56	48	40	32
24	16	8							

Keep On Observing (KOO):

I like to find out solution of problems, I always remain content, I am always enterprising, I am good at communication, I am courageous, I always speak economically, I never hesitate, I am sober, I am not aggressive and so on....

CYCLE-7

8	16	24	32	40	48	56	64	56	48
40	32	24	16	8					

Keep On Observing (KOO):

I like to find out solution of problems, I always remain content, I am always enterprising, I am good at communication, I am courageous, I always speak economically, I never hesitate, I am sober, I am not aggressive and so on....

CYCLE-8

8	16	24	32	40	48	56	64	72	64
56	48	40	32	24	16	8			

Keep On Observing (KOO):

I like to find out solution of problems, I always remain content, I am always enterprising, I am good at communication, I am courageous, I always speak economically, I never hesitate, I am sober, I am not aggressive and so on....

CYCLE-9

8	16	24	32	40	48	56	64	72	80
72	64	56	48	40	32	24	16	8	

Keep On Observing (KOO):

I like to find out solution of problems, I always remain content, I am always enterprising, I am good at communication, I am courageous, I always speak economically, I never hesitate, I am sober, I am not aggressive and so on....

CYCLE-10

8	16	24	32	40	48	56	64	72	80
88	80	72	64	56	48	40	32	24	16
8									

Keep On Observing (KOO):

I like to find out solution of problems, I always remain content, I am always enterprising, I am good at communication, I am courageous, I always speak economically, I never hesitate, I am sober, I am not aggressive and so on....

CYCLE-11

8	16	24	32	40	48	56	64	72	80
88	96	88	80	72	64	56	48	40	32
24	16	8							

Keep On Observing (KOO):

I like to find out solution of problems, I always remain content, I am always enterprising, I am good at communication, I am courageous, I always speak economically, I never hesitate, I am sober, I am not aggressive and so on....

CYCLE-12

8	16	24	32	40	48	56	64	72	80
88	96	104	96	88	80	72	64	56	48
40	32	24	16	8					

Keep On Observing (KOO):

I like to find out solution of problems, I always remain content, I am always enterprising, I am good at communication, I am courageous, I always speak economically, I never hesitate, I am sober, I am not aggressive and so on....

Let's do an introspective exercise:

Please check what you achieved and able to exercise now in your life

Sr. No.	Qualities/ characteristics	Posses by a mathe-matised mind	Posses by a success full mind	Posses by a happy mind	Posses by a pat-tern	Posses by you		
						Begin-ning	Con-soli-dating	Exer-cising
1	like to find out solution of problems	yes	yes	Yes	yes			
2	remain content	yes	yes	Yes	yes			
3	enterprising	yes	yes	Yes	yes			
4	good at communication	yes	yes	Yes	yes			
5	courageous	yes	yes	Yes	yes			
6	speak economically	yes	yes	Yes	yes			
7	never hesitate	yes	yes	Yes	yes			
8	Sober	yes	yes	Yes	yes			
9	aggressive	no	no	No	no			
10	straight forward	yes	Yes	Yes	yes			
11	daring	yes	yes	Yes	Yes			
12	enthusiastic	yes	yes	Yes	yes			
13	risk taking	yes	calcu-lated	calcu-lated	calcu-lated			
14	bold	yes	yes	Yes	Yes			
15	can take stress	yes	Yes	Yes	yes			
16	dominant	yes	no	No	No			
17	influenced by facts than by feeling	yes	Yes	Yes	yes			
18	Hard working	yes	yes	yes	Yes			
19	easy going never in hurry	yes	yes	Yes	yes			
20	quick decision	yes	yes	yes	Yes			
21	communicative	yes	yes	Yes	yes			
22	free from guilt	yes	yes	yes	yes			
23	never hesitate	yes	yes	yes	yes			
24	Secure	yes	yes	Yes	yes			
25	never act according to others	yes	yes	yes	yes			
26	capable of getting things done	yes	yes	Yes	yes			
27	assertive behaviour	yes	yes	yes	yes			

28	develop their own sets of rules	yes	If required	If required	If required			
29	self disciplined	yes	yes	yes	Yes			
30	abstract thinking	yes	yes	Yes	yes			
31	reliable behaviour	yes	yes	yes	yes			
32	experementive	yes	yes	yes	yes			
33	impulsive	yes	no	no	no			
34	self destructive	no	no	no	no			
35	social	yes	yes	yes	yes			
36	cope with routine life		yes	yes	yes			
37	highly self motivated	yes	yes	Yes	yes			
38	practical	yes	yes	yes	yes			
39	mindful	yes	yes	yes	yes			
40	lost in the world of dreams	no	no	no	no			
41	participating	yes	yes	yes	yes			
42	Cautious	yes	yes	Yes	yes			
43	likes people	yes	yes	yes	yes			
44	open minded	yes	yes	yes	yes			
45	resolve conflicts	yes	yes	Yes	yes			
46	emotionally mature	yes	yes	Yes	yes			
47	realistic	yes	yes	yes	yes			
48	Cheerful	yes	yes	Yes	yes			
49	Intuitive	yes	yes	yes	yes			
50	keep things under control	yes	yes	yes	yes			
51	Competitor of self	yes	yes	Yes	yes			
52	self confident	yes	yes	Yes	yes			
53	Assertive	yes	yes	Yes	yes			
54	Mature	yes	yes	Yes	yes			
55	Relax	yes	yes	Yes	yes			
56	Adaptive	yes	yes	Yes	yes			
57	Flexible	yes	yes	Yes	yes			
58	open to change	yes	yes	Yes	yes			
59	accommodative	yes	yes	Yes	yes			
60	socially active	yes	yes	Yes	yes			
61	cultural interests	yes	yes	Yes	yes			
62	down to earth	yes	yes	Yes	yes			
63	friendly nature	yes	yes	Yes	yes			
64	Sociable	yes	yes	Yes	yes			
65	good reasoning	yes	yes	Yes	yes			
66	intelligent	yes	yes	Yes	yes			
67	hard to fool	yes	yes	Yes	yes			

Express your feeling about your accomplishments through mathyogs9211:

....
....
....
....
....
....
....
....
....
....
....
....
....
....
....
....
....
....
....
....
....
....
....
....
....
....
....
....

CHAPTER-XIII

COUNTING BY NINE'S

Group 9: Counting by nine's

Sr. No.	GROUP IX								
Term	PATTERN-1	PATTERN-2	PATTERN-3	PATTERN-4	PATTERN-5	PATTERN-6	PATTERN-7	PATTERN-8	PATTERN-9
1	1	2	3	4	5	6	7	8	9
2	10	11	12	13	14	15	16	17	18
3	19	20	21	22	23	24	25	26	27
4	28	29	30	31	32	33	34	35	36
5	37	38	39	40	41	42	43	44	45
6	46	47	48	49	50	51	52	53	54
7	55	56	57	58	59	60	61	62	63
8	64	65	66	67	68	69	70	71	72
9	73	74	75	76	77	78	79	80	81
10	82	83	84	85	86	87	88	89	90
11	91	92	93	94	95	96	97	98	99
12	100	101	102	103	104	105	106	107	108

PATTERN: 1

CYCLE-1

1	10	1							

Keep On Observing (KOO):

I like to find out solution of problems, I always remain content, I am always enterprising, I am good at communication, I am courageous, I always speak economically, I never hesitate, I am sober, I am not aggressive and so on....

CYCLE-2

1	10	19	10	1					

Keep On Observing (KOO):

I like to find out solution of problems, I always remain content, I am always enterprising, I am good at communication, I am courageous, I always speak economically, I never hesitate, I am sober, I am not aggressive and so on....

CYCLE-3

1	10	19	28	19	10	1			

Keep On Observing (KOO):

I like to find out solution of problems, I always remain content, I am always enterprising, I am good at communication, I am courageous, I always speak economically, I never hesitate, I am sober, I am not aggressive and so on....

CYCLE-4

1	10	19	28	37	28	19	10	1	

Keep On Observing (KOO):

I like to find out solution of problems, I always remain content, I am always enterprising, I am good at communication, I am courageous, I always speak economically, I never hesitate, I am sober, I am not aggressive and so on....

CYCLE-5

1	10	19	28	37	46	37	28	19	10
1									

Keep On Observing (KOO):

I like to find out solution of problems, I always remain content, I am always enterprising, I am good at communication, I am courageous, I always speak economically, I never hesitate, I am sober, I am not aggressive and so on....

CYCLE-6

1	10	19	28	37	46	55	46	37	28
19	10	1							

Keep On Observing (KOO):

I like to find out solution of problems, I always remain content, I am always enterprising, I am good at communication, I am courageous, I always speak economically, I never hesitate, I am sober, I am not aggressive and so on....

CYCLE-7

1	10	19	28	37	46	55	64	55	46
37	28	19	10	1					

Keep On Observing (KOO):

I like to find out solution of problems, I always remain content, I am always enterprising, I am good at communication, I am courageous, I always speak economically, I never hesitate, I am sober, I am not aggressive and so on....

CYCLE-8

1	10	19	28	37	46	55	64	73	64
55	46	37	28	19	10	1			

Keep On Observing (KOO):

I like to find out solution of problems, I always remain content, I am always enterprising, I am good at communication, I am courageous, I always speak economically, I never hesitate, I am sober, I am not aggressive and so on....

CYCLE-9

1	10	19	28	37	46	55	64	73	82
73	64	55	46	37	28	19	10	1	

Keep On Observing (KOO):

I like to find out solution of problems, I always remain content, I am always enterprising, I am good at communication, I am courageous, I always speak economically, I never hesitate, I am sober, I am not aggressive and so on....

CYCLE-10

1	10	19	28	37	46	55	64	73	82
91	82	73	64	55	46	37	28	19	10
1									

Keep On Observing (KOO):

I like to find out solution of problems, I always remain content, I am always enterprising, I am good at communication, I am courageous, I always speak economically, I never hesitate, I am sober, I am not aggressive and so on....

CYCLE-11

1	10	19	28	37	46	55	64	73	82
91	100	91	82	73	64	55	46	37	28
19	10	1							

PATTERN: 2

CYCLE-1

2	11	2							

Keep On Observing (KOO):

I like to find out solution of problems, I always remain content, I am always enterprising, I am good at communication, I am courageous, I always speak economically, I never hesitate, I am sober, I am not aggressive and so on....

CYCLE-2

2	11	20	11	2					

Keep On Observing (KOO):

I like to find out solution of problems, I always remain content, I am always enterprising, I am good at communication, I am courageous, I always speak economically, I never hesitate, I am sober, I am not aggressive and so on....

CYCLE-3

2	11	20	29	20	11	2			

Keep On Observing (KOO):

I like to find out solution of problems, I always remain content, I am always enterprising, I am good at communication, I am courageous, I always speak economically, I never hesitate, I am sober, I am not aggressive and so on....

CYCLE-4

2	11	20	29	38	29	20	11	2	

Keep On Observing (KOO):

I like to find out solution of problems, I always remain content, I am always enterprising, I am good at communication, I am courageous, I always speak economically, I never hesitate, I am sober, I am not aggressive and so on....

CYCLE-5

2	11	20	29	38	47	38	29	20	11
2									

Keep On Observing (KOO):

I like to find out solution of problems, I always remain content, I am always enterprising, I am good at communication, I am courageous, I always speak economically, I never hesitate, I am sober, I am not aggressive and so on....

CYCLE-6

2	11	20	29	38	47	56	47	38	29
20	11	2							

Keep On Observing (KOO):

I like to find out solution of problems, I always remain content, I am always enterprising, I am good at communication, I am courageous, I always speak economically, I never hesitate, I am sober, I am not aggressive and so on....

CYCLE-7

2	11	20	29	38	47	56	65	56	47
38	29	20	11	2					

Keep On Observing (KOO):

I like to find out solution of problems, I always remain content, I am always enterprising, I am good at communication, I am courageous, I always speak economically, I never hesitate, I am sober, I am not aggressive and so on....

CYCLE-8

2	11	20	29	38	47	56	65	74	65
56	47	38	29	20	11	2			

Keep On Observing (KOO):

I like to find out solution of problems, I always remain content, I am always enterprising, I am good at communication, I am courageous, I always speak economically, I never hesitate, I am sober, I am not aggressive and so on....

CYCLE-9

2	11	20	29	38	47	56	65	74	83
74	65	56	47	38	29	20	11	2	

Keep On Observing (KOO):

I like to find out solution of problems, I always remain content, I am always enterprising, I am good at communication, I am courageous, I always speak economically, I never hesitate, I am sober, I am not aggressive and so on....

CYCLE-10

2	11	20	29	38	47	56	65	74	83
92	83	74	65	56	47	38	29	20	11
2									

Keep On Observing (KOO):

I like to find out solution of problems, I always remain content, I am always enterprising, I am good at communication, I am courageous, I always speak economically, I never hesitate, I am sober, I am not aggressive and so on....

CYCLE-11

2	11	20	29	38	47	56	65	74	83
92	101	92	83	74	65	56	47	38	29
20	11	2							

PATTERN: 3

Keep On Observing (KOO):

I like to find out solution of problems, I always remain content, I am always enterprising, I am good at communication, I am courageous, I always speak economically, I never hesitate, I am sober, I am not aggressive and so on....

CYCLE-1

3	12	3							

Keep On Observing (KOO):

I like to find out solution of problems, I always remain content, I am always enterprising, I am good at communication, I am courageous, I always speak economically, I never hesitate, I am sober, I am not aggressive and so on....

CYCLE-2

3	12	21	12	3					

Keep On Observing (KOO):

I like to find out solution of problems, I always remain content, I am always enterprising, I am good at communication, I am courageous, I always speak economically, I never hesitate, I am sober, I am not aggressive and so on....

CYCLE-3

3	12	21	30	21	12	3			

Keep On Observing (KOO):

I like to find out solution of problems, I always remain content, I am always enterprising, I am good at communication, I am courageous, I always speak economically, I never hesitate, I am sober, I am not aggressive and so on....

CYCLE-4

3	12	21	30	39	30	21	12	3	

Keep On Observing (KOO):

I like to find out solution of problems, I always remain content, I am always enterprising, I am good at communication, I am courageous, I always speak economically, I never hesitate, I am sober, I am not aggressive and so on....

CYCLE-5

3	12	21	30	39	48	39	30	21	12
3									

Keep On Observing (KOO):

I like to find out solution of problems, I always remain content, I am always enterprising, I am good at communication, I am courageous, I always speak economically, I never hesitate, I am sober, I am not aggressive and so on....

CYCLE-6

3	12	21	30	39	48	57	48	39	30
21	12	3							

Keep On Observing (KOO):

I like to find out solution of problems, I always remain content, I am always enterprising, I am good at communication, I am courageous, I always speak economically, I never hesitate, I am sober, I am not aggressive and so on....

CYCLE-7

3	12	21	30	39	48	57	66	57	48
39	30	21	12	3					

Keep On Observing (KOO):

I like to find out solution of problems, I always remain content, I am always enterprising, I am good at communication, I am courageous, I always speak economically, I never hesitate, I am sober, I am not aggressive and so on....

CYCLE-8

3	12	21	30	39	48	57	66	75	66
57	48	39	30	21	12	3			

Keep On Observing (KOO): I

like to find out solution of problems, I always remain content, I am always enterprising, I am good at communication, I am courageous, I always speak economically, I never hesitate, I am sober, I am not aggressive and so on....

CYCLE-9

3	12	21	30	39	48	57	66	75	84
75	66	57	48	39	30	21	12	3	

Keep On Observing (KOO):

I like to find out solution of problems, I always remain content, I am always enterprising, I am good at communication, I am courageous, I always speak economically, I never hesitate, I am sober, I am not aggressive and so on....

CYCLE-10

3	12	21	30	39	48	57	66	75	84
93	84	75	66	57	48	39	30	21	12
3									

Keep On Observing (KOO):

I like to find out solution of problems, I always remain content, I am always enterprising, I am good at communication, I am courageous, I always speak economically, I never hesitate, I am sober, I am not aggressive and so on....

CYCLE-11

3	12	21	30	39	48	57	66	75	84
93	102	93	84	75	66	57	48	39	30
21	12	3							

PATTERN: 4

Keep On Observing (KOO):

I like to find out solution of problems, I always remain content, I am always enterprising, I am good at communication, I am courageous, I always speak economically, I never hesitate, I am sober, I am not aggressive and so on....

CYCLE-1

4	13	4							

Keep On Observing (KOO):

I like to find out solution of problems, I always remain content, I am always enterprising, I am good at communication, I am courageous, I always speak economically, I never hesitate, I am sober, I am not aggressive and so on....

CYCLE-2

4	13	22	13	4					

Keep On Observing (KOO):

I like to find out solution of problems, I always remain content, I am always enterprising, I am good at communication, I am courageous, I always speak economically, I never hesitate, I am sober, I am not aggressive and so on....

CYCLE-3

4	13	22	31	22	13	4			

Keep On Observing (KOO):

I like to find out solution of problems, I always remain content, I am always enterprising, I am good at communication, I am courageous, I always speak economically, I never hesitate, I am sober, I am not aggressive and so on....

CYCLE-4

4	13	22	31	40	31	22	13	4	

Keep On Observing (KOO):

I like to find out solution of problems, I always remain content, I am always enterprising, I am good at communication, I am courageous, I always speak economically, I never hesitate, I am sober, I am not aggressive and so on....

CYCLE-5

4	13	22	31	40	49	40	31	22	13
4									

Keep On Observing (KOO):

I like to find out solution of problems, I always remain content, I am always enterprising, I am good at communication, I am courageous, I always speak economically, I never hesitate, I am sober, I am not aggressive and so on....

CYCLE-6

4	13	22	31	40	49	58	49	40	31
22	13	4							

eep On Observing (KOO):

I like to find out solution of problems, I always remain content, I am always enterprising, I am good at communication, I am courageous, I always speak economically, I never hesitate, I am sober, I am not aggressive and so on....

CYCLE-7

4	13	22	31	40	49	58	67	58	49
40	31	22	13	4					

Keep On Observing (KOO):

I like to find out solution of problems, I always remain content, I am always enterprising, I am good at communication, I am courageous, I always speak economically, I never hesitate, I am sober, I am not aggressive and so on....

CYCLE-8

4	13	22	31	40	49	58	67	76	67
58	49	40	31	22	13	4			

Keep On Observing (KOO):

I like to find out solution of problems, I always remain content, I am always enterprising, I am good at communication, I am courageous, I always speak economically, I never hesitate, I am sober, I am not aggressive and so on....

CYCLE-9

4	13	22	31	40	49	58	67	76	85
76	67	58	49	40	31	22	13	4	

Keep On Observing (KOO):

I like to find out solution of problems, I always remain content, I am always enterprising, I am good at communication, I am courageous, I always speak economically, I never hesitate, I am sober, I am not aggressive and so on....

CYCLE-10

4	13	22	31	40	49	58	67	76	85
94	85	76	67	58	49	40	31	22	13
4									

Keep On Observing (KOO):

I like to find out solution of problems, I always remain content, I am always enterprising, I am good at communication, I am courageous, I always speak economically, I never hesitate, I am sober, I am not aggressive and so on....

CYCLE-11

4	13	22	31	40	49	58	67	76	85
94	103	94	85	76	67	58	49	40	31
22	13	4							

PATTERN: 5

Keep On Observing (KOO):

I like to find out solution of problems, I always remain content, I am always enterprising, I am good at communication, I am courageous, I always speak economically, I never hesitate, I am sober, I am not aggressive and so on....

CYCLE-1

5	14	5							

Keep On Observing (KOO):

I like to find out solution of problems, I always remain content, I am always enterprising, I am good at communication, I am courageous, I always speak economically, I never hesitate, I am sober, I am not aggressive and so on....

CYCLE-2

5	14	23	14	5					

Keep On Observing (KOO):

I like to find out solution of problems, I always remain content, I am always enterprising, I am good at communication, I am courageous, I always speak economically, I never hesitate, I am sober, I am not aggressive and so on....

CYCLE-3

5	14	23	32	23	14	5			

Keep On Observing (KOO):

I like to find out solution of problems, I always remain content, I am always enterprising, I am good at communication, I am courageous, I always speak economically, I never hesitate, I am sober, I am not aggressive and so on....

CYCLE-4

| 5 | 14 | 23 | 32 | 41 | 32 | 23 | 14 | 5 | |

Keep On Observing (KOO):

I like to find out solution of problems, I always remain content, I am always enterprising, I am good at communication, I am courageous, I always speak economically, I never hesitate, I am sober, I am not aggressive and so on....

CYCLE-5

| 5 | 14 | 23 | 32 | 41 | 50 | 41 | 32 | 23 | 14 |
| 5 | | | | | | | | | |

Keep On Observing (KOO):

I like to find out solution of problems, I always remain content, I am always enterprising, I am good at communication, I am courageous, I always speak economically, I never hesitate, I am sober, I am not aggressive and so on....

CYCLE-6

| 5 | 14 | 23 | 32 | 41 | 50 | 59 | 50 | 41 | 32 |
| 23 | 14 | 5 | | | | | | | |

Keep On Observing (KOO):

I like to find out solution of problems, I always remain content, I am always enterprising, I am good at communication, I am courageous, I always speak economically, I never hesitate, I am sober, I am not aggressive and so on....

CYCLE-7

5	14	23	32	41	50	59	68	59	50
41	32	23	14	5					

Keep On Observing (KOO):

I like to find out solution of problems, I always remain content, I am always enterprising, I am good at communication, I am courageous, I always speak economically, I never hesitate, I am sober, I am not aggressive and so on....

CYCLE-8

5	14	23	32	41	50	59	68	77	68
59	50	41	32	23	14	5			

Keep On Observing (KOO):

I like to find out solution of problems, I always remain content, I am always enterprising, I am good at communication, I am courageous, I always speak economically, I never hesitate, I am sober, I am not aggressive and so on....

CYCLE-9

5	14	23	32	41	50	59	68	77	86
77	68	59	50	41	32	23	14	5	

Keep On Observing (KOO):

I like to find out solution of problems, I always remain content, I am always enterprising, I am good at communication, I am courageous, I always speak economically, I never hesitate, I am sober, I am not aggressive and so on....

CYCLE-10

5	14	23	32	41	50	59	68	77	86
95	86	77	68	59	50	41	32	23	14
5									

Keep On Observing (KOO):

I like to find out solution of problems, I always remain content, I am always enterprising, I am good at communication, I am courageous, I always speak economically, I never hesitate, I am sober, I am not aggressive and so on....

CYCLE-11

5	14	23	32	41	50	59	68	77	86
95	104	95	86	77	68	59	50	41	32
23	14	5							

PATTERN: 6

CYCLE-1

6	15	6							

Keep On Observing (KOO):

I like to find out solution of problems, I always remain content, I am always enterprising, I am good at communication, I am courageous, I always speak economically, I never hesitate, I am sober, I am not aggressive and so on....

CYCLE-2

6	15	24	15	6					

Keep On Observing (KOO):

I like to find out solution of problems, I always remain content, I am always enterprising, I am good at communication, I am courageous, I always speak economically, I never hesitate, I am sober, I am not aggressive and so on....

CYCLE-3

6	15	24	33	24	15	6			

Keep On Observing (KOO):

I like to find out solution of problems, I always remain content, I am always enterprising, I am good at communication, I am courageous, I always speak economically, I never hesitate, I am sober, I am not aggressive and so on....

CYCLE-4

6	15	24	33	42	33	24	15	6	

Keep On Observing (KOO):

I like to find out solution of problems, I always remain content, I am always enterprising, I am good at communication, I am courageous, I always speak economically, I never hesitate, I am sober, I am not aggressive and so on....

CYCLE-5

6	15	24	33	42	51	42	33	24	15
6									

Keep On Observing (KOO):

I like to find out solution of problems, I always remain content, I am always enterprising, I am good at communication, I am courageous, I always speak economically, I never hesitate, I am sober, I am not aggressive and so on....

CYCLE-6

6	15	24	33	42	51	60	51	42	33
24	15	6							

Keep On Observing (KOO):

I like to find out solution of problems, I always remain content, I am always enterprising, I am good at communication, I am courageous, I always speak economically, I never hesitate, I am sober, I am not aggressive and so on....

CYCLE-7

6	15	24	33	42	51	60	69	60	51
42	33	24	15	6					

Keep On Observing (KOO):

I like to find out solution of problems, I always remain content, I am always enterprising, I am good at communication, I am courageous, I always speak economically, I never hesitate, I am sober, I am not aggressive and so on....

CYCLE-8

6	15	24	33	42	51	60	69	78	69
60	51	42	33	24	15	6			

Keep On Observing (KOO):

I like to find out solution of problems, I always remain content, I am always enterprising, I am good at communication, I am courageous, I always speak economically, I never hesitate, I am sober, I am not aggressive and so on....

CYCLE-9

6	15	24	33	42	51	60	69	78	87
78	69	60	51	42	33	24	15	6	

Keep On Observing (KOO):

I like to find out solution of problems, I always remain content, I am always enterprising, I am good at communication, I am courageous, I always speak economically, I never hesitate, I am sober, I am not aggressive and so on....

CYCLE-10

6	15	24	33	42	51	60	69	78	87
96	87	78	69	60	51	42	33	24	15
6									

Keep On Observing (KOO):

I like to find out solution of problems, I always remain content, I am always enterprising, I am good at communication, I am courageous, I always speak economically, I never hesitate, I am sober, I am not aggressive and so on....

CYCLE-11

6	15	24	33	42	51	60	69	78	87
96	105	96	87	78	69	60	51	42	33
24	15	6							

PATTERN: 7

CYCLE-1

7	16	7							

Keep On Observing (KOO):

I like to find out solution of problems, I always remain content, I am always enterprising, I am good at communication, I am courageous, I always speak economically, I never hesitate, I am sober, I am not aggressive and so on....

CYCLE-2

7	16	25	16	7					

Keep On Observing (KOO):

I like to find out solution of problems, I always remain content, I am always enterprising, I am good at communication, I am courageous, I always speak economically, I never hesitate, I am sober, I am not aggressive and so on....

CYCLE-3

7	16	25	34	25	16	7			

Keep On Observing (KOO):

I like to find out solution of problems, I always remain content, I am always enterprising, I am good at communication, I am courageous, I always speak economically, I never hesitate, I am sober, I am not aggressive and so on....

CYCLE-5

7	16	25	34	43	34	25	16	7	

Keep On Observing (KOO):

I like to find out solution of problems, I always remain content, I am always enterprising, I am good at communication, I am courageous, I always speak economically, I never hesitate, I am sober, I am not aggressive and so on....

CYCLE-5

7	16	25	34	43	52	43	34	25	16
7									

Keep On Observing (KOO):

I like to find out solution of problems, I always remain content, I am always enterprising, I am good at communication, I am courageous, I always speak economically, I never hesitate, I am sober, I am not aggressive and so on....

CYCLE-6

7	16	25	34	43	52	61	52	43	34
25	16	7							

Keep On Observing (KOO):

I like to find out solution of problems, I always remain content, I am always enterprising, I am good at communication, I am courageous, I always speak economically, I never hesitate, I am sober, I am not aggressive and so on....

CYCLE-7

7	16	25	34	43	52	61	70	61	52
43	34	25	16	7	.				

Keep On Observing (KOO):

I like to find out solution of problems, I always remain content, I am always enterprising, I am good at communication, I am courageous, I always speak economically, I never hesitate, I am sober, I am not aggressive and so on....

CYCLE-8

7	16	25	34	43	52	61	70	79	70
61	52	43	34	25	16	7			

Keep On Observing (KOO):

I like to find out solution of problems, I always remain content, I am always enterprising, I am good at communication, I am courageous, I always speak economically, I never hesitate, I am sober, I am not aggressive and so on....

CYCLE-9

7	16	25	34	43	52	61	70	79	88
79	70	61	52	43	34	25	16	7	

Keep On Observing (KOO):

I like to find out solution of problems, I always remain content, I am always enterprising, I am good at communication, I am courageous, I always speak economically, I never hesitate, I am sober, I am not aggressive and so on....

CYCLE-10

7	16	25	34	43	52	61	70	79	88
97	88	79	70	61	52	43	34	25	16
7									

Keep On Observing (KOO):

I like to find out solution of problems, I always remain content, I am always enterprising, I am good at communication, I am courageous, I always speak economically, I never hesitate, I am sober, I am not aggressive and so on....

CYCLE-11

7	16	25	34	43	52	61	70	79	88
97	106	97	88	79	70	61	52	43	34
25	16	7							

PATTERN: 8

CYCLE-1

8	17	8							

Keep On Observing (KOO):

I like to find out solution of problems, I always remain content, I am always enterprising, I am good at communication, I am courageous, I always speak economically, I never hesitate, I am sober, I am not aggressive and so on....

CYCLE-2

8	17	26	17	8					

Keep On Observing (KOO):

I like to find out solution of problems, I always remain content, I am always enterprising, I am good at communication, I am courageous, I always speak economically, I never hesitate, I am sober, I am not aggressive and so on....

CYCLE-3

8	17	26	35	26	17	8			

Keep On Observing (KOO):

I like to find out solution of problems, I always remain content, I am always enterprising, I am good at communication, I am courageous, I always speak economically, I never hesitate, I am sober, I am not aggressive and so on....

CYCLE-4

8	17	26	35	44	35	26	17	8	

Keep On Observing (KOO):

I like to find out solution of problems, I always remain content, I am always enterprising, I am good at communication, I am courageous, I always speak economically, I never hesitate, I am sober, I am not aggressive and so on....

CYCLE-5

8	17	26	35	44	53	44	35	26	17
8									

Keep On Observing (KOO):

I like to find out solution of problems, I always remain content, I am always enterprising, I am good at communication, I am courageous, I always speak economically, I never hesitate, I am sober, I am not aggressive and so on....

CYCLE-6

8	17	26	35	44	53	62	53	44	35
26	17	8							

Keep On Observing (KOO):

I like to find out solution of problems, I always remain content, I am always enterprising, I am good at communication, I am courageous, I always speak economically, I never hesitate, I am sober, I am not aggressive and so on....

CYCLE-7

8	17	26	35	44	53	62	71	62	53
44	35	26	17	8					

Keep On Observing (KOO):

I like to find out solution of problems, I always remain content, I am always enterprising, I am good at communication, I am courageous, I always speak economically, I never hesitate, I am sober, I am not aggressive and so on....

CYCLE-8

8	17	26	35	44	53	62	71	80	71
62	53	44	35	26	17	8			

Keep On Observing (KOO):

I like to find out solution of problems, I always remain content, I am always enterprising, I am good at communication, I am courageous, I always speak economically, I never hesitate, I am sober, I am not aggressive and so on....

CYCLE-9

8	17	26	35	44	53	62	71	80	89
80	71	62	53	44	35	26	17	8	

Keep On Observing (KOO):

I like to find out solution of problems, I always remain content, I am always enterprising, I am good at communication, I am courageous, I always speak economically, I never hesitate, I am sober, I am not aggressive and so on....

CYCLE-10

8	17	26	35	44	53	62	71	80	89
98	89	80	71	62	53	44	35	26	17
8									

Keep On Observing (KOO):

I like to find out solution of problems, I always remain content, I am always enterprising, I am good at communication, I am courageous, I always speak economically, I never hesitate, I am sober, I am not aggressive and so on....

CYCLE-11

8	17	26	35	44	53	62	71	80	89
98	107	98	89	80	71	62	53	44	35
26	17	8							

PATTERN: 9

Keep On Observing (KOO):

I like to find out solution of problems, I always remain content, I am always enterprising, I am good at communication, I am courageous, I always speak economically, I never hesitate, I am sober, I am not aggressive and so on....

CYCLE-1

9	18	9							

Keep On Observing (KOO):

I like to find out solution of problems, I always remain content, I am always enterprising, I am good at communication, I am courageous, I always speak economically, I never hesitate, I am sober, I am not aggressive and so on....

CYCLE-2

9	18	27	18	9					

Keep On Observing (KOO):

I like to find out solution of problems, I always remain content, I am always enterprising, I am good at communication, I am courageous, I always speak economically, I never hesitate, I am sober, I am not aggressive and so on....

CYCLE-3

9	18	27	36	27	18	9			

Keep On Observing (KOO):

I like to find out solution of problems, I always remain content, I am always enterprising, I am good at communication, I am courageous, I always speak economically, I never hesitate, I am sober, I am not aggressive and so on....

CYCLE-4

9	18	27	36	45	36	27	18	9	

Keep On Observing (KOO):

I like to find out solution of problems, I always remain content, I am always enterprising, I am good at communication, I am courageous, I always speak economically, I never hesitate, I am sober, I am not aggressive and so on....

CYCLE-5

9	18	27	36	45	54	45	36	27	18
9									

Keep On Observing (KOO):

I like to find out solution of problems, I always remain content, I am always enterprising, I am good at communication, I am courageous, I always speak economically, I never hesitate, I am sober, I am not aggressive and so on....

CYCLE-6

9	18	27	36	45	54	63	54	45	36
27	18	9							

Keep On Observing (KOO):

I like to find out solution of problems, I always remain content, I am always enterprising, I am good at communication, I am courageous, I always speak economically, I never hesitate, I am sober, I am not aggressive and so on....

CYCLE-7

9	18	27	36	45	54	63	72	63	54
45	36	27	18	9					

Keep On Observing (KOO):

I like to find out solution of problems, I always remain content, I am always enterprising, I am good at communication, I am courageous, I always speak economically, I never hesitate, I am sober, I am not aggressive and so on....

CYCLE-8

9	18	27	36	45	54	63	72	81	72
63	54	45	36	27	18	9			

Keep On Observing (KOO):

I like to find out solution of problems, I always remain content, I am always enterprising, I am good at communication, I am courageous, I always speak economically, I never hesitate, I am sober, I am not aggressive and so on....

CYCLE-9

9	18	27	36	45	54	63	72	81	90
81	72	63	54	45	36	27	18	9	

Keep On Observing (KOO):

I like to find out solution of problems, I always remain content, I am always enterprising, I am good at communication, I am courageous, I always speak economically, I never hesitate, I am sober, I am not aggressive and so on....

CYCLE-10

9	18	27	36	45	54	63	72	81	90
99	90	81	72	63	54	45	36	27	18
9									

Keep On Observing (KOO):

I like to find out solution of problems, I always remain content, I am always enterprising, I am good at communication, I am courageous, I always speak economically, I never hesitate, I am sober, I am not aggressive and so on....

CYCLE-11

9	18	27	36	45	54	63	72	81	90
99	108	99	90	81	72	63	54	45	36
27	18	9							

Keep On Observing (KOO):

I like to find out solution of problems, I always remain content, I am always enterprising, I am good at communication, I am courageous, I always speak economically, I never hesitate, I am sober, I am not aggressive and so on....

Let's do an introspective exercise:

Please check what you achieved and able to exercise now in your life

Sr. No.	Qualities/ characteristics	Posses by a mathematised mind	Posses by a successfull mind	Posses by a happy mind	Posses by a pattern	Posses by you		
						Beginning	Consolidating	Exercising
1	like to find out solution of problems	yes	yes	Yes	yes			
2	remain content	yes	yes	Yes	yes			
3	enterprising	yes	yes	Yes	yes			
4	good at communication	yes	yes	Yes	yes			
5	courageous	yes	yes	Yes	yes			
6	speak economically	yes	yes	Yes	yes			
7	never hesitate	yes	yes	Yes	yes			
8	Sober	yes	yes	Yes	yes			
9	aggressive	no	no	No	no			
10	straight forward	yes	Yes	Yes	yes			
11	daring	yes	yes	Yes	Yes			
12	enthusiastic	yes	yes	Yes	yes			
13	risk taking	yes	calculated	calculated	calculated			
14	bold	yes	yes	Yes	Yes			
15	can take stress	yes	Yes	Yes	yes			
16	dominant	yes	no	No	No			
17	influenced by facts than by feeling	yes	Yes	Yes	yes			
18	Hard working	yes	yes	yes	Yes			
19	easy going never in hurry	yes	yes	Yes	yes			
20	quick decision	yes	yes	yes	Yes			
21	communicative	yes	yes	Yes	yes			
22	free from guilt	yes	yes	yes	yes			
23	never hesitate	yes	yes	yes	yes			
24	Secure	yes	yes	Yes	yes			
25	never act according to others	yes	yes	yes	yes			
26	capable of getting things done	yes	yes	Yes	yes			
27	assertive behaviour	yes	yes	yes	yes			

28	develop their own sets of rules	yes	If required	If required	If required			
29	self disciplined	yes	yes	yes	Yes			
30	abstract thinking	yes	yes	Yes	yes			
31	reliable behaviour	yes	yes	yes	yes			
32	experementive	yes	yes	yes	yes			
33	impulsive	yes	no	no	no			
34	self destructive	no	no	no	no			
35	social	yes	yes	yes	yes			
36	cope with routine life		yes	yes	yes			
37	highly self motivated	yes	yes	Yes	yes			
38	practical	yes	yes	yes	yes			
39	mindful	yes	yes	yes	yes			
40	lost in the world of dreams	no	no	no	no			
41	participating	yes	yes	yes	yes			
42	Cautious	yes	yes	Yes	yes			
43	likes people	yes	yes	yes	yes			
44	open minded	yes	yes	yes	yes			
45	resolve conflicts	yes	yes	Yes	yes			
46	emotionally mature	yes	yes	Yes	yes			
47	realistic	yes	yes	yes	yes			
48	Cheerful	yes	yes	Yes	yes			
49	Intuitive	yes	yes	yes	yes			
50	keep things under control	yes	yes	yes	yes			
51	Competitor of self	yes	yes	Yes	yes			
52	self confident	yes	yes	Yes	yes			
53	Assertive	yes	yes	Yes	yes			
54	Mature	yes	yes	Yes	yes			
55	Relax	yes	yes	Yes	yes			
56	Adaptive	yes	yes	Yes	yes			
57	Flexible	yes	yes	Yes	yes			
58	open to change	yes	yes	Yes	yes			
59	accommodative	yes	yes	Yes	yes			
60	socially active	yes	yes	Yes	yes			
61	cultural interests	yes	yes	Yes	yes			
62	down to earth	yes	yes	Yes	yes			
63	friendly nature	yes	yes	Yes	yes			
64	Sociable	yes	yes	Yes	yes			
65	good reasoning	yes	yes	Yes	yes			
66	intelligent	yes	yes	Yes	yes			
67	hard to fool	yes	yes	Yes	yes			

Express your feeling about your accomplishments through mathyogs9211:

....
....
....
....
....
....
....
....
....
....
....
....
....
....
....
....
....
....
....
....
....
....
....
....
....
....
....
....

CHAPTER-XIV

COUNTING BY TEN'S

Group 10: Counting by ten's

Sr. No.	GROUP X									
Term	PATTERN-1	PATTERN-2	PATTERN-3	PATTERN-4	PATTERN-5	PATTERN-6	PATTERN-7	PATTERN-8	PATTERN-9	PATTERN-10
1	1	2	3	4	5	6	7	8	9	10
2	11	12	13	14	15	16	17	18	19	20
3	21	22	23	24	25	26	27	28	29	30
4	31	32	33	34	35	36	37	38	39	40
5	41	42	43	44	45	46	47	48	49	50
6	51	52	53	54	55	56	57	58	59	60
7	61	62	63	64	65	66	67	68	69	70
8	71	72	73	74	75	76	77	78	79	80
9	81	82	83	84	85	86	87	88	89	90
10	91	92	93	94	95	96	97	98	99	100

PATTERN-1

CYCLE-1

1		11		1							

Keep On Observing (KOO):

I like to find out solution of problems, I always remain content, I am always enterprising, I am good at communication, I am courageous, I always speak economically, I never hesitate, I am sober, I am not aggressive and so on....

CYCLE-2

1		11		21		11		1							

Keep On Observing (KOO):

I like to find out solution of problems, I always remain content, I am always enterprising, I am good at communication, I am courageous, I always speak economically, I never hesitate, I am sober, I am not aggressive and so on....

CYCLE-3

1		11		21		31		21		11		1					

Keep On Observing (KOO):

I like to find out solution of problems, I always remain content, I am always enterprising, I am good at communication, I am courageous, I always speak economically, I never hesitate, I am sober, I am not aggressive and so on....

CYCLE-4

1	11	21	31	41	31	21	11	1	

Keep On Observing (KOO):

I like to find out solution of problems, I always remain content, I am always enterprising, I am good at communication, I am courageous, I always speak economically, I never hesitate, I am sober, I am not aggressive and so on....

CYCLE-5

1	11	21	31	41	51	41	31	21	11
1									

Keep On Observing (KOO):

I like to find out solution of problems, I always remain content, I am always enterprising, I am good at communication, I am courageous, I always speak economically, I never hesitate, I am sober, I am not aggressive and so on....

CYCLE-6

1	11	21	31	41	51	61	51	41	31
21	11	1							

Keep On Observing (KOO):

I like to find out solution of problems, I always remain content, I am always enterprising, I am good at communication, I am courageous, I always speak economically, I never hesitate, I am sober, I am not aggressive and so on....

CYCLE-7

1	11	21	31	41	51	61	71	61	71
61	51	41	31	21	11	1			

Keep On Observing (KOO):

I like to find out solution of problems, I always remain content, I am always enterprising, I am good at communication, I am courageous, I always speak economically, I never hesitate, I am sober, I am not aggressive and so on....

CYCLE-8

1	11	21	31	41	51	61	71	81	71
61	51	41	31	21	11	1			

Keep On Observing (KOO):

I like to find out solution of problems, I always remain content, I am always enterprising, I am good at communication, I am courageous, I always speak economically, I never hesitate, I am sober, I am not aggressive and so on....

CYCLE-9

1	11	21	31	41	51	61	71	81	91
81	71	61	51	41	31	21	11	1	

PATTERN: 2

Keep On Observing (KOO):

I like to find out solution of problems, I always remain content, I am always enterprising, I am good at communication, I am courageous, I always speak economically, I never hesitate, I am sober, I am not aggressive and so on....

CYCLE-1

2	12	2							

Keep On Observing (KOO):

I like to find out solution of problems, I always remain content, I am always enterprising, I am good at communication, I am courageous, I always speak economically, I never hesitate, I am sober, I am not aggressive and so on....

CYCLE-2

2	12	22	12	2					

Keep On Observing (KOO):

I like to find out solution of problems, I always remain content, I am always enterprising, I am good at communication, I am courageous, I always speak economically, I never hesitate, I am sober, I am not aggressive and so on....

CYCLE-3

2	12	22	32	22	12	2			

Keep On Observing (KOO):

I like to find out solution of problems, I always remain content, I am always enterprising, I am good at communication, I am courageous, I always speak economically, I never hesitate, I am sober, I am not aggressive and so on....

CYCLE-4

2	12	22	32	42	32	22	12	2	

Keep On Observing (KOO):

I like to find out solution of problems, I always remain content, I am always enterprising, I am good at communication, I am courageous, I always speak economically, I never hesitate, I am sober, I am not aggressive and so on....

CYCLE-5

2	12	22	32	42	52	42	32	22	12
2									

Keep On Observing (KOO):

I like to find out solution of problems, I always remain content, I am always enterprising, I am good at communication, I am courageous, I always speak economically, I never hesitate, I am sober, I am not aggressive and so on....

CYCLE-6

2	12	22	32	42	52	62	52	42	32
22	22	2							

Keep On Observing (KOO):

I like to find out solution of problems, I always remain content, I am always enterprising, I am good at communication, I am courageous, I always speak economically, I never hesitate, I am sober, I am not aggressive and so on....

CYCLE-7

2	12	22	32	42	52	62	72	62	72
62	52	42	32	22	12	2			

Keep On Observing (KOO):

I like to find out solution of problems, I always remain content, I am always enterprising, I am good at communication, I am courageous, I always speak economically, I never hesitate, I am sober, I am not aggressive and so on....

CYCLE-8

2	12	22	32	42	52	62	72	82	72
62	52	42	32	22	12	2			

Keep On Observing (KOO):

I like to find out solution of problems, I always remain content, I am always enterprising, I am good at communication, I am courageous, I always speak economically, I never hesitate, I am sober, I am not aggressive and so on....

CYCLE-9

2	12	22	32	42	52	62	72	82	92
82	72	62	52	42	32	22	12	2	

419

Keep On Observing (KOO):

I like to find out solution of problems, I always remain content, I am always enterprising, I am good at communication, I am courageous, I always speak economically, I never hesitate, I am sober, I am not aggressive and so on....

PATTERN: 3

CYCLE-1

3	13	3							

Keep On Observing (KOO):

I like to find out solution of problems, I always remain content, I am always enterprising, I am good at communication, I am courageous, I always speak economically, I never hesitate, I am sober, I am not aggressive and so on....

CYCLE-2

3	13	23	13	3					

Keep On Observing (KOO):

I like to find out solution of problems, I always remain content, I am always enterprising, I am good at communication, I am courageous, I always speak economically, I never hesitate, I am sober, I am not aggressive and so on....

CYCLE-3

3	13	23	33	23	13	3			

Keep On Observing (KOO):

I like to find out solution of problems, I always remain content, I am always enterprising, I am good at communication, I am courageous, I always speak economically, I never hesitate, I am sober, I am not aggressive and so on....

CYCLE-4

3	13	23	33	43	33	23	13	3	

Keep On Observing (KOO):

I like to find out solution of problems, I always remain content, I am always enterprising, I am good at communication, I am courageous, I always speak economically, I never hesitate, I am sober, I am not aggressive and so on....

CYCLE-5

3	13	23	33	43	53	43	33	23	13
3									

Keep On Observing (KOO):

I like to find out solution of problems, I always remain content, I am always enterprising, I am good at communication, I am courageous, I always speak economically, I never hesitate, I am sober, I am not aggressive and so on....

CYCLE-6

3	13	23	33	43	53	63	53	43	33
23	13	3							

Keep On Observing (KOO):

I like to find out solution of problems, I always remain content, I am always enterprising, I am good at communication, I am courageous, I always speak economically, I never hesitate, I am sober, I am not aggressive and so on....

CYCLE-7

3	13	23	33	43	53	63	73	63	53
43	33	23	13	3					

Keep On Observing (KOO):

I like to find out solution of problems, I always remain content, I am always enterprising, I am good at communication, I am courageous, I always speak economically, I never hesitate, I am sober, I am not aggressive and so on....

CYCLE-8

3	13	23	33	43	53	63	73	83	73
63	53	43	33	23	13	3			

Keep On Observing (KOO):

I like to find out solution of problems, I always remain content, I am always enterprising, I am good at communication, I am courageous, I always speak economically, I never hesitate, I am sober, I am not aggressive and so on....

CYCLE-9

3	13	23	33	43	53	63	73	83	93
83	73	63	53	43	33	23	13	1	

Keep On Observing (KOO):

I like to find out solution of problems, I always remain content, I am always enterprising, I am good at communication, I am courageous, I always speak economically, I never hesitate, I am sober, I am not aggressive and so on....

PATTERN: 4

CYCLE-1

4	14	4							

Keep On Observing (KOO):

I like to find out solution of problems, I always remain content, I am always enterprising, I am good at communication, I am courageous, I always speak economically, I never hesitate, I am sober, I am not aggressive and so on....

CYCLE-2

4	14	24	14	4					

Keep On Observing (KOO):

I like to find out solution of problems, I always remain content, I am always enterprising, I am good at communication, I am courageous, I always speak economically, I never hesitate, I am sober, I am not aggressive and so on....

CYCLE-3

4	14	24	34	24	14	4			

Keep On Observing (KOO):

I like to find out solution of problems, I always remain content, I am always enterprising, I am good at communication, I am courageous, I always speak economically, I never hesitate, I am sober, I am not aggressive and so on....

CYCLE-4

| 4 | 14 | 24 | 34 | 44 | 34 | 24 | 14 | 4 | |

Keep On Observing (KOO):

I like to find out solution of problems, I always remain content, I am always enterprising, I am good at communication, I am courageous, I always speak economically, I never hesitate, I am sober, I am not aggressive and so on....

CYCLE-5

| 4 | 14 | 24 | 34 | 44 | 54 | 44 | 34 | 24 | 14 |
| 4 | | | | | | | | | |

Keep On Observing (KOO):

I like to find out solution of problems, I always remain content, I am always enterprising, I am good at communication, I am courageous, I always speak economically, I never hesitate, I am sober, I am not aggressive and so on....

CYCLE-6

| 4 | 14 | 24 | 34 | 44 | 54 | 64 | 54 | 44 | 34 |
| 24 | 14 | 4 | | | | | | | |

Keep On Observing (KOO):

I like to find out solution of problems, I always remain content, I am always enterprising, I am good at communication, I am courageous, I always speak economically, I never hesitate, I am sober, I am not aggressive and so on....

CYCLE-7

4	14	24	34	44	54	64	74	64	74
64	54	44	34	24	14	4			

Keep On Observing (KOO):

I like to find out solution of problems, I always remain content, I am always enterprising, I am good at communication, I am courageous, I always speak economically, I never hesitate, I am sober, I am not aggressive and so on....

CYCLE-8

4	14	24	34	44	54	64	74	84	74
64	54	44	34	24	14	4			

Keep On Observing (KOO):

I like to find out solution of problems, I always remain content, I am always enterprising, I am good at communication, I am courageous, I always speak economically, I never hesitate, I am sober, I am not aggressive and so on....

CYCLE-9

4	14	24	34	44	54	64	74	84	94
84	74	64	54	44	34	24	14	4	

Keep On Observing (KOO):

I like to find out solution of problems, I always remain content, I am always enterprising, I am good at communication, I am courageous, I always speak economically, I never hesitate, I am sober, I am not aggressive and so on....

PATTERN: 5

CYCLE-1

5	15	5							

Keep On Observing (KOO):

I like to find out solution of problems, I always remain content, I am always enterprising, I am good at communication, I am courageous, I always speak economically, I never hesitate, I am sober, I am not aggressive and so on....

CYCLE-2

5	15	25	15	5					

Keep On Observing (KOO):

I like to find out solution of problems, I always remain content, I am always enterprising, I am good at communication, I am courageous, I always speak economically, I never hesitate, I am sober, I am not aggressive and so on....

CYCLE-3

5	15	25	35	25	15	5			

Keep On Observing (KOO):

I like to find out solution of problems, I always remain content, I am always enterprising, I am good at communication, I am courageous, I always speak economically, I never hesitate, I am sober, I am not aggressive and so on....

CYCLE-4

5	15	25	35	45	35	25	15	5	

Keep On Observing (KOO):

I like to find out solution of problems, I always remain content, I am always enterprising, I am good at communication, I am courageous, I always speak economically, I never hesitate, I am sober, I am not aggressive and so on....

CYCLE-5

5	15	25	35	45	55	45	35	25	15
5									

Keep On Observing (KOO):

I like to find out solution of problems, I always remain content, I am always enterprising, I am good at communication, I am courageous, I always speak economically, I never hesitate, I am sober, I am not aggressive and so on....

CYCLE-6

5	15	25	35	45	55	65	55	45	35
25	15	5							

Keep On Observing (KOO):

I like to find out solution of problems, I always remain content, I am always enterprising, I am good at communication, I am courageous, I always speak economically, I never hesitate, I am sober, I am not aggressive and so on....

CYCLE-7

5	15	25	35	45	55	65	75	65	75
65	55	45	35	25	15	5			

Keep On Observing (KOO):

I like to find out solution of problems, I always remain content, I am always enterprising, I am good at communication, I am courageous, I always speak economically, I never hesitate, I am sober, I am not aggressive and so on....

CYCLE-8

5	15	25	35	45	55	65	75	85	75
65	55	45	35	25	15	5			

Keep On Observing (KOO):

I like to find out solution of problems, I always remain content, I am always enterprising, I am good at communication, I am courageous, I always speak economically, I never hesitate, I am sober, I am not aggressive and so on....

CYCLE-9

5	15	25	35	45	55	65	75	85	95
85	75	65	55	45	35	25	15	5	

Keep On Observing (KOO):

I like to find out solution of problems, I always remain content, I am always enterprising, I am good at communication, I am courageous, I always speak economically, I never hesitate, I am sober, I am not aggressive and so on....

PATTERN: 6

CYCLE-1

6	16	6							

Keep On Observing (KOO): I like to find out solution of problems, I always remain content, I am always enterprising, I am good at communication, I am courageous, I always speak economically, I never hesitate, I am sober, I am not aggressive and so on....

CYCLE-2

6	16	26	16	6					

Keep On Observing (KOO):

I like to find out solution of problems, I always remain content, I am always enterprising, I am good at communication, I am courageous, I always speak economically, I never hesitate, I am sober, I am not aggressive and so on....

CYCLE-3

6	16	26	36	26	16	6			

Keep On Observing (KOO):

I like to find out solution of problems, I always remain content, I am always enterprising, I am good at communication, I am courageous, I always speak economically, I never hesitate, I am sober, I am not aggressive and so on....

CYCLE-4

6	16	26	36	46	36	26	16	6	

Keep On Observing (KOO):

I like to find out solution of problems, I always remain content, I am always enterprising, I am good at communication, I am courageous, I always speak economically, I never hesitate, I am sober, I am not aggressive and so on....

CYCLE-5

6	16	26	36	46	56	46	36	26	16
6									

Keep On Observing (KOO):

I like to find out solution of problems, I always remain content, I am always enterprising, I am good at communication, I am courageous, I always speak economically, I never hesitate, I am sober, I am not aggressive and so on....

CYCLE-6

6	16	26	36	46	56	66	56	46	36
26	16	6							

Keep On Observing (KOO):

I like to find out solution of problems, I always remain content, I am always enterprising, I am good at communication, I am courageous, I always speak economically, I never hesitate, I am sober, I am not aggressive and so on....

CYCLE-7

6	16	26	36	46	56	66	76	66	76
66	56	46	36	26	16	6			

Keep On Observing (KOO):

I like to find out solution of problems, I always remain content, I am always enterprising, I am good at communication, I am courageous, I always speak economically, I never hesitate, I am sober, I am not aggressive and so on....

CYCLE-8

6	16	26	36	46	56	66	76	86	76
66	56	46	36	26	16	6			

Keep On Observing (KOO):

I like to find out solution of problems, I always remain content, I am always enterprising, I am good at communication, I am courageous, I always speak economically, I never hesitate, I am sober, I am not aggressive and so on....

CYCLE-9

6	16	26	36	46	56	66	76	86	96
86	76	66	56	46	36	26	16	6	

Keep On Observing (KOO):

I like to find out solution of problems, I always remain content, I am always enterprising, I am good at communication, I am courageous, I always speak economically, I never hesitate, I am sober, I am not aggressive and so on....

PATTERN: 7

CYCLE-1

7	17	7							

Keep On Observing (KOO):

I like to find out solution of problems, I always remain content, I am always enterprising, I am good at communication, I am courageous, I always speak economically, I never hesitate, I am sober, I am not aggressive and so on....

CYCLE-2

7	17	27	17	7					

Keep On Observing (KOO):

I like to find out solution of problems, I always remain content, I am always enterprising, I am good at communication, I am courageous, I always speak economically, I never hesitate, I am sober, I am not aggressive and so on....

CYCLE-3

7	17	27	37	27	17	7			

Keep On Observing (KOO):

I like to find out solution of problems, I always remain content, I am always enterprising, I am good at communication, I am courageous, I always speak economically, I never hesitate, I am sober, I am not aggressive and so on....

CYCLE-4

7	17	27	37	47	37	27	17	7	

Keep On Observing (KOO):

I like to find out solution of problems, I always remain content, I am always enterprising, I am good at communication, I am courageous, I always speak economically, I never hesitate, I am sober, I am not aggressive and so on....

CYCLE-5

7	17	27	37	47	57	47	37	27	17
7									

Keep On Observing (KOO):

I like to find out solution of problems, I always remain content, I am always enterprising, I am good at communication, I am courageous, I always speak economically, I never hesitate, I am sober, I am not aggressive and so on....

CYCLE-6

7	17	27	37	47	57	67	57	47	37
27	17	7							

Keep On Observing (KOO):

I like to find out solution of problems, I always remain content, I am always enterprising, I am good at communication, I am courageous, I always speak economically, I never hesitate, I am sober, I am not aggressive and so on....

CYCLE-7

7	17	27	37	47	57	67	77	67	77
67	57	47	37	27	17	7			

Keep On Observing (KOO):

I like to find out solution of problems, I always remain content, I am always enterprising, I am good at communication, I am courageous, I always speak economically, I never hesitate, I am sober, I am not aggressive and so on....

CYCLE-8

7	17	27	37	47	57	67	77	87	77
67	57	47	37	27	17	7			

Keep On Observing (KOO):

I like to find out solution of problems, I always remain content, I am always enterprising, I am good at communication, I am courageous, I always speak economically, I never hesitate, I am sober, I am not aggressive and so on....

CYCLE-9

7	17	27	37	47	57	67	77	87	97
87	77	67	57	47	37	27	17	7	

Keep On Observing (KOO):

I like to find out solution of problems, I always remain content, I am always enterprising, I am good at communication, I am courageous, I always speak economically, I never hesitate, I am sober, I am not aggressive and so on....

PATTERN: 8

CYCLE-1

8	18	8							

Keep On Observing (KOO):

I like to find out solution of problems, I always remain content, I am always enterprising, I am good at communication, I am courageous, I always speak economically, I never hesitate, I am sober, I am not aggressive and so on....

CYCLE-2

8	18	28	18	8					

Keep On Observing (KOO):

I like to find out solution of problems, I always remain content, I am always enterprising, I am good at communication, I am courageous, I always speak economically, I never hesitate, I am sober, I am not aggressive and so on....

CYCLE-3

8	18	28	38	28	18	8			

Keep On Observing (KOO):

I like to find out solution of problems, I always remain content, I am always enterprising, I am good at communication, I am courageous, I always speak economically, I never hesitate, I am sober, I am not aggressive and so on....

CYCLE-4

8	18	28	38	48	38	28	18	8	

Keep On Observing (KOO):

I like to find out solution of problems, I always remain content, I am always enterprising, I am good at communication, I am courageous, I always speak economically, I never hesitate, I am sober, I am not aggressive and so on....

CYCLE-5

8	18	28	38	48	58	48	38	28	18
8									

Keep On Observing (KOO):

I like to find out solution of problems, I always remain content, I am always enterprising, I am good at communication, I am courageous, I always speak economically, I never hesitate, I am sober, I am not aggressive and so on....

CYCLE-6

8	18	28	38	48	58	68	58	48	38
28	18	8							

Keep On Observing (KOO):

I like to find out solution of problems, I always remain content, I am always enterprising, I am good at communication, I am courageous, I always speak economically, I never hesitate, I am sober, I am not aggressive and so on....

CYCLE-7

8	18	28	38	48	58	68	78	68	58
48	38	28	18	8					

Keep On Observing (KOO):

I like to find out solution of problems, I always remain content, I am always enterprising, I am good at communication, I am courageous, I always speak economically, I never hesitate, I am sober, I am not aggressive and so on....

CYCLE-8

8	18	28	38	48	58	68	78	88	78
68	58	48	38	28	18	8			

Keep On Observing (KOO):

I like to find out solution of problems, I always remain content, I am always enterprising, I am good at communication, I am courageous, I always speak economically, I never hesitate, I am sober, I am not aggressive and so on....

CYCLE-9

8	18	28	38	48	58	68	78	88	98
88	78	68	58	48	38	28	18	8	

Keep On Observing (KOO):

I like to find out solution of problems, I always remain content, I am always enterprising, I am good at communication, I am courageous, I always speak economically, I never hesitate, I am sober, I am not aggressive and so on....

PATTERN: 8

CYCLE-1

9	19	9							

Keep On Observing (KOO):

I like to find out solution of problems, I always remain content, I am always enterprising, I am good at communication, I am courageous, I always speak economically, I never hesitate, I am sober, I am not aggressive and so on....

CYCLE-2

9	19	29	19	9					

Keep On Observing (KOO):

I like to find out solution of problems, I always remain content, I am always enterprising, I am good at communication, I am courageous, I always speak economically, I never hesitate, I am sober, I am not aggressive and so on....

CYCLE-3

9	19	29	39	29	19	9			

Keep On Observing (KOO):

I like to find out solution of problems, I always remain content, I am always enterprising, I am good at communication, I am courageous, I always speak economically, I never hesitate, I am sober, I am not aggressive and so on....

CYCLE-4

| 9 | 19 | 29 | 39 | 49 | 39 | 29 | 19 | 9 | |

Keep On Observing (KOO):

I like to find out solution of problems, I always remain content, I am always enterprising, I am good at communication, I am courageous, I always speak economically, I never hesitate, I am sober, I am not aggressive and so on....

CYCLE-5

9	19	29	39	49	59	49	39	29	19
9									

Keep On Observing (KOO):

I like to find out solution of problems, I always remain content, I am always enterprising, I am good at communication, I am courageous, I always speak economically, I never hesitate, I am sober, I am not aggressive and so on....

CYCLE-6

9	19	29	39	49	59	69	59	49	39
29	19	9							

Keep On Observing (KOO):

I like to find out solution of problems, I always remain content, I am always enterprising, I am good at communication, I am courageous, I always speak economically, I never hesitate, I am sober, I am not aggressive and so on....

CYCLE-7

9	19	29	39	49	59	69	79	69	59
49	39	29	19	9					

Keep On Observing (KOO):

I like to find out solution of problems, I always remain content, I am always enterprising, I am good at communication, I am courageous, I always speak economically, I never hesitate, I am sober, I am not aggressive and so on....

CYCLE-8

9	19	29	39	49	59	69	79	89	79
69	59	49	39	29	19	9			

Keep On Observing (KOO):

I like to find out solution of problems, I always remain content, I am always enterprising, I am good at communication, I am courageous, I always speak economically, I never hesitate, I am sober, I am not aggressive and so on....

CYCLE-9

9	19	29	39	49	59	69	79	89	99
89	79	69	59	49	39	29	19	9	

Keep On Observing (KOO):

I like to find out solution of problems, I always remain content, I am always enterprising, I am good at communication, I am courageous, I always speak economically, I never hesitate, I am sober, I am not aggressive and so on....

PATTERN: 9

CYCLE-1

10	20	10							

Keep On Observing (KOO):

I like to find out solution of problems, I always remain content, I am always enterprising, I am good at communication, I am courageous, I always speak economically, I never hesitate, I am sober, I am not aggressive and so on....

CYCLE-2

10	20	30	20	10					

Keep On Observing (KOO):

I like to find out solution of problems, I always remain content, I am always enterprising, I am good at communication, I am courageous, I always speak economically, I never hesitate, I am sober, I am not aggressive and so on....

CYCLE-3

10	20	30	40	30	20	10			

Keep On Observing (KOO):

I like to find out solution of problems, I always remain content, I am always enterprising, I am good at communication, I am courageous, I always speak economically, I never hesitate, I am sober, I am not aggressive and so on....

CYCLE-4

10	20	30	40	50	40	30	20	10	9

Keep On Observing (KOO):

I like to find out solution of problems, I always remain content, I am always enterprising, I am good at communication, I am courageous, I always speak economically, I never hesitate, I am sober, I am not aggressive and so on....

CYCLE-5

10	20	30	40	50	60	50	40	30	20
10									

Keep On Observing (KOO):

I like to find out solution of problems, I always remain content, I am always enterprising, I am good at communication, I am courageous, I always speak economically, I never hesitate, I am sober, I am not aggressive and so on....

CYCLE-6

10	20	30	40	50	60	70	60	50	40
30	20	10							

Keep On Observing (KOO):

I like to find out solution of problems, I always remain content, I am always enterprising, I am good at communication, I am courageous, I always speak economically, I never hesitate, I am sober, I am not aggressive and so on....

CYCLE-7

10	20	30	40	50	60	70	80	70	60
50	40	30	20	10					

Keep On Observing (KOO):

I like to find out solution of problems, I always remain content, I am always enterprising, I am good at communication, I am courageous, I always speak economically, I never hesitate, I am sober, I am not aggressive and so on....

CYCLE-8

10	20	30	40	50	60	70	80	90	80
70	60	50	40	30	20	10			

Keep On Observing (KOO):

I like to find out solution of problems, I always remain content, I am always enterprising, I am good at communication, I am courageous, I always speak economically, I never hesitate, I am sober, I am not aggressive and so on....

CYCLE-9

10	20	30	40	50	60	70	80	90	100
90	80	70	60	50	40	30	20	10	

Keep On Observing (KOO):

I like to find out solution of problems, I always remain content, I am always enterprising, I am good at communication, I am courageous, I always speak economically, I never hesitate, I am sober, I am not aggressive and so on....

Let's do an introspective exercise:

Please check what you achieved and able to exercise now in your life

Sr. No.	Qualities/ characteristics	Posses by a mathematised mind	Posses by a successfull mind	Posses by a happy mind	Posses by a pattern	Posses by you		
						Beginning	Consolidating	Exercising
1	like to find out solution of problems	yes	yes	Yes	yes			
2	remain content	yes	yes	Yes	yes			
3	enterprising	yes	yes	Yes	yes			
4	good at communication	yes	yes	Yes	yes			
5	courageous	yes	yes	Yes	yes			
6	speak economically	yes	yes	Yes	yes			
7	never hesitate	yes	yes	Yes	yes			
8	Sober	yes	yes	Yes	yes			
9	aggressive	no	no	No	no			
10	straight forward	yes	Yes	Yes	yes			
11	daring	yes	yes	Yes	Yes			
12	enthusiastic	yes	yes	Yes	yes			
13	risk taking	yes	calculated	calculated	calculated			
14	bold	yes	yes	Yes	Yes			
15	can take stress	yes	Yes	Yes	yes			
16	dominant	yes	no	No	No			
17	influenced by facts than by feeling	yes	Yes	Yes	yes			
18	Hard working	yes	yes	yes	Yes			
19	easy going never in hurry	yes	yes	Yes	yes			
20	quick decision	yes	yes	yes	Yes			
21	communicative	yes	yes	Yes	yes			
22	free from guilt	yes	yes	yes	yes			
23	never hesitate	yes	yes	yes	yes			
24	Secure	yes	yes	Yes	yes			
25	never act according to others	yes	yes	yes	yes			
26	capable of getting things done	yes	yes	Yes	yes			
27	assertive behaviour	yes	yes	yes	yes			

28	develop their own sets of rules	yes	If required	If required	If required			
29	self disciplined	yes	yes	yes	Yes			
30	abstract thinking	yes	yes	Yes	yes			
31	reliable behaviour	yes	yes	yes	yes			
32	experimentive	yes	yes	yes	yes			
33	impulsive	yes	no	no	no			
34	self destructive	no	no	no	no			
35	social	yes	yes	yes	yes			
36	cope with routine life		yes	yes	yes			
37	highly self motivated	yes	yes	Yes	yes			
38	practical	yes	yes	yes	yes			
39	mindful	yes	yes	yes	yes			
40	lost in the world of dreams	no	no	no	no			
41	participating	yes	yes	yes	yes			
42	Cautious	yes	yes	Yes	yes			
43	likes people	yes	yes	yes	yes			
44	open minded	yes	yes	yes	yes			
45	resolve conflicts	yes	yes	Yes	yes			
46	emotionally mature	yes	yes	Yes	yes			
47	realistic	yes	yes	yes	yes			
48	Cheerful	yes	yes	Yes	yes			
49	Intuitive	yes	yes	yes	yes			
50	keep things under control	yes	yes	yes	yes			
51	Competitor of self	yes	yes	Yes	yes			
52	self confident	yes	yes	Yes	yes			
53	Assertive	yes	yes	Yes	yes			
54	Mature	yes	yes	Yes	yes			
55	Relax	yes	yes	Yes	yes			
56	Adaptive	yes	yes	Yes	yes			
57	Flexible	yes	yes	Yes	yes			
58	open to change	yes	yes	Yes	yes			
59	accommodative	yes	yes	Yes	yes			
60	socially active	yes	yes	Yes	yes			
61	cultural interests	yes	yes	Yes	yes			
62	down to earth	yes	yes	Yes	yes			
63	friendly nature	yes	yes	Yes	yes			
64	Sociable	yes	yes	Yes	yes			
65	good reasoning	yes	yes	Yes	yes			
66	intelligent	yes	yes	Yes	yes			
67	hard to fool	yes	yes	Yes	yes			

Express your feeling about your accomplishments through mathyoga9211:

....
....
....
....
....
....
....
....
....
....
....
....
....
....
....
....
....
....
....
....
....
....
....
....
....
....
....

Printed in the United States
By Bookmasters